THE
GREAT
BAHAMAS
HURRICANE OF 1866

THE STORY OF ONE OF THE GREATEST AND DEADLIEST HURRICANES TO EVER IMPACT THE BAHAMAS

WAYNE NEELY

iUNIVERSE, INC.
BLOOMINGTON

The Great Bahamas Hurricane of 1866
The Story of One of the Greatest and Deadliest
Hurricanes to Ever Impact the Bahamas

The front cover illustrated picture shows the damaged ruins of the Trinity Methodist Church
after the Great Bahamas Hurricane of 1866. This image was taken from photographs by Mr.
W. Davenport. It was opened for public worship in April, 1865. The Great Bahamas Hurricane
of 1866 destroyed it, however, it was rebuilt and reopened in 1869 and again destroyed in 1886
by another hurricane.

iUniverse books may be ordered through booksellers or by contacting:

iUniverse
1663 Liberty Drive
Bloomington, IN 47403
www.iuniverse.com
1-800-Authors (1-800-288-4677)

ISBN: 978-1-4620-1102-5 (sc)
ISBN: 978-1-4620-1103-2 (dj)
ISBN: 978-1-4620-1104-9 (ebk)

Printed in the United States of America

iUniverse rev. date: 4/22/2011

Contents

DEDICATION

This book is dedicated first and foremost to all of the victims of the *Great Bahamas Hurricane of 1866.* By telling of their stories of heroism and tragedy in the midst of such a devastating hurricane; it is my hope and desire that their stories will forever be told in the archives of the Bahamian History. Furthermore, it is my hope that their stories will live on for future generations of Bahamians to read about and to appreciate why this storm was regarded as 'One of the Greatest and Deadliest Hurricanes of the Bahamas.'

To my dad and mom Lofton and Francita Neely. Thanks for the great love and support you've showed me over the years.

To Ray, Stephanie, Leroy, Neil, Rupert, Barbara, Susan, Dwight, Peter, William, and Darnell without your tremendous help and support, this book and my previous books would not have been possible and I owe all of you a great debt of gratitude.

To Mr. Les Brown who at a conference held here in the Bahamas through his own unique way and method reminded me to: - 1) "Pass it on"; 2) "It is important how you use your down time"; 3) "Someone's opinion of you doesn't have to become a reality"; and 4) "In the time of adversity Expand!" And to Dr. Myles Munroe who always reminds me to 1) "Die empty!" 2) "To pursue my purpose!" and 3) "Maximize My Potential." I listened to them and this book is the end result...Thank you Mr. Les Brown and Dr. Myles Munroe for your invaluable contribution to my life.

Booker T. Washington once said, "Success is to be measured not so much by the position that one has reached in life as by the obstacles which he has overcome while trying to succeed."

Dr. Martin Luther King Jr. once said, "Faith is taking the first step even when you don't see the whole staircase."

Mahatma Gandhi once said, "You must be the change you want to see in the world!" and "There are 2 types of people in this world, those that take the credit and those that actually do the work. Take my advice and follow the latter, as there is a lot less competition there."

PREFACE

As I have researched the history of Bahamian hurricanes over the years, I've discovered that hurricanes make history because they forever change the lives of men, women and especially the children who survive them. Natural disasters become etched into a collective memory bank when they throw people's lives into disarray and the natural world overwhelms our daily routines. Having grown up in the Bluff, South Andros, I too have vivid memories of notable Bahamian hurricanes especially Hurricane David in 1979. I remember going out after the storm and looking at and being amazed by the many large trees uprooted by the storm and looking at the damage it did to my grandmother's house. At the time, I do not think I realized the lesson of impermanence; however, I now know that is what we take home from these major events. Our lives are fragile, our world is vulnerable, and we are subject to constant changes and some are grander than others, especially when it comes to major hurricanes. We must learn from the past and try to live in harmony with the natural world. The Bahamas's geographic location persuades us to be more aware of past hurricanes since history guarantees that they will come again with the same or greater fury. We can identify patterns and commonalities between storms just as human history helps us learn from our society's disasters.

Hurricane, just say the word and some of the adjectives that come to mind are, powerful, devastating, destructive, and frightening. They all have one thing in common and that is that they add up to the most powerful weather forces on this planet. Human affairs and meteorology intertwine to weave the history of tropical cyclones here in the Bahamas. The first people on record to live in the Bahamas were the Lucayan Indians who reckoned time by the cycles of their lives and of the seasons. Sadly, they left no written records of the tempests they survived beyond folklores and fables that faded in a generation or two. Then came Christopher Columbus who encountered several hurricanes which sank several of his ships and he encountered a hurricane right here in the

Bahamas during one of his later voyages to the New World. With the coming of the Europeans, written records, first in meticulous Spanish and then in English, began but generally only of major storms which sank numerous ships or devastated these early settlements.

The quantitative record of the North Atlantic hurricanes began in 1851, and actually started to be reliable just before the turn of the 20th century. Against the background of rampant development, hurricane landfalls varied in multi-decadal cycles. During the first three decades of the 20th century, the Bahamas experienced an above average of five to six hurricanes per decade. Then in the 1940s, the incidence decreased. During the 1950s there were really no major hurricanes to occur however, the 1960s saw two major hurricanes (notably Donna in 1960 and Betsy in 1965) which made a direct hit on the Bahamas. There was a lull in hurricanes in the 1970s and 1980s, but sadly it returned with even greater fury in the 1990s with Hurricane Andrew in 1992 and Hurricane Floyd in 1999 and they became two of the Bahamas and the region's most enduring and notable hurricanes. Now the atmosphere and oceans appear to have entered a new and more ominous hurricane phase with increased hurricane activity. However, the trend of escalating hurricane damages sustained over the more recent years have been attributed to the rapidly expanding Bahamian population and exploding coastal development rather than more frequent or powerful hurricanes.

Natural disasters have played a significant part in the shaping of physical and human nature since the dawn of history. With the exception, however, of some vividly described events by travellers and sailors, detailed attention to their causes and effects have, until recently, been absent with regards to hurricanes. The cataclysmic Great Hurricane of 1780, Hurricane Katrina in 2005, Hurricane Andrew in 1992, Hurricane Mitch in 1998 and many others have all been described in their various ways by travellers, journalists, sea captains and diarists over the many years of their occurrences. All of these major hurricanes have rocked the entire North Atlantic hurricane basin with their incredible ferocity, strength and great devastation over the many years of their occurrences. Here in the Bahamas, this hurricane in 1866 had a similar effect on the islands and the people of the Bahamas.

In this book, readers will learn about the complex set of weather conditions that contribute to hurricanes and about the swiftness and severity of hurricanes. During the early era of the Caribbean, hurricane disasters were simply described but they were not analyzed, but thankfully, today that has changed as meteorologists from all over the world have been probing all aspects of these deadly storms. As the technology of weather has increased over the years, so too has the understanding of them. A detailed hurricane report which was written by then Governor Rawson gave a clear and concise picture of the devastation that this hurricane had on the Bahamas in October 1866. However, it was not fully reported until March of 1868 after information that had been separately collected and assessed from well over 34 sources on both land and at sea. This hurricane considering the era in which it had occurred has been well documented by both Bahamians and other historians doing research on this storm.

The Great Bahamas Hurricane of 1866 swept the entire chain of islands in the Bahamas in early October of 1866, eventually landing in the Bahamian record books as one of the most deadly and enduring Bahamian hurricanes. This storm, after briefly punishing the Virgin Islands, Puerto Rico, the Dominican Republic, and Haiti with mudslides that killed hundreds, this powerful hurricane then edged northwestward and struck the Turks and Caicos Islands where it killed 63 persons and destroyed over 800 houses. It then with even greater ferocity struck the Bahamian Islands as a powerful Category four hurricane. Landfall occurred on several of the major islands, where a massive storm surge washed over the beaches and swept away hundreds of homes and a few persons caught in the storm surge. Coastal communities on many of the Family Islands like, Abaco, Eleuthera, Exuma, Andros and many others caught the brunt of the storm and suffered significant damage and a massive amount of casualties. This hurricane barreled inland and battered these islands with sustained winds of well over 140 miles per hour and even higher gusts that toppled trees, sunk many ships and destroyed vital infrastructures like warehouses, docks and bridges and peeled away rooftops. It then raced northward into the open waters of the Atlantic and affected the island of Bermuda. When it was all over, *The Great Bahamas Hurricane of 1866* had killed more than 387 persons in the Bahamas and left a massive trail of destruction across these islands. But nowhere was its impact more dramatic and pronounced than in the capital city of Nassau itself as you will see later.

Nassau began as a small town sometime between 1648 and 1666. Located on New Providence, originally called *Sayle's Island*, it was first colonized by Bermudians and English some of whom had originally settled on Eleuthera, the isle of Freedom. By 1670, there were over 300 settlers on New Providence, and no doubt they settled where Nassau, or *Charlestown* as it was called, is today. Why did Nassau become the capital city of the Bahamas and not George Town, Exuma or Harbour Island, Eleuthera for instance, which also had many of the attributes of the capital at the time? Nassau had many geographical advantages, its sheltered location, its accessibility to shipping by way of the Providence Channel and its fine harbour. In fact, its early settlers were comprised mainly of men of the sea. The city of Nassau grew from humble beginnings. In the 1660s, it was comprised of only a few dozen shacks. Later in 1695, Proprietary Governor Nicholas Trott laid out Charlestown anew and renamed it Nassau in honour of the Prince of Orange-Nassau, who became William III of England. In that year, the town consisted of 160 houses. Trott also built a fort which he named Nassau. The buildings at this time were mainly wooden with thatched roofs of palmetto leaves. The small buildings huddled around the large sheltered harbour that singled Nassau out as most suitable for the seat of Nassau.

During the early days, the town's development and growth had many ups and downs. From the late 17th century, privateers and pirates increasingly used Nassau as a base from which to plunder and destroy French and Spanish ships. Since the privateers were the only source of prosperity, the community and the Governor turned a blind eye on their activities. Many citizens were involved in piratical dealings. To add to its hardships, the town was attacked several times in the early 18th century. In 1703, it was sacked and plundered by a combined Spanish and French fleet. Being almost totally destroyed, most of the inhabitants fled. Those few who stayed in Nassau *"lived shatteringly in little huts, ready upon any assault to secure themselves in the woods."*

Nassau's development as a modern town began in earnest under the first Royal Governor Woodes Rogers (1718-1721; 1729-1732). Rogers meeting the town in a dilapidated state, he immediately set out to work to rebuild it so that Nassau *"began to have the appearance of a civilized place"* as one writer noted. During his second term of office, Woodes

Rogers called the first General Assembly, and among the 12 Acts passed in the first session, included one "to lay out the town of Nassau." Further expansion of the town took place in the 1740s during the governorship of John Tinker (1738-1758) and during the 1760s under William Shirley's governorship (1758-1768). The latter governor initiated a new survey of the town and reclaimed much of the mosquito-breeding swamp land so that the town could expand eastward. Among the new but yet unpaved streets to be built was Shirley Street, honoring the name of the Governor who created it. Notwithstanding those improvements, Nassau was still a modest town in 1783. The inhabitants were very poor and owned very little property, usually comprising of a few small vessels and a few stone structures and there was no plantation system at all like their other counterparts in the Caribbean. Principally occupied in a sea-faring life of fishing, wrecking, turtling, the early inhabitants also engaged in woodcutting, mainly dye-woods and other varieties such as Madeira and Boxwood. There was no staple crop and very little agriculture. The only produce was a little fruit with some easily-grown products such as, guinea corn, peas, beans, potatoes, yams, plantains and bananas.

The advent of the Loyalists fleeing from the newly independent states of America in the 1780s greatly influenced the growth of the town. Within the first decade of the arrival of the refugees there were new streets built, docks and wharves were improved, a new jail built and a workhouse constructed, and a roofed market-place built. Architecturally, the Loyalists had a great impact on the town. The architectural styles of the Southern States and New England towns were transported to Nassau. Nassau was transformed by the Loyalists. Besides important architectural changes, streets were cleaned, repaired and new ones built. Docks and wharves were improved. New regulations, for example, one prohibiting thatched roofs in Nassau in order to protect home owners against fire and hurricanes, were passed. There was an improvement to cemeteries which were to be enclosed and a regulation passed that stipulated that graves must be at least four feet deep. Architecturally, the Loyalists had a tremendous impact on the town. The American colonists before the Revolutionary War had already established their own variations of Georgian architecture. Most of the materials used in the early southern colonial towns were wood. Stone was rarely used. However, in Nassau, both were employed because they were readily available. In 1783, the houses in Nassau were constructed mainly of wood and lightly built. The Loyalists patterned their houses mainly on the Georgian style, but adapted them to meet the Bahamian climate and economic conditions. They were also designed with devastating hurricanes in mind because the Bahamas was in the direct path of these storms.

In the 1850s, the city of Nassau was hit by an outbreak of the disease cholera. However, Nassau had rebound by this disease and by the 1860s, it was described as a busy town of well over 12,000 inhabitants which were scattered on the southern side of Bay Street and on the northern slopes of the ridge now East Hill and West Hill Streets. By the mid 1860s, some fine Georgian colonial-style homes, such as Graycliff, East Hill and Jacaranda were built. The decades of the 1840s and 1850s witnessed a slow but steady growth of Nassau. However, the pace of development was significantly increased during the 1860s with the outbreak of the American Civil War. The beginning of the conflict coincided with the granting in 1861 of Letters of Patent which raised the parish of Christ Church to the status of a Cathedral and the town of Nassau to the City of Nassau. The fledgling tourist industry was becoming more important, being encouraged by the 1859 contract made between the Bahamas Government and Samuel Cunard for regular steamship service connected between Nassau and New York. Additionally, the Royal Victoria Hotel was built to accommodate winter visitors and it soon became the headquarters of the colourful blockade runners.

The brief prosperity brought on by the war stimulated some significant improvements in the City of Nassau. For the first time, Bay Street was widened and provided with kerbstones and lights. The northern side of Bay Street was reclaimed and warehouses and shops built, including, John S. George on the corner of East and Bay Streets. The old prison on East Street was built towards the end of the blockade period. Sadly, tragedy was again to strike these islands of the Bahamas in 1866, when a massive hurricane struck and ended up destroying any and everything in its path. Among the buildings demolished was the newly constructed Trinity Church which was rebuilt three years later. Fortunately, Nassau and the entire Bahamas recovered very quickly and by 1900 it was described as "a nice-looking town with nice wide and clean streets shaded with cork and almond trees." The town benefited from the development of local industries especially the sponge, pineapple and sisal industries during the 19th century.

Hurricanes are one of nature's most awesome phenomena which occur in the tropical and subtropical areas across the world every year. The majority of these storms happens in the summer and early fall in these tropical and subtropical areas. This is where the sea-surface temperatures are above 26.5oC and the dynamics of the atmosphere are conducive to the formation of these storms. No doubt about it, they are among the most destructive forces in nature. Extreme rainfall, unbelievably high waves, winds of incredible ferocity, nothing can compare to the destructive potential of hurricanes. We are use to reading about hurricanes in the newspapers, on a computer, or even watching film footage of them on the local and international television stations. There is no question about it-they are tremendously exciting and awe inspiring and it is quite easy to see why. They cut right across the mundane and sometimes too predictable routines of our everyday lives, and they fill us with renewed wonder at the sensational power of the forces of nature. Then we feel a twinge of guilt at being excited, because we know, as we read about and watch them, that people are losing their homes, their businesses, their belongings, their well-being, their peace of mind and even their lives. In some powerful hurricanes, entire communities are wiped out and then we feel sorry for the disaster victims. Our responses invariably contain this guilty triple-take of excitement, shame and pity, and we feel we have to suppress our sense of exhilaration because of some natural weather phenomenon which we in this region call hurricanes.

Earth is a unique and dynamic planet. It is the only one in our Solar System that has both an atmosphere and oceans of water, and these have created ideal conditions for life to evolve and flourish. Currents in the atmosphere and oceans transport heat and moisture around the globe, so that life can exist almost everywhere on this planet. These currents also create the weather that we are familiar with today. This changes daily, but in predictable patterns. The pattern of weather in a particular place over a long period of time is its climate. Simply put, weather is what's going on in the atmosphere in any one location at a particular time; fortunately, nothing is as simple as that. The weather we experience at the Earth's surface is caused by a complex set of interrelated factors. Some of these are large-scale events, and affects all parts of the Earth at some time. These include, the impact of solar heating-energy from the sun, in other words the seasons. Other large-scale, global factors include the amount of water vapour and other gases in the atmosphere which influence global temperatures. Additionally, the impact of high and low pressure systems and large scale permanent or periodic ocean currents is of fundamental importance in explaining why we have particular weather and climate on planet Earth.

Understanding weather allows us to plan our days, our vacations, travels, and our crops. As a matter of fact, weather is a complex and dynamic process driven by the sun; the Earth's oceans, rotation, and inclination; and so many other factors that even today many of its mysteries still remain unexplained. To say that weather is an important factor in everyone's life is a huge understatement. Being prepared for what the weather brings can be as simple as turning on the television to catch the early morning weather forecast before heading to work or to the beach, or as complicated as examining long-range forecasts to decide which crops to plant, or when and where to evacuate from an approaching storm. Weather constantly affects people in small ways but can also have major consequences when a hurricane threatens our well-being and livelihoods, or even our lives. It seems inconceivable that when looking at great storms, such as this one in 1866 that something so large and deadly could have a beneficial side. But hurricanes are really just giant heat engines that pick up warmth from the oceans in the warmer latitudes and transport it to colder latitudes, helping to restore or balance the Earth's warm and cool zones, thus giving us as humans the ability to live and survive on an otherwise very volatile planet.

In 1866, the hurricane preparedness technology and tools for tracking hurricanes we use today were in their infancy or virtually non-existent. As such, hurricane preparedness for the Great Bahamas Hurricane of 1866 was lacking, to say the least. We did have some tools available for tracking hurricanes in the mid 1800s, however, the few available instruments such as, thermometers, anemometers and barometers lacked certain sophistication. Back then, we could only detect a hurricane in its later stages after it had hit or devastated some land area in the Caribbean before it struck the Bahamas. As a result, it was very difficult to predict with any degree of accuracy, where and when it might strike or how strong it might be. As such, people were only able to put up hurricane shutters and evacuate from their homes at the last second, and hope for the best. Furthermore, this was in a period where mass communications were not available for storm tracking. Even if we could have known in advance of an approaching hurricane, theoretically, it would have been next to impossible to issue warnings in a timely manner to save lives. As such, hurricane preparations were predictably slim or non-existent.

Compared to the hurricane forecasting technology of today, forecasting in 1866 didn't do much more than wetting a finger and holding it into the wind or simply watching the clouds, birds or other animals reaction to an impending storm. Forecasters now enjoy access to satellites, radars and survey dozens of advanced computer models. They fly into a hurricane in a $50 million jet, dropping instrument packages from over 8 miles up and send data faster than the human eye can follow. They employ everything from special radios to the Internet to warn people of imminent danger. In fact, the geographic range of possible landfalls established when a storm is five days away is now about as wide as forecasters thirty years ago could set for a storm that was three days away from hitting land. Unfortunately, today people have come to expect exactness. They see the dotted line that forecasters use to show the most probable track, and they think that's the 'only' possible track. But what they should be paying more attention to is the "cone of probability or uncertainty" that surrounds the line and grows wider the farther out the forecast goes.

Increasing awareness and preparation, better building codes and the advent of mass communications have significantly dropped the average hurricane deaths from thousands per year in the 1800's and early 1900s to less than 100 a year now. Unfortunately, today the property damage has risen sharply due to many persons living on or near the coast. Today, adjusting for inflation, population growth, and increased property values, hurricane researchers speculate that the 1866 storm, should it follow the same path today, would be one of the costliest Bahamian hurricanes on record, with an estimated value of over $800 million in damage, dwarfing modern day storms such as, Andrew, Floyd, Frances, Jeanne or Wilma. Could another 1866 disaster happen again? The easy answer is no. Now, in the twenty-first century, we receive days of warning that a storm may be heading our way. We can brace our homes or simply run like hell. Could a hurricane still bring great loss of life? Sure it can and it has happened in the past with modern day storms such as, Hurricane Mitch which killed over 10,000 persons in Central America in 1998.

Hurricanes are no novelty to the Bahamas, but the fury of one that occurred in 1866 was definitely memorable. No one at the time who lived through the howling winds and the terror of a sky filled with the flying debris and roofs of the demolished houses ever forgot it. Winds from all best guessed estimates reached at least a Category four or even a Category five intensity on the Saffir-Simpson Scale had it occurred today. Property damages throughout the Bahamas were astounding and at least 387 persons lost their lives as a direct result of this massive and deadly hurricane. In Long Cay, one of the many islands devastated by this storm, the island's salt crop was entirely loss for that year and impacted for years to follow, leaving the residents without a valuable source of income and near starvation. By 9pm to midnight of that night, many houses were either significantly damaged or totally destroyed. After the storm, most of the islands were devoid of ships for all had broken away from their moorings and some had been driven ashore and wrecked while others were simply driven out to sea never to be seen again. The Bahamas was devastated, and its unsheltered inhabitants were reduced to the last extremity of misery and despair.

This book is about a select sub-group of natural disasters which we call hurricanes that often have far-reaching consequences with rippled effects across history. A natural disaster is a climatic or environmental occurrence that either kills or injures people, damages property, or causes great financial loss. Most are unpredictable, spontaneous calamities called "Acts of God." Some, such as fire, may need human intervention to get them started, while others such as hurricanes simply need heat as a catalyst to get them started. All of these disasters were crucial shapers of the world we live in. It is very important to understand why disasters like hurricanes happen. It was all too easy in past centuries to portray hurricanes as chaotic, unforeseen and unforeseeable by some evil god. People were actively encouraged especially by spiritual and community leaders to think of them as acts of punishment by a vengeful god or the

Almighty God. This is a particularly cruel mindset; a family bereaved by a hurricane has to bear the additional grief that some evil god or the Almighty God had deliberately struck their loved ones down and that they must have done something wicked or drastically wrong to deserve such a punishment. As we shall see, the Great Bahamas Hurricane of 1866 did something significant to change that. This hurricane in 1866 brought about an increase in our understanding of the way the world around us works. Nowadays, we have come to accept the fact that hurricanes are foreseeable but some hurricanes such as this enormous storm in 1866 could not have been foreseen whereby avoiding action could have been taken.

FOREWORD

While the devastation of impacts from recent hurricanes such as, Hurricanes Frances and Jeanne (2004) and Hurricane Andrew (1992) are still well-remembered by many residents of the Bahamas, the stories of prior hurricanes that unleashed their full wrath on the Bahamas have long since been forgotten by most people. Wayne Neely does a great service by going back through the historical records and reconstructing the story of the Great Bahamas Hurricane of 1866, which was responsible for nearly 400 deaths and much damage on the islands. Blockade running, a lucrative industry during the Civil War, had recently ended with the cessation of the war, and the combined economic damage from the end of this productive industry and the hurricane provided a huge blow to the economy of the Bahamas.

In addition to covering the societal impacts of the hurricane, he goes into detail describing how these storms were monitored in historical times, including the techniques used to follow these storms in the mid 19th century. Wayne also provides a nice discussion of current scientific knowledge about how hurricanes form, intensify, and dissipate as well as the ways that these storms are currently monitored and predicted. He is a meteorologist with the Bahamian Weather Service and is an acknowledged expert on hurricanes impacting the Bahamas both past and present. I found this book to be a thorough, enjoyable read from cover to cover, and I am sure that you will too.

Dr. Phil Klotzbach
Research Scientist
Department of Atmospheric Science,
Colorado State University.

Dr. Phil Klotzbach has worked with Dr. William Gray on the seasonal hurricane forecasts since 2000 and is currently working as a research scientist in the Department of Atmospheric Science. His research interests include seasonal hurricane prediction and causes of climate change. He received his Ph.D. in Atmospheric Science from Colorado State University (CSU) in 2007. Dr. Klotzbach has been employed in the Department of Atmospheric Science at CSU for the over ten years where he has been the co-author on the Atlantic basin hurricane forecasts with Dr. William Gray. He became first or head author on the seasonal hurricane forecasts in 2006. A marathoner, mountaineer and wunderkind who graduated from college at 18, Klotzbach predicts the fury Nature will unleash during each Atlantic hurricane season as the lead forecaster of the Tropical Meteorology Project at Colorado State University. He has taken over the highly anticipated region wide seasonal hurricane forecast from Professor William Gray. The seasonal hurricane forecast began in 1984 and was spearheaded by William Gray, a world renowned hurricane expert who has studied the storms since the 1950s. Since then, the forecasts have been highly publicized and can even influence insurance rates in hurricane-prone areas throughout the region. They give people an idea of the severity of the upcoming season by estimating the number of storms and the probability of a strong storm reaching the U.S. coastline. Klotzbach and his team release four predictions: one in early December, almost seven months before the hurricane season begins on June 1, followed by updates in early April, late May and early August. In each report, they predict the number of named storms (tropical systems packing winds of at least 39 mph), hurricanes (at least 74 mph) and intense hurricanes (at least 111 mph) for the North Atlantic.

INTRODUCTION

The weather affects each and every one of us at sometime or the other in our everyday lives. A bright, sunny morning can lift our moods; a dark and gloomy day can dampen our spirits. The weather even affects many aspects of our health, hence the expression "feeling under the weather." In some situations, the weather has an even bigger impact on the world. In fact, entire species have come into being, adapted or have become extinct and economies have crashed just because of the change in temperature of a few degrees, or a variation in the amount of rainfall. Being able to predict or forecast the weather is not just a matter of convenience, in the long term our very future may depend on it.

Understanding why seasonal conditions can vary so much from one year to the next can help us see exactly how our way of life is affecting the delicate global systems around us. In the shorter term we need to know how hurricanes arise and what makes them so powerful and deadly and where tornadoes come from for instance, so that we can foresee when they might occur and minimize their potential to cause damage or death. However, the weather is also an endless source of fascination and interest. Primitive people believed that thunderstorms, rainbows, lightning, hurricanes and other weather phenomena were omens sent by the gods and looking at the glory of a rainbow or experiencing the majestic power of a major hurricane, it is easy to see why. We may try to control the weather, to harness its extraordinary forces, yet we are still fascinated at nature's amazing handiwork.

For many of us, the weather is only of interest when it comes to deciding each morning what to wear, or perhaps when and where to take a holiday. Is it cold or hot? Will it rain or be windy? At other times it becomes an issue only when there is something unusual taking place, such as a period of extreme heat or a deadly storm. However, increasingly, we have become interested in the weather as we read about and experience more unusual effects. Media coverage is often very extensive and often scaremongering. This comprehensive book covers all aspects of hurricanes, from how they are formed to how they die out. Methods of all aspects of hurricanes are explained, analyzed and discussed to make you the reader much more knowledgeable about all of the intricacies of hurricanes in general. Understanding hurricanes, tracing their causes and effects, can only enhance our understanding of the Earth and nature, and help us to live in harmony with both.

Hurricanes are possibly the most dramatic, feared and respected of all the common weather events. They can bring heavy rainfall, strong gusty winds, deadly storm surges, sometimes hail, thunderstorms and occasionally tornadoes or even waterspouts, almost any of which can cause significant damage, particularly in coastal areas. As old as the oceans themselves, hurricanes are born each year from the heat of the Tropics. They begin as innocent thunderclouds and evolve into massive storms with violent winds and torrential rains. They may live for days or even weeks and most die off harmlessly over cooler waters. Some track dangerously close to land before veering away just beyond the shoreline. Occasionally these storms make landfall with a violent blast of wind, rain, and storm surge. Other storm systems may be larger and tornadoes sometimes pack more violent winds, but nothing in our atmosphere can match the ferocity and broad-scale destructive force of hurricanes. These seasonal tropical cyclones and their counterparts around the globe are the greatest storms on Earth, killing more people worldwide than all other storms combined.

Through the stunning personal recollections and vivid historical accounts we will revisit the Great Bahamas Hurricane of 1866 as it impacted the Bahamas. There are lesser known hurricanes in the 1800s but none can compare to this mighty storm. Interspersed throughout the book, there are special sections that will help you understand the factors at play when nature unleashes its fury. If you've ever wondered what conditions bring about a hurricane, where and why they form or how much energy is contained in them, you'll find what you seek in this book, illustrated by the most thrilling and vintage pictures of nature gone wild that you will ever see. Hurricanes are natures fury unleashed and they are an incredible beauty to behold, and it's a fascinating topic of study and contemplation. This book allows you to see, learn and think about this great storm. Furthermore, it allows you to be amazed at the wonders and at the same time the fury of nature.

This comprehensive book covers all areas of this great hurricane which impacted the Bahamas in 1866. Prior to this publication we have often heard and read about this great hurricane very briefly from other noted historians (such as, Dr. Gail Saunders, Michael Craton, Jim Lawlor, Nicolette Bethel, Ronald Shaklee, Ronald Lightbourn, Dr. Paul Albury and others), but never has this storm been fully researched and documented so comprehensively before this book. There are those who will argue that I missed out a particular aspect of this storm, over emphasized or neglected another but this storm in my opinion is one of the most memorable hurricanes to affect the Bahamas. You can feel free to disagree or agree with me on this. This book however seeks to provide invaluable information on both hurricanes in general and this great storm which affected the Bahamas in 1866.

My main goal at this time is to provide a historical viewpoint of this hurricane and say what made it in my humble opinion unique and memorable here in the Bahamas. It is written in a non-technical and non-scientific language when and where possible, where the average reader can understand and appreciate what made this storm so great in the annals of Bahamian History. I hope that you enjoy learning about this hurricane as I have enjoyed researching and presenting it to you. This book will attempt to answer some questions that arise from the interest of hurricanes. Its emphasis will be placed on understanding them, that is, on providing the reader with the physical explanations of these amazing atmospheric phenomenons known as *Hurricanes*. As such, its purpose is two fold; first, to give the reader a deeper appreciation of the physical attributes of these storms and what makes them work and second, to impart a historical awareness of this hurricane and how it affected life here in the Bahamas. In the process of communicating this understanding, a considerable amount of descriptive information about the structure of hurricanes and the processes that go on in them will be presented. This book is for the general reader who is interested in knowing when and where this tropical cyclone actually affected the Bahamas and the magnitude of the damage inflicted by this hurricane.

First settled over two hundred years before this hurricane struck, the colony of the Bahamas had progressed little by 1850, and then in fits and starts rather than continuously it slowly developed into a bustling colony. In 1866, the Bahamas was working its way out of a depression which followed the prosperous years of the American Civil War. Blockade running (the act of slipping into the Union-guarded ports of the South in order to supply the Confederate States with the manufactured goods they needed), brought quick, easy money into the country and the country prospered because of this illegal activity. But the era, though great, was also short-lived, and in 1865, three years after the beginning of blockade running, the industry closed when the Confederation was defeated by the North. The colony suffered a sudden economic collapse and needed something desperately to fill this void. This is where sponging and wrecking came into play on the life and existence of the Bahamian way of life.

In the Out Islands, life was greatly affected by this storm because of their large dependence on sailing vessels and sloops for all aspects of their everyday lives. The main sources of income in the Bahamas at the time were, fishing, farming and wrecking and salvaging. But on the island of New Providence, site of the capital, life was difficult. Workers who had migrated from the Out Islands to work in the city were left unemployed. Sadly, the warehouses which were only recently hurriedly erected were left abandoned with the coming of the economic slump. The townspeople, who could no longer be fully satisfied by the meager harvests reaped by the Nassauvian fishermen, were forced to pay high prices for food or live off that which they could grow. Starvation, although uncommon, was near and knocking on the doorsteps of many Bahamians.

Society was deeply segregated and divided into two distinct categories, whites and blacks, and was not united by the depression. The rich white Bahamians and the colonial settlers, who could afford the imports brought in by merchant ships, lived well; but the poor freed black slaves, who were unemployed, were forced to survive on the produce from their small vegetable plots and the few chickens and other farm animals which lived there. The only money they earned came from the fruits they sold at the market; and this depended on the seasons. Nassau was divided geographically to suit the social categories. The freed black slaves inhabited special "coloured" settlements, the most important of which were:- Fox Hill, Headquarters (later to become Grant's Town), Carmichael and Adelaide. All of these communities were located "Over the Hill"-the hot flat "Valley" behind the ridge which ran the entire length of the island. Much of this lowland area was swamp, buzzing with mosquitoes and prone to floods. Sheltered from the sea breezes by the ridge, the "Over the Hill" areas were hot, humid and very uncomfortable. The Bahamas was not prepared for a colossal disaster of this magnitude which would stir up the sea and flood the land, which would sink ships, wreck mansions and sweep away the flimsy shacks of the Valley. Nevertheless, the colony was visited by one. For in October of 1866, a hurricane the likes of which no one had ever been seen before in that era then swept across the entire archipelago. There was simply nothing like this storm with sustained winds of over 140 mph and when it was over 387 persons died and the entire Bahamas as you will see later was devastated.

This great and powerful hurricane in 1866 transformed the normally easygoing Nassau Harbour into a raging, frenzied torrent which swept everything before it. Of the more than 200 vessels in the harbour at the time, sadly only one remained intact. The *Great Bahamas Hurricane of 1866* came only a year after a period of great economic prosperity during the American Civil War. It was the worst hurricane in the history of the Bahamas, devastating the entire chain of islands from Inagua in the south to Grand Bahama in the north. The 'eye' of this deadly hurricane had a massive size of well over 23 miles across in diameter. It passed over the island of New Providence in the early evening of October 1, 1866. Eyewitnesses later reported that *"the ocean rolled completely over Hog Island (now called Paradise Island) into the harbour in surges so enormous that the crest was even with the gallery of the lighthouse, sixty feet above the sea."* In the following days, the Governor reported that 612 houses were destroyed in the city of Nassau alone, and as many badly damaged. More than a thousand people were left homeless. Nassau itself was so devastated that it was unable to send assistance at all to the poor and starving people in the Out Islands, where there were many injuries and deaths. The end of the blockade era had produced an awful slump in the Bahamian economy, and then the hurricane came along and destroyed what was left of the Bahamian economic life.

CHAPTER ONE

THE HISTORY BEHIND THE WORD 'HURRICANE' AND OTHER TROPICAL CYCLONE NAMES

What is a hurricane? Simply put, it is a large, violent storm that originates in a tropical region and features extremely high winds-by definition, in excess of 74 miles per hour. It also brings drenching rains and has the ability to spin off tornadoes. Hurricanes are storms that form between the tropics of Cancer and Capricorn in the Atlantic, Pacific and Indian Oceans. They have different names depending on where they are formed and located. In the Atlantic they are called hurricanes, in the north-west Pacific, typhoons, in the Indian Ocean they are known as tropical cyclones while north of Australia they are sometimes called Willy Willies. However, by any name, they are impressive to behold. To form, hurricanes need sea surface temperatures of 26.5°C or greater, moisture and light winds in the upper atmosphere. The hurricane season in the North Atlantic lasts from June 1 to November 30. Around 80 tropical storms form every year with most of them occurring in the south or south-east of Asia, while here in the North Atlantic we account for only a mere 12 percent of the worldwide total of tropical cyclones. These storms are enormous creatures of nature, often between 120 and 430 miles in diameter. They may last from a few days to a week or more and their tracks are notoriously unpredictable.

A hurricane is a tropical cyclone with winds that exceed 64 knots (74mph) and blow anti-clockwise about the center in the northern hemisphere. A tropical cyclone is a powerful storm system characterized by a low pressure center and numerous severe thunderstorms that produce strong winds and flooding rainfall. A tropical cyclone feeds on the heat released (latent heat) when moist air rises and the water vapour it contains condenses. They are fueled by a different heat mechanism than

1

other cyclonic windstorms such as nor'easters, European windstorms, and polar lows, leading to their classification as "warm core" storm systems. The term 'tropical' simply refers to both the geographic origin of these systems, which forms almost exclusively in tropical regions of the Earth, and their formation in maritime tropical air masses. The term "cyclone" refers to a family of such storms' cyclonic nature, with anti-clockwise rotation in the northern hemisphere and clockwise rotation in the southern hemisphere. Depending on their location and strength, tropical cyclones are referred to by other names, such as hurricanes, typhoons, tropical storms, cyclonic storms, tropical depressions and simply cyclones which all have low atmospheric pressure at their center. A hurricane consists of a mass of organized thunderstorms that spiral in towards the extreme low pressure of the storm's eye or center. The most intense thunderstorms, the heaviest rainfall, and the highest winds occur outside the eye, in the region known as the Eyewall. In the eye itself, the air is warm, winds are light, and skies are generally clear and rain free but can also be cloudy to overcast.

Captain George Nares, a nineteenth century Scottish naval officer and polar explorer, was always on the lookout for hurricanes. "June-too soon," he wrote. "July-stand by; August-look out you must; September-remember; October-all over." Whatever you think about the dynamics of hurricanes-two things can be said about them and that is they are very unpredictable and very destructive. The forces of nature such as, deadly hurricanes have shaped the lives of people from the earliest times. Indeed, the first 'meteorologists' were priests and shamans of ancient communities. All religions recognized the power of the weather elements and most scriptures contain tales about or prophecies foretelling, great natural disasters sometimes visited upon a community because of the sins of its citizens. Ancient peoples often reacted to the weather in a fearful, superstitious manner. They believed that mythological gods controlled the weather elements such as, winds, rain and sun which governed their existence. When weather conditions were favorable, there would be plenty of game to hunt and fish to catch, and crops would yield bountiful harvests. But their livelihood was at the mercy of the wild weather because fierce hurricanes could damage villages of flimsy huts, destroy crops and generate vast floodwaters that could sweep away livestock.

In times of hurricanes, food shortages and starvation were constant threats as crops failed and game animals became scarce when their food supplies dried up due to a hurricane. These ancient tribes as you will see later believed that their weather fortunes were inextricably linked with the moods and actions of their gods. For this reason, they spent a great deal of time and effort appeasing these mythological weather gods. Many of these ancient tribes tried to remain on favorable terms with their deities through a mixture of prayers, rituals, dances and sometimes even human sacrifices. In some cultures such as the Aztecs of Central America, they went so far as to offer up human sacrifices to appease their rain-god Tláloc. In addition, Quetzalcoatl, the all powerful and mighty deity in the ancient Aztec society, whose name means 'Precious Feathered Serpent,' played a critical role; he was the creator of life and controlled devastating hurricanes. The Egyptians celebrated Ra, the Sun God. Thor was the Norse god of thunder and lightning, a god to please so that calm waters would grace their seafaring expeditions. The Greeks had many weather gods, however, it was Zeus who was the most powerful of them all.

The actual origin of the word 'hurricane' and other tropical cyclone names were based on the many religions, cultures, myths, and races of people. In modern cultures, 'myth' has come to mean a story or an idea that is not true. The word 'myth' comes directly from the Greek word 'mythos'(μύθος), whose many meanings include, 'word', 'saying', 'story', and 'fiction.' Today, it is often used any and everywhere and people speak of myths about how to catch or cure the common cold. But the age-old myths about hurricanes in this book were an important part of these people's religion, cultures, and everyday lives. Often they were both deeply spiritual and culturally entertaining and significant. For many of these ancient races, their mythology was their history and there was often little, if any distinction between the two. Some myths were actually based on historical events, such as, devastating hurricanes or even wars but myths often offer us a treasure trove of dramatic tales. The active beings in myths are generally gods and goddesses, heroes and heroines, or animals. Most myths are set in a timeless past before recorded and critical history begins. A myth is a sacred narrative in the sense that it holds religious or spiritual significance for those who tell it, and it contributes to and expresses systems of thought and values. It is a traditional story, typically involving supernatural beings or forces or creatures, which embodies and provides an explanation, aetiology (*origin myths*), or justification for something such as the early history of a society, a religious belief or ritual, or a natural phenomenon.

The United Nation's sub-body, the World Meteorological Organization estimates that in an average year, about 80 of these tropical cyclones kills up to 15,000 people worldwide and cause an estimate of several billion dollars worth of property damage alone. Meteorologists have estimated that between 1600 to today, hurricanes have caused well over 200,000 deaths in this region alone and over 8 million deaths worldwide. Hurricanes, Typhoons and Cyclones are all the same kind of violent storms originating over warm tropical ocean waters and are called by different names all over the world. From the Timor Sea to as far as northwestern Australia they are called Cyclones or by the Australian colloquial term of 'Willy-Willies' from an old Aboriginal word (derived from whirlwind). In the Bay of Bengal and the Indian Ocean, they are simply called Cyclones (an English name based on a Greek word meaning "coil" as in "coil of a snake" because the winds that spiral within them resembles the coil of a snake) and are not named even to this day.

They are called Hurricanes (derived from a Carib or Arawak Indian word) in the Gulf of Mexico, Central and North America, the Caribbean and Eastern North Pacific Oceans (east of the International Dateline). A Hurricane is the name given to these intense storms of tropical origin, with sustained winds exceeding 64 knots (74 miles per hour). In the Indian Ocean all the way to Mauritius and along the Arabian Coasts they are known as 'Asifa-t.' In Mexico and Central America hurricanes are also known as El Cordonazo and in Haiti, they are known as Tainos. While they are called Typhoons[originating from the Chinese word 'Ty-Fung' (going back to as far as the Song (960-1278) and Yuan (1260-1341) dynasties) translated to mean 'Big or Great Wind'...] in the Western North Pacific and in the Philippines and the South China Sea (west of the International Dateline) they are known as 'Baguios' or 'Chubasco'(or simply a Typhoon).

In Japan they are known as 'Repus,' or by the more revered name of a Typhoon. The word "taifū" (台風) in Japanese means *Typhoon*; the first character meaning "pedestal" or "stand"; the second character meaning wind. The Japanese term for "divine wind" is Kamikaze(神風). The Kamikaze, were a pair or series of typhoons that were said to have saved Japan from two Mongol invasion fleets under Kublai Khan which attacked Japan in 1274 and again in 1281. The latter is said to have been the largest attempted naval invasion in history whose scale was only recently eclipsed in modern times by the D-Day invasion by the allied forces into Normandy in 1944. This was the term that was given to the typhoon winds that came up and blew the Mongol invasion fleet off course and destroyed it as it was poised to attack Japan.

On October 29, 1274, the first invasion began. Some 40,000 men, including about 25,000 Mongolians, 8,000 Korean troops, and 7,000 Chinese seamen, set sail from Korea in about 900 ships to attack Japan. With fewer troops and inferior weapons, the Japanese were far outmatched and overwhelmed and were sure to be defeated. But at nightfall just as they were attacking the Japanese coastal forces, the Korean sailors sensed an approaching typhoon and begged their reluctant Mongol commanders to put the invasion force back at sea or else it would be trapped on the coast and its ships destroyed at anchor by this typhoon. The next morning, the Japanese were surprised and delighted to see the Mongol fleet struggling to regain the open ocean in the midst of a great typhoon. The ships sadly, were no match for this great storm, and many foundered or were simply dashed to bits and pieces on the rocky coast. Nearly 13,000 men perished in this storm mostly by drowning. This Mongol fleet had been decimated by a powerful typhoon as it was poised to attack Japan.

With the second storm, even as Kublai Khan was mounting his second Japanese offensive, he was waging a bitter war of conquest against southern China, whose people had resisted him for 40 years. But finally, in 1279, the last of the southern providences, Canton, fell to the Mongol forces, and China was united under one ruler for the first time in three hundred years. Buoyed by success, Kublai again tried to bully Japan into submission by sending his emissaries to the Japanese asking them to surrender to his forces. But this time the Japanese executed his emissaries, enraging him even further and thereby paving the way for a second invasion. Knowing this was inevitable; the Japanese went to work building coastal fortifications, including a massive dike around Hakozaki Bay, which encompasses the site of the first invasion.

The second Mongol invasion of Japan assumed staggering proportions. One armada consisted of 40,000 Mongols, Koreans, and north Chinese who were to set sail from Korea, while a second, larger force of some 100,000 men was to set out from various ports in south China. The invasion plan called for the two armadas to join forces in the spring before the summer typhoon season, but unfortunately the southern force was late, delaying the invasion until late June 1281. The Japanese defenders held back the invading forces for six weeks until on the fifteenth and sixteenth of August, history then repeated itself when a gigantic typhoon decimated the Mongol fleet poised to attack Japan again.

As a direct result of these famous storms, the Japanese came to think of the typhoon as a 'divine wind,' or 'kamikaze,' sent by their gods to deliver their land from the evil invaders. Because they needed another intervention to drive away the Allied fleet in WWII, they gave this name to their Japanese suicide pilots as nationalist propaganda. In the Japanese Shinto religion, many forces of nature are worshipped as gods, known as 'kami' are represented as human figures. The Japanese god of thunder is often depicted as a strong man beating his drum. The Japanese called it Kamikaze, and the Mongols never ever returned to attack Japan again because of their personal experiences with these two great storms. In popular Japanese myths at the time, the god Raijin was the god who turned the storms against the Mongols. Other variations say that the god Fūjin or Ryūjin caused the destructive kamikaze. This use of *kamikaze* has come to be the common meaning of the word in English.

Whatever name they are known by in different regions of the world, they refer to the same weather phenomena a *'Tropical Cyclone.'* They are all the same severe tropical storms that share the same fundamental characteristics aside from the fact that they rotate clockwise in the southern hemisphere and counterclockwise in the northern hemisphere. However, by World Meteorological Organization International Agreement, the term tropical cyclone is the general term given to all hurricane-type storms that originate over tropical waters. The term cyclone, used by meteorologists, refers to an area of low pressure in which winds move counterclockwise in the northern hemisphere around the low pressure center and are usually associated with bad weather, heavy rainfall and strong wind speeds. Whereas, a tropical cyclone was the name first given to these intense circular storms by Englishman Captain Henry Piddington (1797-1848) who was keenly interested in storms affecting India and spent many years collecting information on ships caught in severe storms in the Indian Ocean. He would later become the President of the Marine Courts of Inquiry in Calcutta, India and used the term tropical cyclone to refer to a tropical storm which blew the freighter *'Charles Heddles'* in circles for nearly a week in Mauritius in February of 1845. In his book *'Sailor's Hornbook for the Laws of Storms in All Parts of the World,'* published in 1855, he called these storms cyclones, from the Greek word for coil of a snake. He called these storm tropical cyclones because it expressed sufficiently what he described as the 'tendency to move in a circular motion.'

The word cyclone is from the Greek word 'κύκλος', meaning 'circle' or Kyklos meaning 'coils of the snake', describing the rotating movement of the storm. An Egyptian word 'Cykline' meaning to 'to spin' has also been cited as a possible origin. In Greek mythology, Typhoeus or Typhōn was the son of Tartarus and Gaia. He was a monster with many heads, a man's body, and a coiled snake's tail. The king of the gods and god of the sky and weather, Zeus, fought a great battle with Typhoeus and finally buried him under Mount Etna. According to legend, he was the source of the powerful storm winds which caused widespread devastation, loss of many lives and numerous shipwrecks. The Greek word 'typhōn' meaning 'whirlwind' comes from this legend, another possible source for the origin of the English word 'typhoon.' The term is most often used for cyclones occurring in the Western Pacific Ocean and Indian Ocean. In addition, the word is an alteration of the Arabic word, tūfān, meaning hurricane, and the Greek word, typhōn, meaning violent storm and an Egyptian word 'Cykline' meaning to 'to spin.'

The history of the word typhoon presents a perfect example of the long journey that many words made in coming to the English Language vocabulary. It travelled from Greece to Arabia to India, and also arose independently in China, before assuming its current form in our language. The Greek word typhōn, used both as the name of the father of the winds and a common noun meaning "whirlwind, typhoon," was borrowed into Arabic during the Middle Ages, when Arabic learning both preserved and expanded the classical heritage and passed it on to

Europe and other parts of the world. In the Arabic version of the Greek word, it was passed into languages spoken in India, where Arabic-speaking Muslim invaders had settled in the eleventh century. Thus the descendant of the Arabic word, passing into English through an Indian language and appearing in English in forms such as touffon and tūfān, originally referred specifically to a severe storm in India.

The modern form of typhoon was also influenced by a borrowing from the Cantonese variety of Chinese, namely the word 'Ty-Fung', and respelled to make it look more like Greek. 'Ty-Fung', meaning literally "great wind," was coincidentally similar to the Arabic borrowing and is first recorded in English guise as tuffoon in 1699. The Cantonese tai-fung and the Mandarin ta-feng are derived from the word jufeng. It is also believed to have originated from the Chinese word 'jufeng.' 'Ju' can mean either 'a wind coming from four directions' or 'scary'; 'feng' is the generic word for wind. Arguably the first scientific description of a tropical cyclone and the first appearance of the word jufeng in the literature is contained in a Chinese book called Nan Yue Zhi (Book of the Southern Yue Region), written around A.D. 470. In that book, it is stated that *"Many Jufeng occur around Xi'n County. Ju is a wind (or storm) that comes in all four directions. Another meaning for Jufeng is that it is a scary wind. It frequently occurs in the sixth and seventh month (of the Chinese lunar calendar; roughly July and August of the Gregorian calendar). Before it comes it is said that chickens and dogs are silent for three days. Major ones may last up to seven days and minor ones last one or two days. These are called heifeng (meaning black storms/winds) in foreign countries."*

European travellers to China in the sixteenth century took note of a word sounding like typhoon being used to denote severe coastal windstorms. On the other hand, typhoon was used in European texts and literature around 1500, long before systematic contact with China was established. It is possible that the European use of this word was derived from Typhon, the draconian earth demon of Greek Legend. The various forms of the word from these different countries coalesced and finally became typhoon, a spelling that officially first appeared in 1819 in Percy Bysshe Shelley's play 'Prometheus Unbound.' This play was concerned with the torments of the Greek mythological figure Prometheus and his suffering at the hands of Zeus. By the early eighteenth century, typhon and typhoon were in common use in European literature, as in the famous poem *Summer* by Scottish poet James Thomson (1700-1748):

> *Beneath the radiant line that grits the globe,*
> *The circling Typhon, whirled from point to point.*
> *Exhausting all the rage of all the sky,*
> *And dire Ecnephia, reign.*

In Yoruba mythology, *Oya*, the female warrior, was the goddess of fire, wind and thunder. When she became angry, she created tornadoes and hurricanes. Additionally, to ward off violent and tropical downpours, Yoruba priests in southwestern Nigeria held ceremonies around images of the thunder and lightning god Sango to protect them from the powerful winds of hurricanes. In ancient Egyptian legend, Set was regarded as the god of storms. He was associated with natural calamities like hurricanes, thunderstorms, lightning, earthquakes and eclipses. In Iroquois mythology, Ga-oh was the wind giant, whose house was guarded by several animals, each representing a specific type of wind. The Bear was the north wind who brought winter hurricanes, and he was also capable of crushing the world with his storms or destroying it with his cold air. In Babylonian mythology, Marduk, the god of gods, defeated the bad tempered dragon goddess Tiamat with the help of a hurricane. When the other gods learned about Tiamat's plans to destroy them, they turned to Marduk for help. Armed with a bow and an arrow, strong winds and a powerful hurricane, Marduk captured Tiamat and let the hurricane winds fill her jaws and stomach. Then he shot an arrow into her belly and killed her and then became the lord of all the gods.

The Meso-American and Caribbean Indians worshipped many gods. They had similar religions based on the worship mainly agricultural and natural elements gods, even though the gods' names and the symbols for them were a bit different. People asked their gods for good weather, lack of hurricanes, abundant crops and good health or for welfare. The main Inca god was the creator god *Viracocha*. His assistants were the gods of the Earth and the sea. As farming occupied such an important place in the region, the 'Earth mother' or 'Earth goddess' was particularly important. The Aztecs, Mayas, Taínos and other Indians adopted many gods from other civilizations. As with the Mayans, Aztecs and Taínos, each god was connected with some aspects of nature or natural forces and in each of these religions, hurricanes or the fear of them and the respect for them played a vital part of their worship. The destructive power of storms like hurricanes inspires both fear and fascination and it is no surprise that humans throughout time have tried to control these storms. Ancient tribes were known to make offerings to the weather gods to appease them. People in ancient times believed that these violent storms were brought on by angry weather gods. In some cultures, the word for hurricane means 'storm god', 'evil spirit', 'devil' or 'god of thunder and lightning.'

The word *hurricane* comes to us via the early Spanish explorers of the New World, who were told by the Indians of this region of an evil god capable of inflicting strong winds and great destruction on their lives and possessions. The natives of the Caribbean and Central America had a healthy respect for hurricanes and an uncanny understanding of nature. In the legends of the Mayan civilizations of Central America and the Taínos of the Caribbean, these gods played an important role in their Creation. According to their beliefs and myths, the wicked gods Huracán, Hurrikán, Hunraken, and Jurakan annually victimized and savagely ravaged their homes, inflicting them with destructive winds, torrential rainfall and deadly floods. These natives were terrified whenever these gods made an appearance. They would beat drums, blew conch shells, shouted curses, engage in bizarre rituals and did everything possible to thwart these gods and drive them away. Sometimes they felt they were successful in frightening them off and at other times their fury could not be withstood and they suffered the consequences from an angry god. Some of these natives depicted these fearsome deities on primitive carvings as a hideous creature with swirling arms, ready to release his winds and claim its prey.

There are several theories about the origin of the word *Hurricane*; some people believe it originated from the Caribbean Arawak-speaking Indians. It is believed that these Indians named their storm god 'Huracán' and over time it eventually evolved into the English word *Hurricane*. Others believed that it originated from the fierce group of cannibalistic Indians called the Caribs but according to some historians this seems like the least likely source of this word. Native people throughout the Caribbean Basin linked hurricanes to supernatural forces and had a word for these storms which often had similar spellings but they all signified death and destruction by some evil spirit and the early European colonial explorers to the New World picked up the native names. Actually, one early historian noted that the local Caribbean Indians in preparation for these storms often tied themselves to trees to keep from being blown away from the winds of these storms. According to one early seventeenth-century English account, Indians on St. Christopher viewed 'Hurry-Cano' as a "tempestuous spirit." These ancient Indians of this region personalized the hurricane, believing that it was bearing down on them as punishment by the gods for something they had done-or not done. These days, there is more science and less superstition to these powerful storms of nature called hurricanes. Yet we humanize hurricanes with familiar names, and the big ones become folkloric and iconic characters, their rampages woven into the histories of the Caribbean, North and Central American coastal towns and cities.

A next popular theory about the hurricane's origin is that it came from the Mayan Indians of Mexico who had an ancient word for these storms, called 'Hurrikán' (or 'Huracán'). In Mayan mythology, 'Hurrikán' ("one legged") was a wind, storm and fire god and one of the creator deities who participated in all three attempts of creating humanity. 'Hurrikán' was the Mayan god of big wind, and his image was chiseled into the walls of the Mayan temples. He was one of the three most powerful forces in the pantheon of deities, along with Cabrakán (earthquakes) and Chirakán (volcanoes). He also caused the Great Flood after the first humans angered the gods. He supposedly lived in the windy mists above the floodwaters and repeated "earth" until land came up from the seas. In appearance he has one leg, the other being transformed into a serpent, a zoomorphic snout or long-nose, and a smoking object such as a cigar, torch holder or axe head which pierces a mirror on his forehead.

Actually, the first human historical record of hurricanes can be found in the ancient Mayan hieroglyphics. A powerful and deadly hurricane struck the Northern Yucatán in 1464 wiping out most of the Mayan Indian population of that area. According to Mayan mythology, the Mayan rain and wind god, Chac, sent rain for the crops. But he also sent hurricanes, which destroyed crops and flooded villages. The

Mayans hoped that if they made offerings to Chac (including human sacrifices), the rains would continue to fall, but the hurricanes would cease. Every year the Mayans threw a young woman into the sea as a sacrifice to appease the god Hurrikán and a warrior was also sacrificed to lead the girl to Hurrikán's underwater kingdom. Also, one of the sacrifices in honour of this god was to drown children in wells. In some Maya regions, Chac the god of rain and wind was so important that the facades of their buildings were covered with the masks of Chac. In actual fact, at its peak, it was one of the most densely populated and culturally dynamic societies in the world but still they always built their homes far away from the hurricane prone coast.

By customarily building their major settlements away from the hurricane-prone coastline, the Mayan Indians practiced a method of disaster mitigation that, if rigorously applied today, would reduce the potential for devastation along coastal areas. The only Mayan port city discovered to date is the small to medium sized city of Tulum, on the east coast of the Yucatán Peninsula south of Cancun. Tulum remained occupied when the Spaniards first arrived in the sixteenth century and its citizens were more prepared for the storms than for the Spaniards. As the many visitors to these ruins can see, the ceremonial buildings and grounds of the city were so skillfully constructed that many remain today and withstanding many hurricanes. The Indians of Guatemala called the god of stormy weather 'Hunrakán.' Of course, the Indians did not observe in what period of the year these hurricanes could strike their country; they believed that the devil or the evil spirits sent them whenever they pleased. Their gods were the uncontrollable forces of nature on which their lives were wholly dependent, the sun, the stars, the rains and the storms.

The Taínos were generally considered to be part of the Taíno-Arawak Indians who travelled from the Orinoco-Amazon region of South America to Venezuela and then into the Caribbean Islands of the Dominican Republic, Haiti, the Bahamas, Jamaica, Puerto Rico, and as far west as Cuba. Christopher Columbus called these inhabitants of the western hemisphere 'Indians' because he mistakenly thought he had reached the islands on the eastern side of the Indian Ocean. The word 'Taíno' comes directly from Christopher Columbus because they were the indigenous set of people he encountered on his first voyage to the

Caribbean and they called themselves 'Taíno' meaning 'good' or 'noble' to differentiate themselves from their fierce enemies-the Carib Indians. This name applied to all the Island Taínos including those in the Lesser Antilles. These so-called Indians were divided into innumerable small ethnic groups, each with its own combination of linguistic, cultural, and biological traits.

Locally, the Taínos referred to themselves by the name of their location. For example, those in Puerto Rico referred to themselves as Boricua which means 'people from the island of the valiant noble lords' their island was called Borike'n meaning 'Great land of the valiant noble lord' and those occupying the Bahamas called themselves 'Lucayo' or 'Lucayans' meaning 'small islands.' Another important consequence of their navigation skills and their canoes was the fact that the Taínos had contact with other indigenous groups of the Americas, including the Mayas of Mexico and Guatemala. What is the evidence to suggest that the Taínos had contact with the Mayan culture? There are many similarities between the Mayan god, 'Hurrikán' and Taíno god 'Huracán' also, similarities in their ballgames, and similarities in their social structure and social stratification. Furthermore, the Meso-Indians of Mexico also flattened the heads of their infants in a similar fashion to the Island based Arawaks and their relatives.

The Taíno Indians believed in two supreme gods, one male, and the other female. They also believed that man had a soul and after death he would go to a paradise called *Coyaba* where the natural weather elements such as droughts and hurricanes would be forgotten in an eternity of feasting and dancing. In the Taíno Indians culture, they believed in a female zemí (spirit) named Guabancex who controlled hurricanes among other things but when angered she sent out her herald Guataba to order all the other zemis to lend her their winds and with this great power she made the winds and the waters move and cast houses to the ground and uprooted trees.

Representations of Guabancex portrayed her head as the eye of the storm, with twisting arms symbolizing the swirling winds. The international symbol that we use today for hurricanes was derived from this zemi. The various likenesses of this god invariably consist of a head of an indeterminate gender with no torso, two distinctive arms spiraling out from its sides. Most of these images exhibit cyclonic (counterclockwise) spirals. The Cuban ethnologist Fernando Ortiz believes that they were inspired by the tropical hurricanes that have always plagued the Caribbean. If so, the Taínos discovered the cyclonic or vortical nature of hurricanes many hundreds of years before the descendents of European settlers did. How they may have made this deduction remains a mystery to this day.

The spiral rain bands so well known to us from satellites and radars were not officially 'discovered' until the meteorological radar was developed during World War II, and they are far too big to be discerned by eye from the ground. It is speculated that these ancient people surveyed the damage done by the hurricane and, based on the direction by which the trees fell, concluded that the damage could only have been done by rotating winds. Or perhaps they witnessed tornadoes or waterspouts, which are much smaller phenomena whose rotation is readily apparent, and came to believe that all destructive winds are rotary. They also believed that sickness, or misfortunes such as devastating hurricanes were the works of malignant or highly displeased zemis and good fortune was a sign that the zemis were pleased. To keep the zemis pleased, great public festivals were held to propitiate the tribal zemis, or simply in their honour. On these occasions everyone would be well-dressed in elaborate outfits and the cacique would lead a parade beating a wooden drum. Gifts of the finest cassava were offered to the zemis in hopes that the zemis would protect them against the four chief scourges of the Taínos existence: fire, sickness, the Caribs and most importantly devastating hurricanes.

The language of the Taínos was not a written one, and written works from them are very scarce. Some documentation of their lifestyles may be found in the writings of Spanish priests such as, Bartholomew de Las Casas in Puerto Rico and the Dominican Republic during the early 16th century. Some of the Taíno origin words were borrowed by the Spanish and subsequently found its way into the English Language, and are modern day reminders of this once proud and vigorous race of people. These words include; avocado, potato, buccaneer, cay, manatee, maize, guava, *barbacoa* (barbecue), *cacique* (chief), jamaca (hammock), Tabacú (tobacco), caniba (cannibal), *canoa* (canoe), Iguana (lizard), and *huracán* or *huruká* (hurricane). Interestingly, two of the islands in the Bahamas, Inagua and Mayaguana both derived their names from the

Arawak word 'Iguana.' Bimini (meaning "two small islands" in English), another island here in the Bahamas also got it's name from these Indians; however most of the other islands here in the Bahamas were also given Indian names but they have been changed over the many years and centuries by various groups of people who settled or passed through the Bahamas. However, for the early Spanish explorers, the islands of the Bahamas were of no particular economic value, so therefore they established only temporary settlements mainly to transport the peaceful Indians to be used as their slaves in East Hispaniola and Cuba to mine the valuable deposits of gold and silver and to dive for pearls.

Jurakán is the phonetic name given by the Spanish settlers to the god of chaos and disorder that the Taíno Indians in Puerto Rico (and also the Carib and Arawak Indians elsewhere in the Caribbean) believed controlled the weather, particularly hurricanes. From this we derive the Spanish word *huracán* and eventually the English word *hurricane*. As the spelling and pronunciation varied across various indigenous groups, there were many alternative names along the way. For example, many West Indian historians and indigenous Indians called them by the various names including, Juracán, furacan, furican, haurachan, herycano, hurachano, hurricano, and so on. The term makes an early appearance in William Shakespeare's King Lear (Act 3, Scene 2). Being the easternmost of the Greater Antilles, Puerto Rico is often in the path of many of the North Atlantic tropical storms and hurricanes which tend to come ashore on the east coast of the island. The Taínos believed that Juracán lived at the top of a rainforest peak called El Yunque (literally, the anvil but truly derived from the name of the Taíno god of order and creation, Yuquiyú) from where he stirred the winds and caused the waves to smash against the shore.

In the Taíno culture, it was said that when the hurricane was upon them, these people would shut themselves up in their leaky huts and shouted and banged drums and blew shell trumpets to keep the evil spirits of the hurricane from killing them or destroying their homes and crops. According to Taíno legend, the goddess Atabei first created the Earth, the sky, and all the celestial bodies. The metaphor of the sacred waters was included because the Taínos attributed religious and mythical qualities to water. For example, the goddess, Atabei, was associated with water. She was also the goddess of water. Yocahú, the supreme deity, was also associated with water. Both of these deities are called *Bagua*, which is water, the source of life. This image of water as a sacred entity was central to their beliefs. They were at the mercy of water for their farming. Without rain, they would not be able to farm their *conucos*.

These Indians prayed to the twin gods of rain and fair weather so that they would be pleased and prayed to these gods to keep the evil hurricane away from their farms and homes. To continue her (Atabei) work, she bore two sons, Yucaju and Guacar. Yucaju created the sun and moon to give light, and then made plants and animals to populate the Earth. Seeing the beautiful fruits of Yucaju's work, Guacar became jealous and began to tear up the Earth with powerful winds, renaming himself Jurakan, the god of destruction. Yucaju then created Locuo, a being intermediate between a god and a man, to live in peaceful harmony with the world. Locuo, in turn, created the first man and woman, Guaguyona and Yaya. All three continued to suffer from the powerful winds and floods inflicted by the evil god Jurakán. It was said that the god Jurakán, was perpetually angry and ruled the power of the hurricane. He became known as the god of strong winds, hence the name today of hurricane. He was feared and revered and when the hurricanes blew, the Taínos thought they had displeased Jurakán. Jurakán would later become *Huracán* in Spanish and *Hurricane* in English.

The origin of the name "Bahamas" is unclear in the history of these islands. Some historians believe it may have been derived from the Spanish word *baja mar*, meaning lands of the '*shallow seas*'; or the Lucayan Indian word for the island of Grand Bahama, *ba-ha-ma* meaning '*large upper middle land*.' The seafaring Taíno people moved into the uninhabited Southeastern Bahamas from the islands of Hispaniola and Cuba sometime around 1000-800 A.D. These people came to be known as the Lucayans. According to various historians, there were estimated reports of well over 20,000 to 30,000+ Lucayans living in the Bahamas at the time of World famous Spanish Explorer Christopher Columbus's arrival in 1492. Christopher Columbus first landfall in the New World was on an island called San Salvador which is generally accepted to be present-day San Salvador (also known as Watlings Island) in the Southeastern Bahamas. The Lucayans called this island Guanahaní but Columbus renamed it as San Salvador (Spanish for "Holy Saviour"). However, Columbus's discovery of this island of San Salvador is a very controversial and debatable topic among historians, scientists and lay-people alike. Even to this day, some of them still suggest that Columbus made his landfall on some other island in the Bahamas such as, Rum Cay, Samana Cay, Cat Island and some even suggested he landed as far south as the Turks and Caicos Islands. However, it still remains a matter of great debate and mystery within the archeological and scientific community. Regrettably, that question may never be solved, as Columbus's original log book has been lost for centuries, and the only evidence is in the edited abstracts made by Father Bartholomew Las Casas.

In the Bahamas, Columbus made first contact with the Lucayans and exchanged goods with them. The Lucayans-a word that meant 'meal-eaters' in their own language, from their dependence upon cassava flour made from bitter manioc root as their staple starch food. They were sub-Taínos of the Bahamas and believed that all of their islands were once part of the mainland of America but had been cut off by the howling winds and waves of the hurricanes and they referred to these storms as huruká. The Lucayans (the Bahamas being known then as the Lucayan Islands) were Arawakan People who lived in the Bahamas at the time of Christopher Columbus landfall on October 12, 1492. Sometime between 1000-800 A.D. the Taínos of Hispaniola pressured by over-population and trading concerns migrated into the southeastern islands of the Bahamas. The Taínos of Cuba moved into the northwestern Bahamas shortly afterwards. They are widely thought to be the first Amerindians encountered by the Spanish.

Early historical accounts describe them as a peaceful set of people and they referred to themselves as 'Lucayos,' 'Lukku Kairi' or 'Lukku-Cairi' meaning 'small islands' or 'island people' because they referred to themselves by the name of their location. The Lucayans spoke the Ciboney dialect of the Taíno language. This assumption was made from the only piece of speech that was recorded phonetically and has been passed down to us. Las Casas informs us that the Arawaks of the Greater Antilles and Lucayans were unable to understand one another, 'here'(in Hispaniola), he wrote *they do not call gold 'caona' as in the main part of the island, nor 'nozay' as on the islet of Guanahani(San Salvador)*

17

but tuob.' This brief hint of language difference tends to reinforce the theory that the Bahama Islands were first settled by people coming from eastern Cuba of the sub-Taíno culture.

Before Columbus arrived to the Bahamas, there were about 20,000 to 30,000+ Lucayans living here, but because of slavery, diseases such as smallpox and yellow fever (to which they had no immunity), and other hardships brought about by the arrival of the Europeans, by 1517, they were virtually non-existent. As a matter of fact, when Spanish Conquistador Ponce de Leon visited these islands in 1513 in search of the magical 'Fountain of Youth,' he found no trace of these Lucayan Indians, with the exception of one elderly Indian woman. These Indians of the Caribbean and Central America lived in one of the most hurricane prone areas of the earth; as a result most of them built their temples, huts, pyramids and houses well away from the hurricane prone coastline because of the great fear and respect which they had for hurricanes.

Many early colonists in the Caribbean took solace by displaying a Cord of Saint Francis of Assisi, a short length of rope with three knots with three turns apiece, in their boats, churches and homes as a protective talisman during the hurricane season. Various legends and lore soon developed regarding Saint Francis and his connection with nature, including tropical weather and hurricanes. According to tradition, if these residents untied the first knot of the cord, winds would pick up but only moderately. Winds of 'half a gale' resulted from untying the second knot. If all three knots were untied, winds of hurricane strength were produced. Today, some descendants of African slaves in the West Indies still tie knots in the leaves of certain trees and hang them in their homes to ward off hurricanes.

Similar accounts also emerged from encounters with the Carib Indians. In old historical accounts these Indians were referred to by various names such as, *'Caribs' 'Charaibes' 'Charibees'* and *'Caribbees'* and they were a mysterious set of people who migrated from the Amazon jungles of South America. They were a tribe of warlike and cannibalistic Indians who migrated northwards into the Caribbean in their canoes overcoming and dominating an earlier race of peaceful set of people called the Arawaks. While Columbus explored all parts of the West Indies, his successors colonized only those parts inhabited by the Arawak or Taíno Indians, avoiding the Carib inhabited islands because they lacked gold but most importantly because the Carib Indians were too difficult to subjugate. Ironically, the region became known as the Caribbean, named after these fierce Indians. Their practice of eating their enemies so captured the imagination of the Europeans that the Caribbean Sea was also named after these Indians. The English word 'cannibal' is derived from one of the terms, 'Caniba' used by the Arawaks to refer to the Caribs eating the flesh of their enemies. Their raids were made over long distances in large canoes and had as one of their main objectives was to take the Arawak women as their captives, wives and slaves. While on the other hand, the captured Arawak men were tortured and killed and then barbecued and eaten during an elaborate ceremony because it was believed that if they did this, they would obtain their enemies personal power and control their spirits. The French traveller Charles de Rochefort wrote that when these Caribs Indians heard the thunder clap, they would *"make all the haste they can to their little houses, and sit down on low stools about the fire, covering their faces and resting their heads on their hands and knees, and in that posture they fall a weeping and say…Maboya is very angry with them: and they say the same when there happens a Hurricane."*

The Caribs were terrified of spilling fresh water into the sea because they believed that it aroused the anger of hurricanes. They had no small stone gods but believed in good and powerful bad spirits called 'Maboya' which caused all the misfortunes of their lives. They even wore carved amulets and employed medicine men to drive the evil Maboya away. When a great and powerful storm began to rise out of the sea, the Caribs blew frantically into the air to chase it away and chewed manioc bread and spat it into the wind for the same purpose. When that was no use, they gave way to panic and crouched in their communal houses moaning, with their arms held over their heads. They felt that they were reasonably safe there because they fortified their houses with corner posts dug deep into the ground. They also believed that beyond the Maboya were great spirits, the male sun, and the female moon. They believed that the spirits of the stars controlled the weather. They also believed in a bird named Savacou which was sent out by the angry Maboya to call up the hurricane, and after this task was finished this bird would then be transformed into a star.

According to a noted English Historian John Oldmixon of the late 1600's and early 1700's, he reported that the Carib Indians excelled in forecasting hurricanes. Writing about a hurricane which occurred in 1740 on the island of St. Christopher he said:- *"Hurricanes are still frequent here, and it was some time since the custom of both the English and French inhabitants in this and the other Charibbees-Islands, to send about the month of June, to the native Charibbees of Dominica and St. Vincent, to know whether there would be any hurricanes that year; and about 10 or 12 Days before the hurricane came they constantly sent them word, and it was rarely failed."* According to Carib Indians 'Signs or Prognosticks,' a hurricane comes *"on the day of the full change, or quarters of the moon. If it will come on the full moon, you being in the change, then observe these signs. That day you will see the skies very turbulent, the sun more red than at other times, a great calm, and the hills clear of clouds or fogs over them, which in the high-lands are seldom so. In the hollows of the earth or wells, there will be great noise, as if you were in a great storm; the stars at night will look very big with Burs about them, the North-West sky smelling stronger than at other times, as it usually does in violent storms; and sometimes that day for an hour or two, the winds blows very hard westerly, out of its usual course. On the full moon you have the same signs, but a great Bur about the moon, and many about the moon, and many about the sun. The like signs must be taken notice of on the quarter-days of the moon."*

According to several elderly Carib Indians, who stated that hurricanes had become more frequent in the recent years following the arrival of the Europeans to the Caribbean, which they viewed as punishment for their interactions with the Europeans. In actual fact, as early as 1630s, English colonists reported that Carib Indians knew when storms would strike by the number of rings that appeared around the moon: three rings meant the storm would arrive in three days, two rings meant two days and one ring meant the storm would arrive in one day. Of course, the connection between such signs and the onset of hurricanes was indeed a very unreliable way to predict the onset of hurricanes. The Carib Indians while raiding islands in the Caribbean would kill off the Arawak men and take the Arawak women as wives and mothers to their children. Actually, when the Europeans came to the Caribbean, they surprisingly found that many Carib women spoke the Taíno language because of the large number of female Taíno captives among them. So it is speculated that a word like 'hurricane' was passed into the Carib speech and this was how these fierce people learned about the terror of these savage storms. Native Indians of the West Indies often engaged in ritual purifications and sacrifices and offered songs and dances to help ward off hurricanes.

An Aztec myth tells that when the gods created the world, it was dark and cold. The youngest of the gods sacrificed himself to create a sun. But it was like him, weak, dim and feeble. Only when more powerful gods offered themselves did the sun blaze into life and shine brightly on them. However, there was one disadvantage, and that was that these gods needed constant fuel, human lives and the Aztecs obliged. They offered tens of thousands of human sacrifices a year, just to make sure that the sun rose each morning and to prevent natural disasters such as, devastating hurricanes from destroying their communities and villages. The Aztec god Tezcatlipoca (meaning Lord of the Hurricane) was believed to have special powers over the hurricane winds, as did the Palenque god Tahil (Obsidian Mirror) and the Quiché Maya sky god Huracán. The Aztec god Tezcatlipoca was feared for his capricious nature and the Aztecs called him Yaotl (meaning 'Adversary'). Tonatiuh was the Aztec Sun god and the Aztecs saw the sun as a divinity that controlled the weather, including hurricanes and consequently, all human life form. The Aztecs of Mexico, in particular built vast temples to the sun God Tonatiuh, and made bloody sacrifices of both human and animal, to persuade him to shine brightly on them and in particular not send any destructive hurricanes their way and to allow prosperity for their crops. When they built these temples, they were constructed according to the Earth's alignment with the sun but most importantly they were always constructed with hurricanes in mind and away from the hurricane prone coastline.

The Aztec people considered Tonatiuh the leader of Tollán, their heaven. He was also known as the fifth sun, because the Aztecs believed that he was the sun that took over when the fourth sun was expelled from the sky. Mesoamerican creation narratives proposed that before the current world age began there were a number of previous creations, the Aztecs account of the five suns or world ages revealed that in each of the five creations the Earth's inhabitants found a more satisfactory staple food than eaten by their predecessors. In the era of the first sun, which was governed by Black Tezcatlipoca, the world was inhabited by a race of giants who lived on acorns. The second sun, whose presiding god was a serpent god called Quetzatzalcóatl was believed to be the creator of life and in control of the vital rain-bearing winds, and he saw the emergence of a race of primitive humans who lived on the seeds of the mesquite tree.

After the third age, which was ruled by Tláloc, in which people lived on plants that grew on water, such as the water lily, people returned to a diet of wild seeds in the fourth age of Chalchiúhtlicue. It was only in the fifth and current age, an age subject to the sun god Tonatiuh that the people of Mesoamerica learned how to plant and harvest maize. According to their cosmology, each sun was a god with its own cosmic era. According to the Aztecs, they were still in Tonatiuh's era and according to the Aztec creation mythology, the god demanded human sacrifice as a tribute and without it he would refuse to move through the sky, hold back on the rainfall for their crops and would send destructive hurricanes their way. It is said that some 20,000 people were sacrificed each year to Tonatiuh and other gods, though this number however, is thought to be highly inflated either by the Aztecs, who wanted to inspire fear in their enemies, or the Spaniards, who wanted to speak ill of the Aztecs. The Aztecs were fascinated by the sun so they worshiped and carefully observed it, and had a solar calendar second only in accuracy to the Mayans.

It was Captain Fernando de Oviedo who gave these storms their modern name when he wrote *"So when the devil wishes to terrify them, he promises them the 'Huracan,' which means tempest."* The Portuguese word for them is Huracao which is believed to have originated from the original Taíno word Huracán. The Native American Indians had a word for these powerful storms, which they called 'Hurucane' meaning 'evil spirit of the wind.' When a hurricane approached the Florida coast, the medicine men of the North American Indians worked frantic incantations to drive the evil hurricane away. The Seminole Indians of Florida were actually, the first to flee from a storm, citing the blooming of the Florida Everglades saw grass. They believed that only 'an atmospheric condition' such as a major hurricane would cause the pollen to bloom on the sawgrass several days before a hurricane's arrival, giving the native Indians an advanced warning of the impending storm.

Many other sub-culture Indians had similar words for these powerful storms which they all feared and respected greatly. For example, the Galibi Indians called these hurricanes Yuracan, Giuana Indians called them Yarukka and other similar Indian names were Hyrorokan, aracan, urican, huiranvucan, Yurakon, Yuruk or Yoroko. As hurricanes were becoming more frequent in the Caribbean, many of the colonists and natives of this region had various words and spellings all sounding phonetically similar for these powerful storms. The English called them, 'Hurricanes', 'Haurachana', 'Uracan', 'Herocano', 'Harrycane', 'Tempest', and 'Hyrracano.' The Spanish called them 'Huracán'and 'Furicane'and the Portuguese called them, 'Huracao' and 'Furicane.' The French had for a long time adapted the Indian word called 'Ouragan' and the Dutch referred to them as 'Orkan.' These various spellings were used until the word 'hurricane' was finally settled on in the English Language.

Christopher Columbus on his first voyage managed to avoid encountering any hurricanes but it wasn't until some of his later voyages that he encountered several hurricanes that disrupted these voyages to the New World. Based on his first voyage before encountering any hurricanes, Columbus concluded that the weather in the New World is benign: *"In all the Indies, I have always found May-like weather,"* he commented. Although sailing through hurricane-prone waters during the most dangerous months, he did not have any serious hurricane encounters on his early voyage. However, on his final voyages, Christopher Columbus himself weathered at least three of these dangerous storms. Columbus provided the earliest account of a hurricane in a letter written to Queen Isabella in 1494. In this letter he wrote, *"Eyes never beheld the seas so high, angry and covered by foam. We were forced to keep out in this bloody ocean, seething like a pot of hot fire. Never did the sky look more terrible; for one whole day and night it blazed like a furnace. The flashes came with such fury and frightfulness that we all thought the ships would be blasted. All this time the water never ceased to fall from the sky."*

By June of 1494, the small town of Isabella, founded by Columbus on Hispaniola, became the first European settlement destroyed by a hurricane. The Spaniards who accompanied Columbus on his four voyages to the New World took back to Europe with them a new concept of what a severe storm could be and, naturally, a new word of Indian origin. It seems that the Indian word was pronounced 'Furacán' or 'Furacánes' during the early years of discovery and colonization of America. Peter Martyr, one of the earliest historians of the New World, said that they were called by the natives 'Furacanes', although the plural is obviously Spanish. The Rev. P. du Tertre, (1667) in his great work of the middle of the seventeenth century, wrote first 'ouragan', and later 'houragan.'

After 1474 some changes in the Spanish language were made. For instance, words beginning with 'h' were pronounced using the 'f consonant.' The kingdoms of Aragon and Castile were united in 1474, before the discovery of America, and after that time some changes in the Spanish language were made. One of them involved words beginning with the letter 'h.' In Aragon they pronounced such words as 'f'. As Menéndez Pidal said, 'Aragon was the land of the 'f', but the old Castilian lost the sound or pronunciation, so that Spanish Scholar Nebrija (Nebrija wrote a grammar of the Castilian language, and is credited as the first published grammar of any Romance language) wrote, instead of the lost 'f', an aspirated 'h.' Menéndez wrote concerning the pronunciation of the word 'hurricane' and its language used by Fernando Colón, son of Christopher Columbus "Vacillation between 'f' and 'h' is very marked predominance of the 'h.' And so, the 'h' became in Spanish a silent letter, as it still is today." Father Bartholomew Las Casas, referring to one of these storms wrote: *"At this time the four vessels brought by Juan Aguado were destroyed in the port (of Isabella) by a great tempest, called by the Indians in their language 'Furacán.' Now we call them hurricanes, something that almost all of us have experienced at sea or on land..."* In fact, Las Casas, outraged by the brutal treatment of the Indians on Hispaniola, declared that the wrath of the hurricane which struck Hispaniola was the judgment of God on the city and the men who had committed such sins against humanity. All other European languages coined a word for the tropical cyclone, based on the Spanish 'Huracán.' Gonzalo Fernandez de Oviedo (Oviedo y Valdes, 1851, Book VI, Ch. III) is more explicit in his writings concerning the origin of the word 'hurricane.' He says: *"Hurricane, in the language of this island, properly means an excessively severe storm or tempest; because, in fact, it is only a very great wind and a very great and excessive rainfall, both together or either these two things by themselves."* Oviedo further noted that the winds of the *'Huracán'* were so *"fierce that they topple houses and uproot many large trees."*

Even in the English Language the word 'hurricane' evolved through several variations, for example, William Shakespeare mentioned it in his play 'King Lear' where he wrote *"Blow, winds, and crack your cheeks! Rage! Blow! You catracts and hurricanes, spout till you have drench'd out steeples, drown'd the cocks!"* Girolamo Benzoni, in 1565 in his Book *History of the New World* he mentioned his encounter with a hurricane in Hispaniola which at the time he referred to it as *'Furacanum'*: *"In those days a wondrous and terrible disaster occurred in this country. At sunrise such a horrible, strong wind began that the inhabitants of the island thought they had never seen or heard anything like it before. The raging storm wind (which the Spaniards called Furacanum) came with great violence, as if it wanted to spit heaven and earth apart from one another, and hurl everything to the ground...The people were as a whole so despairing because of their great fear that they run here and there, as if they were senseless and mad, and did not know what they did...The strong and frightful wind threw some entire houses and capitals including the people from the capital, tore them apart in the air and threw them down to the ground in pieces. This awful weather did such noticeable damage in such a short time that not three ships stood secure in the sea harbour or came through the storm undamaged. For the anchors, even if they were yet strong, were broken apart through the strong force of the wind and all the masts, despite their being new, were crumpled. The ships were blown around by the wind, so that all the people in them were drowned. For the most part the Indians had crawled away and hidden themselves in holes in order to escape such disaster."*

As stated earlier, Christopher Columbus did not learn on his first voyage, the voyage of discovery, of the existence of such terrible 'tempests' or 'storms.' He had the exceptional good fortune of not being struck by any of them during this voyage. The Indians, while enjoying pleasant weather had no reason to speak about these storms to a group of strangers who spoke a language which they could not understand. Naturally, Columbus did not say one word about these awful storms in his much celebrated letter *"The letter of Columbus on the Discovery of*

America." However, on his second voyage things were quite different. After arriving on November 3, 1493, at an island in the Lesser Antilles which he named Dominica, Columbus sailed northward and later westward, to Isabella Hispaniola, the first city in the New World, at the end of January, 1494. Then in June of that year, 1494, Isabella was struck by a hurricane, the first time that European men had seen such a terrible storm. Surely, for the first time, they heard the Taíno Indians, very much excited; extending their arms raised upward into the air and shouting: *"Furacán! Furacán!"* when the storm commenced. We can indeed say that it was that moment in history, when the word *'Hurricane'* suddenly appeared to the Europeans. Columbus was not at that time in Isabella because he was sailing near the Isle of Pines, Cuba. So his companions of the ships *Marigalante* and *Gallega* were the first white men to hear these words, which were of Indian origin and about a phenomenon of the New World. Knowledge of 'Furacanes,' both the word and the terrifying storms it described, remained limited to Spanish speakers until 1555, when Richard Eden translated Columbus's ship report and other Spanish accounts of the New World, making it the first time it appeared in the English vocabulary.

In October of 1495, probably in the second half of the month, another hurricane struck Isabella, which was much stronger than the first. It finally gave Columbus, who was there at the time, the opportunity of knowing what a hurricane was and of its destructive ability. It also gave him the opportunity of hearing the Indians shouting the same word with fear and anxiety on their faces, on the account of these terrible storms of the tropics, which they believed were caused by evil spirits. Columbus reported in his log: *"The tempest arose and worried me so that I knew not where to turn; eyes never beheld the seas so high, angry, and covered with foam…Never did the sky look more terrible. The people were so worn out, that they longed for death to end their terrible suffering."* Christopher Columbus would later declare that *"nothing but the service of God and the extension of the monarchy"* would induce him to expose himself to such danger from these storms again. 'The Niña' was the only vessel which was the smallest, oldest and the most fragile at the time but amazingly withstood that hurricane, the two other ships of Columbus, 'The San Juan' and 'The Cordera,' were in the harbour and were lost or badly damaged by this hurricane. Columbus gave orders to have one repaired and another ship known as *India* constructed out of the wreck of the ones which had been destroyed, making it the first ship to be built in the Caribbean by Europeans.

In 1502 during his fourth voyage, Columbus warned the Governor Don Nicolas de Orvando of Santo Domingo of an approaching hurricane, but he was ignored; as a result a Spanish treasure fleet set sailed and lost 21 of 30 ships with 500 men. Columbus had a serious disagreement with the bureaucrats appointed by Spain to govern the fledgling colonies in the Caribbean to extract gold, pearl and other precious commodities from the native Indians. Among the more unfriendly of these exploiters was Don Nicolas de Orvando, the Governor of Hispaniola, with whom Columbus had been forbidden to have any contact with by the request of his Spanish sovereigns. But as Columbus approached Santa Domingo, he recognized the early signs of an approaching hurricane, such as large ocean swells and a veil of cirrostratus clouds overhead. Concerned for the safety of his men and ships, he sent a message to Governor Orvando begging him to be allowed to seek refuge in Santa Domingo Harbour. Columbus had observed that the Governor was preparing a large fleet of ships to set sail for Spain, carrying large quantities of gold and slaves, and warned him to delay the trip until the hurricane had passed. Refusing both the request and the advice, Orvando read Columbus's note out loud to the crew and residents, who roared with laughter at Columbus's advice. Unfortunately, the laughter was very short-lived and Orvando's ships left port only to their own demise when 21 of the 30 ships were lost in a hurricane between Hispaniola and Puerto Rico. An additional four of them were badly damaged but fortunately they were able to return to port where they too eventually sunk. Only one ship, the *Aguja*, made it to Spain, and that one, no doubt to Orvando's intense distress, was carrying what little remained of Columbus's own gold.

Meanwhile, Columbus, anticipating strong winds from the north from this hurricane, positioned his fleet in a harbour on the south side of Hispaniola. On the 13th of June, the storm hit with ferocious northeast winds. Even with the protection of the mountainous terrain to the windward side, the fleet struggled. In Columbus's own words, *"The storm was terrible and on that night the ships were parted from me. Each one of them was reduced to an extremity, expecting nothing save death; each one of them was certain the others were lost."* The anchors held only on Columbus's ship; the others were dragged out to sea, where their crews fought for their lives. Nevertheless, the fleet survived with only minimal damage. Almost 18 months later, Columbus returned to Santo Domingo, only to discover that it had been largely destroyed by the hurricane.

When the Europeans first attempted to create settlements in the Caribbean and the Americas, they quickly learned about these storms. As time passed and these settlers learned more about their new homeland, they experienced these storms on such a regular basis that they became accustomed to them. Eventually, they began calling them equinoctial storms, as the storms would normally hit in the weeks around the period of the fall equinox, which in the northern hemisphere occurs in late September. English explorers and privateers soon contributed their own accounts of encounters with these storms. In 1513 Juan Ponce de León completed the first recorded cruise along the Florida coast and came ashore near present-day St. Augustine to claim Florida for Spain. Famous for his unsuccessful search for the magical Fountain of Youth, he might have discovered Florida earlier had it not been for the ravages of hurricanes. In August of 1508, he was struck by two hurricanes within two weeks. The first drove his ship onto the rocks near the Port of Yuna, Hispaniola, and the second left his ship aground on the southwest coast of Puerto Rico. Soon after Hernando Cortés found treasures of gold and silver in the newly discovered lands of West, expeditions to retrieve the riches of the New World for Spain began in earnest. In 1525 Cortés lost the first ship he sent to Mexico in a severe hurricane, along with its crew of over seventy persons. Famous English explorer Sir John Hawkins wrote his own encounters with these storms. Sir John Hawkins wrote that he left Cartagena in late July 1568 *"Hoping to have escaped the time of their stormes…which they call Furicanos."* Hawkins did not leave soon enough, and he and his ships were bashed by an *"extreme storme"* as he referred to it, lasting several days.

English Explorer Sir Francis Drake encountered several major hurricanes while sailing the dangerous seas of the Americas and the Atlantic Ocean and in most cases these encounters changed the course of West Indian and American history. Sir Francis Drake, who travelled the seas of the globe in quest of glory and plunderage, nearly lost his fleet on the Outer Banks of Carolina. One of his most famous encounters was with a major hurricane which occurred while he was anchored near the ill-fated Roanoke colony in present day North Carolina in June of 1586. His ships were anchored just off the banks while he checked on the progress of Sir Walter Raleigh's colonists on Roanoke Island. The hurricane lasted for three days, scattering Drake's fleet and nearly destroying many of his ships. There was no greater thorn in the side of the Spanish than Francis Drake. His exploits were legendary, making him a hero to the English but a simple pirate to the Spaniards and for good reasons because he often robbed them of their valuable treasures. To the Spanish, he was known as *El Draque*, "the Dragon"; "Draque" is the Spanish pronunciation of "Drake." As a talented sea captain and navigator, he attacked their fleets and took their ships and treasures. He raided their settlements in America and played a major role in the defeat of the greatest fleet ever assembled, the "Spanish Armada."

No other English seaman brought home more wealth or had a bigger impact on English history than Drake. At the age of 28 he was trapped in a Mexican port by Spanish war ships. He had gone there for repairs after an encounter with one of his first major hurricanes at sea. Drake escaped but some of the sailors left behind were so badly treated by the Spanish that he swore revenge. He returned to the area in 1572 with two ships and 73 men. Over the next fifteen months he raided Spanish towns and their all important Silver train across the isthmus from Panama. Other English accounts reported ships damaged or lost in storms characterized by extreme wind and rain, some of which were definitely hurricanes. The English (including Drake and Hawkins) had a great respect for hurricanes, to such an extent that, as the hurricane season was understood to be approaching, more and more pirates went home or laid up their ships in some sheltered harbour until the last hurricane had passed and was replaced by the cool air of old man winter.

Probably those that first discovered the period of the year in which hurricanes developed were Spanish priest, officers of the navy or army, or civilians that had lived for a long time in the Caribbean. By the end of the sixteenth century they should have already known the approximate period that these hurricanes occurred. The Roman Catholic Church knew early on that the hurricane season extended at least from August to October because the hierarchy ordered that in all of the churches in the Caribbean to say a special prayer to protect them from these deadly hurricanes. The prayer which had to be said was: *'Ad repellendas tempestates,'* translated to mean '*for the repelling of the hurricanes or tempests.*' It was also ordered that the prayer should be said in Puerto Rico during August and September and in Cuba in September and October. This indicates that it was known that hurricanes were more frequent in those islands during the months mentioned. Eventually, West Indian colonists through first hand experiences with these storms gradually learned that hurricanes struck the Caribbean within a well-defined season. Initially, those early colonists believed that hurricanes could strike at any time of the year, but by the middle of the seventeenth century most of them recognized that there was a distinct hurricane season. This was because the hurricanes simply occurred too frequent within a particular time period for them to remain strange and unusual in their eyes. Numerous letters and reports written by colonists specifically discussed the period between July and October as the *'time of hurricanes.'*

The geography of hurricanes challenged the concept of these storms as 'national judgments or divine favor' by which God spoke to a specific group of people or country. Individual storms routinely struck various islands colonized by different European powers. For example, in 1707 a hurricane devastated the English Leeward Islands, the Dutch Islands of Saba and St. Eustatius, and the French Island of Guadeloupe. In 1674, a Dutch attack on the French Islands was thwarted by a hurricane, which also caused significant damage in the English Leeward Islands and in Barbados. The presence of hurricanes made colonists question their ability to transform the hostile environment of the Caribbean and by extension their ability to establish successful and stable societies here. But hurricanes raised other questions as well: What caused them? What forces gave rise to such powerful and dangerous storms? For some-probably a significant majority during the first several decades of the seventeenth century-they believed that these storms came directly from the hands of God. They interpreted hurricanes as 'wondrous events,' divine judgments for human sins. Others linked hurricanes to various natural processes, including shifting wind patterns. The explosion of various natural processes, including shifting wind patterns, the explosion of various chemicals in the atmosphere, and the celestial movement of the planets and stars.

CHAPTER TWO

THE NAMING OF HURRICANES

Atlantic Tropical Cyclone Names

2011	2012	2013	2014	2015	2016
Arlene	Alberto	Andrea	Arthur	Ana	Alex
Bret	Beryl	Barry	Bertha	Bill	Bonnie
Cindy	Chris	Chantal	Cristobal	Claudette	Colin
Don	Debby	Dorian	Dolly	Danny	Danielle
Emily	Ernesto	Erin	Edouard	Erika	Earl
Franklin	Florence	Fernand	Fay	Fred	Fiona
Gert	Gordon	Gabrielle	Gonzalo	Grace	Gaston
Harvey	Helene	Humberto	Hanna	Henri	Hermine
Irene	Isaac	Ingrid	Isaias	Ida	Igor
Jose	Joyce	Jerry	Josephine	Joaquin	Julia
Katia	Kirk	Karen	Kyle	Kate	Karl
Lee	Leslie	Lorenzo	Laura	Larry	Lisa
Maria	Michael	Melissa	Marco	Mindy	Matthew
Nate	Nadine	Nestor	Nana	Nicholas	Nicole
Ophelia	Oscar	Olga	Omar	Odette	Otta
Philippe	Patty	Pablo	Paulette	Peter	Paula
Rina	Rafael	Rebekah	Rene	Rose	Richard
Sean	Sandy	Sabastien	Sally	Sam	Shary
Tammy	Tony	Tanya	Teddy	Teresa	Tomas
Vince	Valerie	Van	Vicky	Victor	Virginie
Whitney	William	Wendy	Wilfred	Wanda	Walter

Information Courtesy of NOAA.

Hurricanes are the only weather disasters that have been given their own iconic names, such as, Hurricane Andrew, Gilbert, Katrina, Camille or Mitch. No two hurricanes are the same but like people; they share similar characteristics but yet still they have their own unique stories to tell. The naming of storms or hurricanes has undergone various stages of development and transformation. Initially, the word 'Hurricane' accompanied by the year of occurrence was used, for example, *'the Great Hurricane of 1780'* which killed over 22,000 persons in Martinique, Barbados and St. Eustatius. Another example was *'the Great Storm of 1703'* whose incredible damage of the British Isles was expertly detailed by Robinson Crusoe's author, Daniel Defoe. The naming scheme was substituted by a numbering system (e.g. Hurricane #1, #2, #3 of 1929 etc…) however; this became too cumbersome and confusing, especially when disseminating information about two or more storms within the same geographical area or location.

For the major hurricanes of this region, they were often named after the particular country or city they devastated. This was especially true for severe hurricanes which made their landing somewhere in the Caribbean. Three notable examples were, *'the Dominican Republic Hurricane of 1930'* which killed over 8,000 persons in the Dominican Republic, *'the Pointe-a-Pitre Hurricane of 1776'* which devastated the country of Guadeloupe and killed over 6,000 persons and devastated it's largest city and economic capital of Pointe-a-Pitre. Third was *'the Great Nassau Hurricane of 1926'* which devastated the city of Nassau in the Bahamas during the 1926 North Atlantic hurricane season. In some cases they were even named after the holiday on which they occurred, for example, *'the Great Labour Day Hurricane of 1935.'* The Great Labour Day Hurricane of 1935 was the strongest tropical cyclone during the 1935 North Atlantic hurricane season. This compact and intense hurricane caused extensive damage in the Bahamas and the upper Florida Keys. To this day, *the Great Labour Day Hurricane of 1935* is the strongest and most intense hurricane on record to ever have struck the United States in terms of barometric pressure. *The Great Labour Day Hurricane of 1935* was one of the strongest recorded hurricane landfalls worldwide. It was the only hurricane known to have made landfall in the United States with a minimum central pressure below 900 Mbar; only two others have struck the United States with winds of Category 5 strength on the Saffir-Simpson Scale. It remains the third-strongest North Atlantic hurricane on record, and it was only surpassed by Hurricane Gilbert (888Mbar) in 1988 and Hurricane Wilma (882Mbar) in 2005. In total, at least 408 people were killed by this hurricane.

In some cases they were named after the ship which experienced that particular storm. Two notable examples were: - '*The Racer's Storm of 1837*' and '*The Sea Venture Hurricane of 1609.*' The *1837 Racer's Storm* was a very powerful and destructive hurricane in the 19th century, causing 105 deaths and heavy damage to many cities on its 2,000+ mile path. *The Racer's Storm* was the 10th known tropical storm in the 1837 North Atlantic hurricane season. *The Racer's Storm* was named after the British war ship *HMS Racer* which encountered the storm in the extreme northwest Caribbean on September 28th. Another example was *The Sea Venture Hurricane of 1609*. In July 28th of 1609, a fleet of seven tall ships, with two pinnaces in tow carrying 150 settlers and supplies from Plymouth, England to Virginia to relieve the starving Jamestown colonists was struck by a hurricane while en route there. They had been sent by the Virginia Company of London to fortify the Jamestown settlement. Sir George Somers mission was to resupply the six hundred or so pioneers who a year before had settled in the infant British colonial settlement of King James's Town, sited in one of the estuaries south of the Potomac River. *The Sea Venture* was grounded at Bermuda which for some time was called *Somers Island* after the ship's captain, Admiral Sir George Somers. After being struck by this hurricane, *The Sea Venture* sprung a leak and everyone on board worked frantically to save this ship and their lives by trying to pump the water out of the hull of the ship. They tried to stem the flow of water coming into the ship by stuffing salt beef and anything else they could find to fit into the leaks of the ship. After this proved futile most of the crew simply gave up hope, falling asleep where they could, exhausted and aching from their relentless but futile efforts. But just as they were about to give up and face the grim reality that they would be loss to the unforgiving Atlantic Ocean, they spotted the island of Bermuda. Somers skillfully navigated the floundering *Sea Venture* onto a reef about half a mile to the leeward side of Bermuda. They used the ship's long boat to ferry the crew and passengers ashore.

The passengers of the shipwrecked *Sea Venture* became Bermuda's first inhabitants and their stories helped inspire William Shakespeare's writing of his final play '*The Tempest*' making it perhaps the most famous hurricane in early American history. *"And another storm brewing,"* William Shakespeare wrote in *The Tempest*. *"I hear it sing in the wind."* Most of those venturing to the New World had no knowledge of the word or the actual storm. The lead ship, the three-hundred-ton *Sea Venture*, was the largest in the fleet and carried Sir Thomas Gates, the newly appointed governor of the colony, and Sir Georges Somers, admiral of the Virginia Company. It is interesting to note that Shakespeare did not name his play *'The Hurricane.'* He actually did know the word *"hurricano"* because it appears in two earlier plays, *King Lear* and *Troilus and Cressida.* Maybe he recognized that such a title would be confusing and unfamiliar to most of his audience, so he chose a more familiar word *'The Tempest'* instead. Though the island was uninhabited, Spaniards had visited Bermuda earlier and set ashore wild pigs. The shipwrecked passengers fed on those wild pigs, fish, berries and other plentiful game on the island. Although they yearned to stay in that island paradise, they managed to make two vessels *Patience* and the *Deliverance* out of what was left of the *Sea Venture* and ten months later they set sailed for Jamestown. However, some persons remained on the island and became the first colonists of that island, including Admiral Sir George Somers who initially left with the other Jamestown passengers but eventually returned and died on that island.

In some instances, hurricanes were named after important persons within this region; one such storm was, the *'Willoughby Gale of 1666.'* The word *'gale'* during these colonial times was often interchanged with the word 'hurricane' but they often meant the same thing-a hurricane and not the official term we now use today for the definition of a 'meteorological gale.' This storm was named after the British Governor of Barbados, Lord Francis Willoughby who lost his life aboard the flagship *Hope* along with over 2,000 of his troops in his fleet during this hurricane. He was appointed Governor of Barbados by Charles II in May of 1650 and attempted to negotiate the strained politics of that island, which also experienced a division between the Royalists and Parliamentarians. His last act on behalf of the English Crown came in July 1666 when, having learned of the recent French seizure of St. Kitts, he formed a relief force of two Royal Navy Frigates, twelve other large vessels (including commandeered merchant ships), a fire ship, and a ketch, bearing over 2,000 men.

Lord Willoughby had planned to proceed north to Nevis, Montserrat, and Antigua to gather further reinforcements before descending on the

French. Leaving Barbados on July 28, his fleet waited for the French just off the coast of Martinique and Guadeloupe, where he sent a frigate to assault the harbour and ended up capturing two French merchant vessels on August 4. This success could not be exploited however, as that night most of his force was destroyed by a strong hurricane, including the flagship *Hope*, from which Willoughby drowned in this ship during the storm. This hurricane occurred in 1666 and was a very intense storm which struck the islands of St. Kitts, Guadeloupe, and Martinique. The fleet was actually caught by surprise by this hurricane after leaving Barbados en-route to St. Kitts and Nevis to aid the colonists there to help battle against the French attacks. After the storm, only two vessels from this fleet were ever heard from again and the French captured some of these survivors. All of the vessels and boats on the coast of Guadeloupe were dashed to pieces. For a period in the late seventeenth century, some colonists referred to especially powerful and deadly hurricanes as "Willoughby Gales." Personal names were also used elsewhere in this region, for example, *'Saxby's Gale'* which occurred in Canada in 1869, and was named after a naval officer who was thought to have predicted it.

Another example was, the *Daniel Defoe Hurricane of 1703* which occurred in November of 1703 and moved from the Atlantic across to southern England. It was made famous by an obscure political pamphleteer, Daniel Defoe. It was six years before he wrote the world famous book *Robinson Crusoe*. At the time the hurricane struck, he needed money so the storm gave him the idea of collecting eye-witness accounts of the storm and publishing it in a pamphlet. He printed and sold this pamphlet under the very strange and exceptionally long title of *'The storm or collection of the Most Remarkable Casualties and Disasters which happened in the late Dreadful Tempest both by Sea and Land.'* In total, around 8,000 sailors lost their lives, untold numbers perished in the floods on shore, and 14,000 homes, 400 windmills and 16,000 sheep were destroyed. Some of the windmills burned down, because they turned so fast in the fierce winds that friction generated enough heat to set them on fire. The damage in London alone was estimated to have cost £2 million (at 18th century prices).

An additional example was, the *Benjamin Franklin Hurricane of October 1743*, which affected the Northeastern United States and

New England, brought gusty winds and rainy conditions as far as Philadelphia, and produced extensive flooding in Boston. This was the first hurricane to be measured accurately by scientific instruments. John Winthrop, a professor of natural philosophy at Harvard College, measured the pressure and tides during the storm passage. This storm, which wasn't particularly powerful but was memorable because it garnered the interest of future patriot and one of the founders of the United States, Benjamin Franklin, who believed the storm was coming in from Boston. He was wrong, because it was actually going to Boston. From this information, he surmised that the storm was travelling in a clockwise manner from the southwest to northeast. Putting two and two together, Franklin concluded that the low pressure system was causing the storm to move in this manner.

One aspect of the Earth's general circulation is that storms are not stationary; they move, and in somewhat predictable ways. Until the mid-eighteenth century, it had been generally assumed that storms were born, played out, and died in a single location and that they did not move across the Earth's surface. Benjamin Franklin had planned to study a lunar eclipse one evening in September 1743, but the remnants of this hurricane ruined his evening. This was a big disappointment to him, because he had been looking forward to this lunar eclipse that this storm had obscured. His curiosity aroused, Franklin gathered additional details about the storm by reading the Boston newspapers and learned that the storm had moved up the Atlantic seaboard and against the surface winds. He learned that this hurricane struck Boston a day later, sending flood tides sweeping over the docks, destroying boats, and submerging waterfront streets. In the succeeding months he collected additional reports from travellers and newspapers from Georgia to Nova Scotia, and satisfied himself that at least in this part of the world, storms have a tendency to take a northeasterly path up the Atlantic Coast. Thus science took the first step toward a basic understanding of hurricanes and their movements.

Benjamin Franklin is also popularly known for his off the wall weather experiment years later where during a thunderstorm, in 1752, he carried out a dangerous experiment to demonstrate that a thunderstorm generates electricity. He flew a kite, with metal objects attached to its string, high in the sky into a thunderstorm cloud (Cumulonimbus).

The metal items produced sparks, proving that electricity had passed along the wet string. After discovering that bolts of lightning were in fact electricity, with this knowledge Franklin developed the lightning rod to allow the lightning bolt to travel along the rod and safely into the ground. This discovery by Franklin is still used even to this day all over the world. A year later after Benjamin Franklin's famous kite flight, Swedish physicist G.W. Richmann conducted a similar experiment following Franklin's instructions to the letter, and as fate would have it, he was struck by a lightning which killed him instantly. Sailing home from France on the fifth of September, 1789, after his great years as a US Ambassador, Benjamin Franklin experienced a storm which may have been the same storm which devastated Dominica. He was eighty years old and suffering from "the Stone" but was busy observing the temperatures of the sea water, which would eventually lead to his discovery of the Gulf Stream.

Finally, there was the *Alexander Hamilton Hurricane of 1772*, which he experienced growing up as a boy living in the Caribbean on the island of St. Kitts in the Leeward Islands. This was an extremely powerful and deadly hurricane. He later on in life became the confidential aide to George Washington and his greatness rests on his Federalist influence on the American Constitution and much as on his financial genius as the first United States Secretary of the Treasury. Today he is featured on the U.S. ten dollar bill and he is one of two non-presidents featured on currently issued U.S. bills. The other is Benjamin Franklin who is found on the U.S. $100 bill. A westward moving hurricane hit Puerto Rico on August 28. It continued through the Caribbean, hitting Hispaniola on the 30th and later Jamaica. It moved northwestward through the Gulf of Mexico, and hit just west of Mobile, Alabama on the 4th. Many ships were destroyed in the Mobile area, and its death toll was very severe. In Pensacola, it destroyed most of the wharves. The most devastation occurred in the vicinity of Mobile and the Pasca Oocola River. All shipping at the Mouth of the Mississippi was driven into the marshes; this included the ship *El Principe de Orange* from which only 6 survived.

This storm was famously described by Alexander Hamilton, who was living on the island of St. Croix at the time, and wrote a letter about it to his father in St. Kitts. The letter was so dramatic and moving that it was published in newspapers locally on the island and first in New York and then in other states (please see my book- *'Rediscovering Hurricanes'* -for a complete copy of this letter), and the locals on St. Kitts raised enough money to have him brought to America to receive a formal education to make good use of his intellectual abilities. This was because, this letter created such a sensation that some planters of St. Kitts, in the midst of the hurricane devastation, took up a collection to send him to America for better schooling because they saw in him great potential. By 1774 he was a student at King's College, now Columbia University, in New York. On St. Kitts, the damage was considerable and once again, many houses were flattened, and there were several fatalities and many more injuries. Total damage from this storm alone was estimated at £500,000 on St. Kitts. The second storm struck just three days later causing even more significant damage to the few remaining houses on this island already battered by the previous storm in 1772.

Several claimants have been put forth as the originators of the modern tropical cyclone 'naming' system. However, it was forecaster Clement Lindley Wragge, an Australian meteorologist who in 1887 began giving women's names, names from history and mythology and male names, especially names of politicians who offended him to these storms before the end of the 19th century. He was a colourful and controversial meteorologist in charge of the Brisbane, Australia Government weather office. He initially named the storms after mythological figures, but later named them after politicians he didn't like. For example, Wragge named some of these storms using biblical names such as, Ram, Raken, Talmon, and Uphaz or the ancient names of Xerxes and Hannibal. Wragge even nicknamed one storm Eline, a name that he thought was reminiscent of *'dusty maidens with liquid eyes and bewitching manners.'* Most ingeniously, he gained a measure of personal revenge by naming some of the nastiest storms with politicians' names such as, Drake, Barton, and Deakin. By properly naming a hurricane, he was able to publicly describe a politician (perhaps a politician who was not too generous with the weather-bureau appropriations) as *'causing great distress'* or *'wandering aimlessly about the Pacific.'* By naming these storms after these hated politicians he could get a degree of revenge on them without suffering any repercussions from them. During his last days in office, he fought with the Australian Government over the right to issue national forecasts and he lost, and was fired in 1902.

For a while, hurricanes in the West Indies were often named after the particular Saint's Day on which the hurricane occurred. As Christianity took hold in the West Indies, the naming system of storms here in the Caribbean was based on the Catholic tradition of naming these storms with the 'Saint' of the day (e.g. San Ciprian on September 26th). This system for naming them was haphazard and not really a system at all. Powerful hurricanes hitting especially the Spanish speaking islands of the Caribbean got Catholic Saints' names. According to Historian Alejandro Tapia, the first hurricane to be named with the Saint of the day was the *Hurricane of San Bartolomé* which devastated Puerto Rico and the Dominican Republic on August 24th and 25th of 1568. The earlier tropical cyclones were simply designated by historians' years later after their passages.

One example of a great storm named after a Saint of the day was, *'Hurricane San Felipe'* which struck Puerto Rico on 13th September 1876. Another example was *'Hurricane San Felipe the Second'* which occurred strangely enough on the very same date 52 years later on 13th September of 1928 and was responsible for well over 3,433 deaths. Another hurricane which was named the *'Hurricane of Santa Elena'* struck Puerto Rico on 18th August, 1851 and caused massive casualties. Then there was the *'Hurricane of Santa Ana'* (in English, Saint Anne) which struck Puerto Rico and Guadeloupe on 26th July of 1825, the date of the feast in honour of the Mother of the Blessed Virgin, which killed over 1,300 persons. In addition, there was the *'Hurricane of San Ciriaco'* which killed 3,369 persons in Puerto Rico on 8th August of 1899 (feast day of Saint Cyriacus) and remains one of the longest duration tropical storms(28 days) to hit the Caribbean or anywhere in the world.

The tradition of naming storms after the Saint of the day officially ended with Hurricane Betsy in 1956 which is still remembered as the *'Hurricane of Santa Clara.'* However, years later with the passage of Hurricane Donna in 1960, the storm was recognized as the *'Hurricane of San Lorenzo.'* At this time, only the major hurricanes were given names so most storms especially the minor storms before 1950 in the North Atlantic never received any kind of special designation. This is why this hurricane in 1866 was never named but was simply referred to as *'The Great Bahamas Hurricane of 1866'* after the country it devastated. The word 'Great' simply meant that the hurricane was a powerful storm and that it had sustained winds of 136 mph or greater and a minimum central pressure of 28.00 inches or less (see later chapter on the classification of hurricanes).

Later, latitude-longitude positions were used. At first they listed these storms by the latitude and longitude positions where they were first reported. This was cumbersome, slow, open to error and confusing. For example, a name like *'Hurricane 12.8ºN latitude and 54.7ºW longitude'* was very difficult to remember, and it would be easy to confuse this storm with another that was seen two months later, but almost at the same location. In addition, this posed another significant problem, in the 1940's when meteorologists began airborne studies of tropical cyclones, ships and aircrafts communicated mainly in Morse code. This was fine for the letters of the alphabet, but it was awkward at dealing with numbers because it was slow and caused confusion among its users.

In this region, these early storms were often referred to as *Gales, Severe Gales, Equinoctial Storms,* or *Line Storms*. The latter two names referred to the time of the year and the location from which these storms were born (referring to the Equatorial line). Gauging the strength and fury of a seventeenth or eighteenth-century storm was quite a difficult task because at the time these colonists had no means of measuring the wind speeds of a hurricane. Contemporaries recognized a hierarchy of winds ranging from *'a stark calm'* to *'a small Gale'* to *'a Top-Sail Gale'* to *'a fret of wind'* and *'a Tempest'*-later replaced by the word 'hurricane'- but such terms offered little help in interpreting the power of hurricanes or differentiating lesser tropical storms from hurricanes. Furthermore, increased development of the built environment over time meant that the potential for damage, even from minor storms, increased as well, making damage estimates a questionable foundation for judging the power of storms.

Experience has shown that using distinctive names in communications is quicker and less subject to error than the cumbersome latitude-longitude identification methods. The idea was that the names should be short, familiar to users, easy to remember and that their use would facilitate communications with millions of people of different ethnic races threatened by the storm. This was because a hurricane can last for a week or more, and there can be more than one storm at a time, so weather forecasters starting naming these storms so that there would be absolutely no confusion when talking about a particular storm. Names are easier to use and facilitate better communications among individuals and meteorologists with language barriers within the same geographical region, such as within the Caribbean, Central America and North America.

The first U.S. named hurricane (unofficially named) was Hurricane George which was the fifth storm in 1947 season. George had top winds of 155 mph as it came ashore around midday on September 17 between Pompano Beach and Delray Beach. The second hurricane unofficially named was Hurricane Bess (named for the outspoken First Lady of the USA, Bess Truman, in 1949). The third storm was nicknamed by the news media 'Hurricane Harry' after the then President of the United States Harry Truman. United States Navy and Air Force meteorologists working in the Pacific Ocean began naming tropical cyclones during World War II, when they often had to track multiple storms. They gave each storm a distinctive name in order to distinguish the cyclones more quickly than listing their positions when issuing warnings.

Towards the end of World War II, two separate United States fleets in the Pacific lacking sufficient weather information about these storms were twice badly damaged when they sailed directly into them resulting in massive causalities. Three ships were sunk, twenty one were badly damaged, 146 planes were blown overboard, and 763 men were lost. One of the results that came out of these tragedies was the fact that all US Army and Navy planes were then ordered to start tracking and studying these deadly storms, so as to prevent similar disasters like those ones from occurring again. During World War II this naming practice became widespread in weather map discussions among forecasters, especially Air Force and Navy meteorologists who plotted the movements of these storms over the wide expanses of the Pacific Ocean. Using the convention of applying 'she' to inanimate objects such as vehicles, these military meteorologists beginning in 1945 in the Northwest Pacific started naming these storms after their wives and girlfriends. However, this practice didn't last too long for whatever reason, but my guess is that those women rejected or took offense to being named after something that was responsible for so much damage and destruction.

An early example of the use of a woman's name for a storm was in the best selling pocketbook novel "Storm" by George R. Stewart, published by Random House in 1941, and has since been made into a major motion picture by Walt Disney further promoting the idea of naming storms. It involved a young meteorologist working in the San Francisco Weather Bureau Office tracking a storm, which he called *Maria*, from its birth as a disturbance in the North Pacific to its death over North America many days later. The focus of the book is a storm named Maria, but pronounced 'Ma-Rye-Ah.' Yes, the song in the famous Broadway show *Paint Your Wagon* named "They Call the Wind Maria" was inspired by this fictional storm. He gave it a name because he said that he could easily say 'Hurricane Maria' rather than, *'the low pressure center which at 6pm yesterday was located at latitude one-seventy four degrees east and longitude forty-three degrees north'* which he considered too long and cumbersome. As Stewart detailed in his novel, *'Not since at any price would the Junior Meteorologist have revealed to the Chief that he was bestowing names-and girls' names-upon those great moving low-pressure areas.'* He unofficially gave the storms in his book women names such as, Lucy, Katherine and Ruth after some girls he knew because he said that they each had a unique personality. It is not known whether George Stewart was indeed the inspiration for the trend toward naming hurricanes which came along later in the decade, but it seems likely.

In 1950 military alphabet names (e.g. Able, Baker, Charley, Dog, Easy, Fox etc...) were adopted by the World Meteorological Organization (WMO) and the first named Atlantic hurricane was Able in 1950. The Joint Army/Navy (JAN) Phonetic Alphabet was developed in 1941 and was used by all branches of the United States military until the promulgation of the NATO phonetic alphabet in 1956, which replaced it. Before the JAN phonetic alphabet, each branch of the armed forces used its own phonetic alphabet, leading to difficulties in inter-branch communications. This naming method was not very popular, and caused a lot of confusion because officials soon realized that this naming convention would cause more problems in the history books if more than one powerful Hurricane Able made landfall and caused extensive damage and death to warrant retirement. This was because hurricanes that have a severe impact on the lives or the economy of a country or region are remembered for generations after the devastation they caused, and some go into weather history, so distinguishing one storm name from another is essential for the history books.

The modern naming convention came about in response to the need for unambiguous radio communications with ships and aircrafts. As air and sea transportation started to increase and meteorological observations improved in number and quality, several typhoons, hurricanes or cyclones might have to be tracked at any given time. To help in their identification, in 1953 the systematic use of only regular women names were used in alphabetical order and this lasted until 1978. The 1953's Alice was the first real human-named storm. At the time they named them after women because these meteorologists reasoned that people might pay more attention to a storm if they envisioned it as a tangible entity, a character, rather than just a bundle of wind. But the use of only women names eventually was rejected as sexist and forecasters finally went with both male and female names. Beginning in 1960, four semi-permanent sets of names were established, to be recycled after four years. This list was expanded to ten sets in 1971, but before making it through the list even once; these sets were replaced by the now familiar 6 sets of men and women names.

This naming practice started in the Eastern Pacific in 1959 and in 1960 for the remainder of the North Pacific. It is interesting to note that in the Northwest Pacific Basin the names, by and large, are not personal names. While there are a few men and women names, the majority of the Northwest Pacific tropical cyclone names are of flowers, animals, birds, trees, or even foods while some are just descriptive adjectives. In addition, the names are not allotted in alphabetical order but are arranged by the contributing nation with the countries being alphabetized. For example, the Cambodians have contributed Naki (a flower), Krovanh (a tree) and Damrey (an elephant). China has submitted names such as Yutu (a mythological rabbit), Longwang (the dragon king and god of rain in Chinese mythology), and Dainmu (the mother of lightning and the goddess in charge of thunder). Micronesian typhoon names include Sinlaku (a legendary Kosrae goddess) and Ewiniar (the Chuuk Storm god).

In the North Atlantic Basin in 1979, gender equality finally reached the naming process of hurricanes when thousands of sexism complaints written to the WMO and feminists groups in the USA and worldwide urged the WMO to add men's names, hence both men and women names were used alternately and this practice is still in use today. That year would also herald the practice of drawing up list of names in advance of the hurricane season and today an alphabetical list of 21 names is used. Hurricane Bob was the first North Atlantic storm named after a man in the 1979 hurricane season, however it was not retired (it would eventually be retired in the 1991 hurricane season). Hurricane David was the second storm named after a man and it was the first male storm to be retired in the North Atlantic Region. This was due to the great death toll and substantial damage it inflicted to the countries of Dominica, the Dominican Republic and the Bahamas during the last week of August and the first week of September in 1979.

Since 1979, the naming list now includes names from non-English speaking countries within this region, such as Dutch, French and Spanish names which also have a large presence here in the Caribbean. This is done to reflect the diversity of the different ethnic languages of the various countries in this region, so the names of Spanish, French, Dutch, and English persons are used in the naming process. The names of storms are now selected by a select committee from member countries of the World Meteorological Organization that falls within that particular region of the world, and we here in the Caribbean comes under Region IV for classification purposes. This committee meets once a year after the hurricane season has passed and before the beginning of the new hurricane season to decide on which names that are to be retired and to replace those names with a new set of names when and where necessary.

The practice of giving different names to storms in different hurricane basins has also led to a few rare circumstances of name-changing storms. For example, in October of 1988, after Atlantic Hurricane Joan devastated Central America, it proceeded to move into the Pacific and became Pacific tropical storm Miriam. Hurricane Joan was a powerful hurricane which caused death and destruction in over a dozen countries in the Caribbean and Central America. Another example was Hurricane Hattie, which was a powerful Category 5 hurricane that pounded Central America on Halloween during the 1961 North Atlantic hurricane season. It caused $370 million in damages and killed around 275 persons. Hattie is the only hurricane on record to have earned three names (Hattie, Simone, Inga) while crossing into different basins twice. Hattie swept across the Caribbean and came ashore in the town of Belize City, British Honduras (now called Belize), on October 31. It was a strong Category 4 hurricane at landfall, having weakened from a Category 5 hurricane just offshore. After making landfall, its remnants crossed over into the Pacific and attained tropical storm status again under the name Simone. In a remarkable turn of events, after Simone itself made landfall, its remnants crossed back over to the Gulf of Mexico, where the storm became Tropical Storm Inga before dissipating. However, it is debatable whether Inga in fact formed from the remnants of Simone at all.

It is interesting to note here that the letters Q, U, X, Y, and Z are not included in the hurricane list because of the scarcity of names beginning with those letters. However, in other regions of the world some of these letters are used, for example; only "Q" and "U" are omitted in the Northeastern Pacific Basin. When a storm causes tremendous damage and death, the name is taken out of circulation and retired for reasons of sensitivity. It is then replaced with a name of the same letter and of the same gender and if possible, the same language as the name being retired (e.g. neither Hurricane Andrew in 1992 nor Hurricane Katrina in 2005 will ever be used again). Since 1950, there were 73 hurricanes which had their names retired. The list includes one tropical storm, Allison of 2001, which caused billions in damage from its heavy rains.

The name used the most (at least with the same spelling is Arlene (seven times), while Frances and Florence have been used seven and six times respectively. However, considering different spellings of the same name, Debbie/Debby has been used seven times, and Anna/Ana has been used eight times. The first name to be called into use five times was Edith, but that name hasn't been used since 1971. After the 1996 season, Lilly has the distinction of being the first 'L' name to be used three times, while Marco is the first 'M' name to be used more than once. The name Kendra was assigned to a system in the 1966 hurricane season, but in post-season analysis it was decided it had not been a bona fide tropical storm. This storm marked the birth of reclassification of storms in the post-hurricane season (Hurricane Andrew was a storm that was reclassified from a Category four hurricane to a Category five hurricane in the off season).

In only three years (2005, 1995, 2010) have names beginning with the letter 'O' and beyond have been used, but there have been several other years in which more than 14 storms have been tracked such as: 1887-19 storms, 1933-21 storms, 1936-16 storms, 1969-18 storms, 1995-19 storms, 2005-28 storms and 2010-19 storms. The 2010 North Atlantic hurricane season has been extremely active, being the most active season since 2005. It must be noted that the 2010 season ties the record with the 1995 North Atlantic hurricane season and the 1887 North Atlantic hurricane season for the third most named storms (19). Furthermore, 2010 also ties the record with the 1969 North Atlantic hurricane season and 1887 for the second most hurricanes (12). The first three of these years were well before the naming of storms began, but 1969 requires an explanation. This was early in the era of complete satellite coverage, and forecasters were still studying the evolution of non-tropical systems (sub-tropical) into warm-core, tropical-type storms. Several systems that year were not named as tropical because they began at higher latitudes and were initially cold-cored.

Formal classification of subtropical(hybrid type) cyclones and public advisories on them began in 1972, and a few years later, a review was made of satellite imagery from the late 60's and early 70's and several of these systems were included as tropical storms. In fact, two of the storms added in 1969 were hurricanes, so 1969 now stands as having 12 hurricanes. Today, subtropical storms are named using the same list as tropical storms and hurricanes. This makes sense because subtropical cyclones often take on tropical characteristics. Imagine how confusing it would be if the system got a new name just because it underwent internal changes. There is no subtropical classification equivalent to a hurricane. The assumption is that once a storm got that strong it would have acquired tropical characteristics and therefore be called a hurricane or would have merged with an extratropical system in the North Atlantic and lost its name altogether. For example, on October 24, 1979, a subtropical storm briefly reached hurricane strength as it neared Newfoundland, Canada. It quickly combined with another low-pressure system but it was never named.

Whenever a hurricane has had a major impact, any country affected by the storm can request that the name of the hurricane be 'retired' by agreement of the World Meteorological Organization (WMO). Prior to 1969, officially, retiring a storm name actually meant that it cannot be reused for at least 10 years, to facilitate historic references, legal actions, insurance claim activities, etc…and to avoid public confusion with another storm of the same name. But today these storms are retired indefinitely and if that happens, a gender name is selected in English, Dutch, Spanish or French for North Atlantic storms. Other than that, the names are repeated every six years. It is interesting to note here that there hasn't been a case in the North Atlantic, where after 10 years of a name being 'retired' it was placed back on the list or re-used. Those hurricanes that have their names retired tend to be exceptionally destructive storms that often become household names in the regions or countries they affected. When that list of names is exhausted, the Greek Alphabet (Alpha, Beta, Gamma, Delta, Epsilon, Zeta, Eta, Theta, Iota, Kappa and Lambda) is used. It must be noted that so far this list has only been used once in either the Pacific or the Atlantic Basins, which was in the North Atlantic hurricane season of 2005. It is important to note here that there were a few subtropical storms which used the Greek Alphabet in the 1970's but they were really not truly tropical in nature.

If a storm forms in the off-season, it will take the next name on the list based on the current calendar date. For example, if a tropical cyclone formed on December 29th, it would take the name from the previous season's list of names. If a storm formed in February, it would be named from the subsequent season's list of names. Theoretically, a hurricane or tropical storm of any strength can have its name retired; retirement is based entirely on the level of damage and death caused by a storm. However, up until 1972 (Hurricane Agnes), there was no Category 1 hurricane which had its name retired, and no named tropical storm had its name retired until 2001 (Tropical Storm Allison). Allison is the only tropical storm to have its name retired without ever having reached hurricane strength. This is at least partially due to the fact that weaker storms tend to cause less damage, and the few weak storms that have had their names retired caused most of their destruction through heavy rainfall rather than winds.

While no request for retirement has ever been turned down, some storms such as Hurricane Gordon in 1994 caused a great deal of death and destruction but nonetheless was not retired as the main country affected-Haiti did not request retirement. Hurricane Gordon in 1994 killed 1,122 persons in Haiti, and 23 deaths in other nations. Damage in the United States was estimated at $400 million, and damages in Haiti and Cuba were severe. Despite the tremendous damage caused, the name 'Gordon' was not retired and was reused in both the 2000 and 2006 North Atlantic hurricane seasons. Since 1950, 73 storms have had their names retired. Of these, two (Carol and Edna) were reused after the storm for which they were retired but were later retroactively retired, and two others (Hilda and Janet) were included on later lists of storm names but were not reused before being retroactively retired. Before 1979, when the first permanent six-year storm names list began, some storm names were simply not used anymore. For example, in 1966, 'Fern' was substituted for 'Frieda,' and no reason was cited.

In the North Atlantic Basin in most cases, a tropical cyclone retains its name throughout its life. However, a tropical cyclone may be renamed in several situations. First, when a tropical storm crosses from the Atlantic into the Pacific, or vice versa, before 2001 it was the policy of National Hurricane Center (NHC) to rename a tropical storm which crossed from Atlantic into Pacific, or vice versa. Examples included Hurricane Cesar-Douglas in 1996 and Hurricane Joan-Miriam in 1988. In 2001, when Iris moved across Central America, NHC mentioned that Iris would retain its name if it regenerated in the Pacific. However, the Pacific tropical depression developed from the remnants of Iris was called Fifteen-E instead. The depression later became Tropical Storm Manuel. NHC explained that Iris had dissipated as a tropical cyclone prior to entering the eastern North Pacific Basin; the new depression was properly named Fifteen-E, rather than Iris. In 2003, when Larry was about to move across Mexico, NHC attempted to provide greater clarity: *"Should Larry remain a tropical cyclone during its passage over Mexico into the Pacific, it would retain its name. However, a new name would be given if the surface circulation dissipates and then regenerates in the Pacific."* Up to now, it is extremely rare for a tropical cyclone to retain its name during the passage from Atlantic to Pacific, or vice versa.

Second, storms are renamed in situations where there are uncertainties of the continuation of storms. When the remnants of a tropical cyclone redevelop, the redeveloping system will be treated as a new tropical cyclone if there are uncertainties of the continuation, even though the original system may contribute to the forming of the new system. One example is the remnants of Tropical Depression #10 reforming into Tropical Depression #12 from the 2005 season which went on to become the powerful and deadly Hurricane Katrina. Another example was a storm which had the most names as stated earlier; in 1961 there was one tropical storm which had three lives and three names. Tropical Storm Hattie developed off the Caribbean Coast of Nicaragua on October 28, 1961, and drifted north and west before crossing Central America at Guatemala. It re-emerged into the Pacific Ocean on November 1 and was re-christened Simone. Two days later it recurved back towards the coastline of Central America and crossed over into the Atlantic via Mexico, re-emerging into the Gulf of Mexico as Inga.

CHAPTER THREE

THE ANATOMY OF HURRICANES

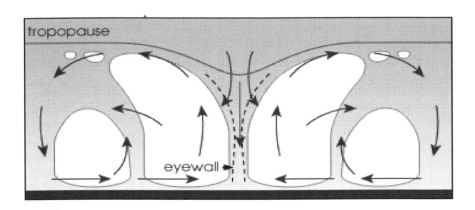

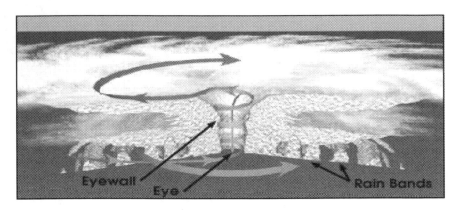

A Cross-sectional view into a hurricane (Courtesy of NOAA). Hurricanes form when the energy released by the condensation of moisture in rising air causes a chain reaction. The air heats up and rises further, which leads to more condensation. The air flowing out of the top of this 'Chimney' drops towards the ground, forming powerful winds. (Graphic by Robert Simmons, NASA GSFC)

From space, hurricanes look stunningly beautiful but the images mask a sequence of terrifying events. Although the rate at which the hurricane moves across the Earth is relatively slow, perhaps only 10-15 mph, the incredible speeds within the hurricane system is perhaps its key feature. A tropical storm becomes a hurricane when it develops sustained wind speeds of 74 mph or more but a major hurricane can cause wind speeds in excess of 155 mph. As the intense rays of the summer sun warms the ocean's surface, evaporation and convection transfer enormous amounts of heat and moisture into the atmosphere, fueling the birth of tropical cyclones. Warm water vapour rises, cools, and condenses, forming billowing clouds, scattered showers, and thunderstorms. Newborn thunderstorms grow and multiply, many produced in passing tropical waves-low-pressure troughs that drift westward through the equatorial waters. Some waves become tropical depressions as thunderstorms build, pressures drop, and low-level circulation develops. If conditions are favorable, a depression can intensify until sustained winds reach 39 mph, at which time it becomes a tropical storm. Once the tropical storm's rotation becomes well organized, its central pressure falls, and sustained winds reach 74 mph, a hurricane is born.

A hurricane's immense power is capable of killing thousands of people and captures the imagination of people all around the world, even those who expect never to experience such a storm. The complex interaction of the forces that create hurricanes and similar storms makes them even more fascinating to those who want to learn a little about how nature works. News images and reports of the recent hurricanes physical and human devastation to many areas of the Caribbean, Central and North America demonstrated to the world not only the power of strong hurricanes, but also the consequences both to individuals and to society of not being prepared to cope with such storms despite ample warnings. While a hurricane lives, the transaction of energy within its circulation is immense. A couple of facts help illustrate the power of hurricanes; first the average hurricane precipitates a trillion gallons of water a day and second, the condensation heat energy released by a hurricane in one day can be equivalent of the energy released by the fusion of 400 20-megaton bombs. To demonstrate this fact, one day's released energy, converted to electricity, could supply the United States' electrical needs for about six months. Hurricane Andrew in 1992 had the equivalent power of an atomic bomb exploding every minute when it made landfall in South Florida. Hurricanes are neither the largest nor strongest storms, but their combination of size and strength definitely makes them the deadliest and most destructive storms on Earth.

Many early ideas and concepts about the origin and structure of hurricanes were well founded in observations and reasons, while others were long held traditions and beliefs. Sometimes there was a connection between traditional ideas and scientific thoughts. For example, most persons before the introduction of modern meteorological offices and instruments, often predicted the onset of a hurricane by observing the tidal changes before the storm, something that is still practiced today but on a more refined and scientific level and it is now referred to as the 'storm surge.' To understand how hurricanes work, and to improve forecasts, meteorologists need detailed information from the heart of the storm. From birth, the hurricane lives in an environment that constantly tries to kill it-and ultimately succeeds. The hurricane tends to survive while it is over warm waters but forces drive the storm ashore or over colder waters beyond the tropics. In these non-nourishing environments it will eventually fade out and die.

During the more recent hurricane seasons, considered to be some of the most active North Atlantic seasons on record, meteorologists investigated hurricanes from top to bottom and from side to side to get as much information about these storms as possible. By using this information, they can gather vital information about the anatomy of hurricanes which can ultimately lead to a greater improvement in hurricane forecasting and evacuation plans, which can ultimately result in saving many more lives and reduced property damages. Known simply as hurricanes in this region and tropical cyclones by meteorologists, they claim more lives and cause more damage each year than any other storm or weather phenomena combined. When a full-blown hurricane strikes, trees are ripped up, power lines are torn down and buildings flattened and totally destroyed by raging winds, gusting up to 200 mph. Large areas are swamped by torrential rainfall, and coastal regions can be completely devastated by the storm surge. Here in the North Atlantic hurricane basin, we are affected by an average of 10 tropical storms per year. Of this total six to eight become hurricanes and two to three of these becomes major hurricanes. However, in some years there are wide variations from these figures. For example, in 2005 there were a record of twenty eight tropical storms and 14 of those became hurricanes, but in 1929 and 1930 there were only three and two hurricanes respectively in those years.

The requirement of relatively high sea-surface temperatures of 26.5°C or greater also makes hurricane occurrences distinctly seasonal. These storms need a tremendous amount of energy, which limits the areas where they can develop. They have to form over the oceans, in locations where the water temperature is greater than the threshold of 26.5°C or greater. If the water temperature is lower, the storm will actually lose energy to the ocean surface. That's why a hurricane weakens when it moves into colder waters or over land areas because its heat gets absorbed by the cooler land mass or water. Because of the great thermal stability of ocean water, sea-surface temperatures reach a seasonal maximum long after the time of the peak solar radiation. Consequently, most North Atlantic hurricanes develop in the late summer and early autumn months; the official hurricane season in the North Atlantic runs from 01st June to 30th November.

The summer solstice, 21st June, marks the official beginning of summer north of the Equator, and is the longest day of the year. It is not, however the hottest day of the year. This is because a phenomenon known as 'seasonal temperature lag,' the hottest time of the year lags behind the time you might logically expect to encounter it. This is because the Earth is slow to absorb and release heat energy, during the late summer months it gets showered with more energy from the sun than it can immediately re-radiate back into space. The temperature keeps building as long as the Earth keeps absorbing more energy than it loses, with the peak coming well after the summer solstice has passed. With the coming of autumn and shorter days, the Earth catches up, and starts radiating heat energy back into space faster than the sun can pour it on. That's when the temperature starts to fall. It continues to fall reaching its lowest point well after the winter solstice, until the next spring when the heat starts building again. This seasonal lag in temperature has a great effect on the formation of hurricanes in the North Atlantic. Ocean waters cover about 75% of the tropics, and this water reflects only about 5% of the solar energy reaching it. The rest is absorbed and this vast quantity of energy that warms both the ocean water and the air above it evaporates large amounts of it to create the typically warm and humid tropical climate, which are ideal conditions for hurricanes to form and thrive.

Hurricanes may reach the Caribbean between June and November, but they are most common in August and September where on average 84 % of these deadly storms occur. The reason for this is simple; in the summer water must be absorbed by three times as much energy as compared to the land, in order to have the same ambient temperature. In addition, the winds must continually perturb the ocean, thereby allowing the colder waters from the deep to mix with the surface waters. This oceanic lag postpones the meteorological onset of summer by a month beyond its astronomical onset, so because of this factor, the warmer months are late July, August and early September rather than in June the astronomical date for summer. In other words, it takes several more weeks for the oceans to reach their warmest temperatures of 26.5 Celsius or greater. Furthermore, the atmospheric circulation in the tropics also reaches its most pronounced and favorable conditions for tropical cyclone development at the same time. As a result of these factors, it is one of the reasons why most of the hurricanes form in late July, August and early September rather than in June.

From a personal perspective, meteorologists have learned that hurricanes don't usually go by the rules of scientific law or statistics because they seem to have a mind of their own at times. Pick up any text book on hurricanes and it will tell you that the one place where hurricanes do not form is in the South Atlantic Ocean. The atmosphere does not provide enough spin near the surface to get them started, the sea surface temperature is not warm enough to support hurricanes and winds higher in the atmosphere tend to shear off any that do make a start. Hence, it was with some amazement that meteorologists from around the world watched the first ever recorded hurricane (officially in the South Atlantic they are called 'cyclones' but for uniformity and clarity I will use the word 'hurricane') to develop off the east coast of Brazil in the last week of March, 2004. Initially the storm did not look much like a hurricane, but gradually it developed some common characteristics with some of its counterparts which develop in the North Atlantic Ocean. It also acquired enough characteristics to convince the majority of the world's tropical cyclone experts that it was indeed a hurricane even though it occurred outside of traditional hurricane basins and was called Hurricane Catarina.

Although hurricanes have created much misery, they can also be beneficial. Hurricanes often provide much-needed rain to drought-stricken coastlines. Their ocean interactions can flush bays of pollutants, restoring the ecosystem's vitality. After the record rainfall from Hurricane Claudette in 1979 in Texas, fish were being caught in the northern industrialized reaches of Galveston Bay that had vanished for several years. Finally, in cruel Darwinian fashion, weak sea life and plants perish during a hurricane, leaving only the strong to survive and reproduce. In this same manner, sometimes hurricanes 'correct' humanity's mistakes. For example, in the early 1900's nonnative foliage, such as Australian pine trees, had been planted on the tip of Key Biscayne, Florida (now the Bill Baggs State Park). These nonnative plants had very few natural enemies in their new environment, and quickly dominated the plant life, resulting in a loss of the natural habitat of that area. However, these Australian nonnative trees lacked the ability to withstand hurricane-force winds because of their shallow roots, and Hurricane Andrew came along and destroyed them all in 1992. It was only then that park officials seized the rare opportunity to replant the park with native foliage.

In the North Atlantic there are four different types of hurricanes that influence us in some way or the other. The first is the Cape Verde Type hurricane which as its name suggests originates off the African Coast in the vicinity of the Cape Verde Islands. Initially it moves in a westerly direction and then in a west-northwest to a northwesterly direction as it makes it way through the Caribbean. The Cape Verde Islands is an archipelago about 400 miles off the West African Coast and are volcanic in nature. It was colonized by Portugal in the fifteenth century and became an independent country in 1975. At one point in their history, these islands served as an outpost station for the movement of African slaves on the 'Middle Passage' to the Americas. This type of hurricane forms over the Atlantic mainly during the early to mid parts of the season, June through mid September months when the easterly waves are most dominant weather features in the Caribbean region. At the beginning and the middle of the hurricane season, storms also tend to form near the Bahamas and this type has come to be known as '*Bahama Busters*' according to world renowned Professor William Gray from Colorado State University. An example of this type was Hurricane Katrina in 2005, which formed just east to the Bahamas and moved initially westward and then northwestward into the Gulf of Mexico and then over Louisiana.

Another type of hurricane is the Gulf of Mexico type, which as its name suggest originates in the Gulf of Mexico and travels northward from its inception and mainly influences Latin America, and the Gulf Coast of the United States. Finally, there is the Western Caribbean type which forms during the early and late parts of the hurricane season and forms in the most favoured location near the Gulf of Honduras or the southern Caribbean Sea mainly in May through June, and mid-September through late November. The formations of these cyclones are due in part to the seasonal movement of the Inter-Tropical Convergence Zone, also known as the Equatorial Trough. From its inception this type of hurricane seems to take a northward movement, which normally takes a track over the island of Cuba and into the Bahamas, the severity of which is influenced by how long the cyclone remains over the mountainous terrain of Cuba.

The nature of hurricanes varies with their age, size and position, but the following features generally characterize most fully developed hurricanes: -

- They are tropical, meaning that they are generated in tropical areas of the ocean near the Equator.
- They are cyclonic, meaning that their winds which weaken with height swirl around a central *eye*. Wind direction is counterclockwise (west to east) in the Northern Hemisphere and clockwise (east to west) in the Southern Hemisphere.
- They are low-pressure systems. The eye of a hurricane is always a low-pressure area and in this area air sinks at the center of the hurricane. The lowest barometric pressures ever recorded on Earth have occurred inside hurricanes.
- The winds swirling around the center of the storm have a sustained speed of at least 74 mph.
- Their main source of energy is from latent heat of condensation

Size:

In the Caribbean, the average diameter of a well-developed hurricane is between 100 to 500 miles, but some have reached diameters of 800 miles. The diameter of the eye, or calm center, of a well-developed hurricane is on average between 10 to 20 miles across. The largest eye ever observed was 56 miles in radius, which was measured from a reconnaissance aircraft during Tropical Cyclone Kerry in the Coral Sea, off the north-east coast of Australia on February 21, 1979. The size of a typical tropical cyclone can vary considerably depending on the extent of the wind and rain fields. Typhoon Tip in October of 1979 is considered the largest tropical cyclone on record at 1350 miles (2170 km) wide. The storm weakened greatly before landfall, but still caused widespread flood damage across most of Japan during the 1979 Pacific typhoon season. Tip is sometimes regarded as the first known 'Super Typhoon.' While Cyclone Tracy in December of 1974 is the smallest tropical cyclone on record at only 60 miles (96 km) wide, it is sometimes referred to as a 'midget' hurricane. Cyclone Tracy was a tropical cyclone which devastated the city of Darwin, Australia, from December 24 to December 25, 1974. After forming over the Arafura Sea, the storm moved southward and affected the city with Category 4 winds on the Australian cyclone intensity scale and the Saffir-Simpson hurricane Scale, although there is evidence to suggest that it had reached category 5 when it made landfall.

Speed:

Like a top spinning swiftly around its axis and 'walking' slowly across the floor, the forward movement of the entire mass of a hurricane is relatively slow compared to the speed of its rotating winds. Hurricanes generally move at a speed of between 10 to 15 miles per hour, but sometimes these storms can go much faster than their average speeds or even remain stationary over one spot for a while. In the Atlantic, the average hurricane moves about 300 to 400 miles a day or about 3,000 miles in its average nine-day life. However, some hurricanes can last three weeks and travel 10,000 miles. The longest-lived tropical storm in the Atlantic Basin history was the third storm of the 1899 season, known as the San Ciriaco Hurricane after a town it devastated on the island of Puerto Rico and was a storm for a total of 33 days from August 3rd until September 4th 1899 (This however, was before the days of satellite coverage so this can never really be officially confirmed). Another example, tropical Storm Ginger in 1971 spun around in the open ocean for 27.25 days in the Atlantic. However, officially the longest lasting and furthest travelling cyclone ever observed was Hurricane/Typhoon John (it crossed the International Date Line twice, it changed status from hurricane to typhoon and back to a hurricane) which lasted a total of 31 days in the 1994 hurricane season.

Movement:

The movements of hurricanes are subject to pressure systems of the surrounding atmosphere, as well as the influence of prevailing winds and of the spinning Earth. While some hurricanes travel in a general curved or parabolic path, others change course quite abruptly. They have been known to reverse direction, zig-zag, turn back around towards the equator, make loops, stall, return to the same area, and move in every direction of the compass. These changes usually occur as the storm passes through areas of light and variable winds between the prevailing easterlies and westerlies. They are also influenced by the presence of highs and lows. High pressure areas act as barriers, and if a high is well developed, its outward-spiraling flow will guide the hurricane around its edges. Low pressures, on the other hand, can tend to draw the hurricane system toward their slowly inward rotating winds. With all these pushes and pulls, the hurricane can follow a seemingly erratic route.

Winds:

Of all the tropical cyclone damaging agents, strong winds are perhaps the best understood of all of them. Damaging winds will accompany any hurricane, no matter what category it is. A hurricane by definition has winds of at least 74 miles per hour. This wind speed alone is enough to cause great damage to poorly constructed signage and knock over some of the sturdiest trees and other vegetation. Obviously, the stronger the hurricane (higher winds), the more potential there is for wind damage to exists. The fierce winds which blow in an anti-clockwise direction around the centre of the central calm in the northern hemisphere may reach 100 to 200 mph. Wind speeds are the greatest near the surface around the central calm or eye. However, when ever a hurricane touches a landmass its wind speed is significantly reduced. Two factors accounts for this abrupt drop in wind speed once a hurricane makes landfall. Over land a hurricane is no longer in contact with its energy source of warm ocean water. Furthermore, the increased surface roughness over land weakens the system. The land surface is rougher than the sea surface so that when a hurricane moves over land, its surface winds are slowed and blow at a greater angle across isobars and toward the storm center. This wind shift causes the storm to begin to fill, that is, the central pressure rises, the horizontal pressure gradient weakens, and the winds slacken. The energy released in a normal hurricane is great. An average hurricane winds are so great that it is equipped with some 1.5 trillion watts of power in its winds which if converted to electricity would be equivalent to about half of the world's entire electrical generating capacity. In fact, in a single day, a hurricane can release the amount of energy necessary to supply all of the United States electrical needs for about six months. One second of a hurricane's energy is equivalent to about ten Hiroshima atomic bombs and in total, a single hurricane during its lifetime can dissipate more energy than that contained in thirty thousand atomic bombs. The hurricane which hit Galveston, Texas, in September, 1900, during its lifespan had sufficient energy to drive all the power stations in the world for four years. A large hurricane stirs up more than a million miles of atmosphere every second.

The force of the wind can quickly decimate the tree population, tear down power lines and utility poles, knock over signs, and may be strong enough to destroy some homes and buildings. Flying debris can also cause damage, and in some cases where people are caught outdoors, injuries and death can prevail. When a hurricane first makes landfall, it is common for tornadoes to form which can cause severe localized wind damage. In most cases, however, wind is a secondary cause of damage. Storm surge is normally the primary cause. The right front quadrant is strongest side of the hurricane, this is the area where there is positive convergence, in this quadrant the winds are typically the strongest, the storm surge is highest, and the possibility of tornadoes are the greatest. The right side of a hurricane is the strongest side because the wind speed and the hurricane speed-of-motion are complimentary there; meaning on this side, the wind blows in the same direction as the storm's forward motion.

On the left side, the hurricane's speed of motion subtracts from the wind speed because the main bulk of the storm is moving away from it. The storm's angle of attack is a key factor in its impact. Just as in an automobile accident, the highest level of destruction is caused by a hurricane hitting the coastline head-on. If a storm travels up the coast, with its left side brushing the seashore, the most dangerous part of the storm stays offshore and the net effect will be much less damage. The worst-case scenario would be a hurricane arriving onshore at high or spring tide. With the ocean level already at its highest point of the day, the storm surge from a Category four or five hurricane can add another 15 to 20 feet of water, with abnormally large waves breaking on top of that. Water weighs around 1,700 pounds per cubic yard, and there are very few structures that can stand up to the force a high storm surge can produce.

The Sea Level Atmospheric Pressure:

The atmospheric pressure is defined as the force per unit area exerted against a surface by the weight of the air above the surface. In the tropics this varies by only about 0.3%, but during the passage of the central low pressure of a hurricane, it may fall by 5% or 10% below the average of 29.2 inches or 989 Millibars. Super Typhoon Tip in the Northwest Pacific on October 12, 1979 had the lowest central pressure ever measured in a tropical cyclone of 870mb and powerful Hurricane Wilma in 2005 had the lowest North Atlantic pressure reading of 882mb.

Clouds:

The solid cumulonimbus or rain clouds, which surrounds the core and within the spiral rainbands, makes up the main part of the hurricane and may extend for a radius of 100 miles around the eye and reach heights of 40,000 to 50,000 feet or more. Within the eye the sky is generally clear and rain-free.

Rainfall:

Virtually all literal use of the word hurricane in literary works evokes violent wind. Yet some of the worst tropical cyclone catastrophes are caused not by winds but by torrential rain (e.g. Hurricane Katrina in 2005). Rainfall associated with hurricanes is both beneficial and harmful. Although the rains contribute to the water needs of the areas traversed by the hurricane, the rains are harmful when the amount is so large as to cause extensive flooding. There are about four factors that determine how much rain will fall in a given place: the amount of water vapour in the air, topography, the vertical extent and duration of the updraft. In fact, some of the most devastating floods are produced by tropical cyclones of sub-hurricane strength. The torrential rainfall which normally accompanies a hurricane can cause serious flooding. A recent and especially tragic example of this is that of Hurricane Mitch of 1998, the deadliest North Atlantic hurricane since the Great Hurricane of 1780. Floods produced by Mitch killed more than 10,000 people in Central America, and the President of Honduras declared that Mitch destroyed 50 years of progress in that country. Whereas, the storm surge and high winds are concentrated near the eye, the rain may extend outward for hundreds of miles away from the center and may last for several days, affecting areas well after the hurricane has diminished or passed over a particular area.

An average of 10 to 15 inches of rain falls over coastal areas during the passage of a well-developed hurricane, but over 20 inches have been recorded and rain may fall at the rate of one inch an hour. In twenty-four hours a record of 32.67 inches of rain fell at Belize City in Belize from Hurricane Keith in 2000, for comparison, the average annual rainfall of Belize is about 74.4 inches. Furthermore, Hurricane Camille dumped over 760 millimeters (30 inches) of rainfall over Central Virginia, drowning 109 persons in the process with flash flooding. For comparison, the average annual rainfall of Central Virginia is about 45.22 inches. The Cedar Key Hurricane of September, 1950, poured nearly 39 inches of rain in 24 hours on Yankeetown, Florida, off the Gulf Coast. This 9-day hurricane traced an unusual double loop in the Cedar Keys area, and the coast from Sarasota northward suffered extensive wind and flood damage. The coastal area inland from Yankeetown to Tampa was flooded for several weeks. In 1963 Pacific Hurricane

Season, Typhoon Gloria dumped in 49.13 inches of rainfall in Baxin, Taiwan. While in the 1967 Pacific Typhoon Season 65.83 inches felled at Xinliao in Taiwan during a 24 hour period from Typhoon Carla. For comparison, the average annual rainfall of Xinliao, Taiwan is about 85 inches. However, Tropical Cyclone Denise in Foc-Foc in the La Reunion Island on the 7th and 8th of January, 1966 holds a world record of 45 inches in just 12 hours and 71.80 inches of rainfall in 24 hours in the same location for the total amount of rainfall over a particular location from a tropical cyclone.

Eye:

This is the most recognizable feature found within a hurricane and is an area at the center of the hurricane consisting of clears skies but can also have scattered to broken to even overcast clouds. Within the eye, the winds are light, the surface pressure is very low and there is almost no rain and it can have a diameter of 20 to 40 miles across. The eye is the warmest part of the hurricane and has the lowest pressure reading. The eye is the calmest part of the storm because the strong surface winds converging towards the center never actually reach the exact center of the storm, but instead form a cylinder of relatively calm air.

Eyewall:

Adjacent to the eye is the eyewall, a ring or wall of intense thunderstorms that whirl around the storm's center and extend upward to almost 50,000 feet above sea level. Within the eyewall, we find the heaviest rainfall and the strongest winds. This is the most dangerous part of the hurricane and the winds in this area may blow up to 155mph and gusting up to 225mph in severe storms. The winds spiral in a counterclockwise direction into the storm's low-pressure center. In several hurricanes, meteorologists have documented a phenomenon called 'eyewall replacement' in which a second eyewall forms around the eye. The inner eyewall collapses and temporarily weakens the storm. The outer eyewall then contracts and takes its place strengthening the storm again.

Spiral Bands:

Long bands of rain clouds that appear to spiral inward to the eyewall, these are called spiral rainbands or feeder bands and can be hundreds of miles across. Surface winds increase in speed as they blow counterclockwise and inward toward the center. These bands become more pronounced as the storm intensifies, and are fed by the warm oceans.

The Height:

A hurricane may be as much as 9 miles or 50,000 feet high. This is equal to almost twice the height of Mount Everest, the highest mountain on Earth.

Storm Surge:

Violent hurricane winds may produce storm surges of up to 45 feet high at sea, and storm surges of over twenty feet may crash against the shores at speeds of up to 40 mph. Long swells may move outwards from the eye of a hurricane for more than 1,000 miles. These long swells are often the first visible signs of an approaching hurricane and are known as the *storm surge*. A storm surge, also called a *hurricane surge*, is the abnormal rise in the sea level caused by wind and pressure forces of a hurricane. It can be extremely devastating, and is in fact a major cause of damage and danger to life during the passage of a hurricane. It is estimated that 75% of all hurricane related deaths and injuries are caused by the storm surge and the remaining 20% of the 25% is simply caused by negligence. For example, persons out of curiosity venturing out into the peak of the storm and being killed by flying debris, or stepping on a live wire and getting electrocuted before the 'all-clear' is given.

The storm surge isn't just another wave pushed ahead of a storm; it acts like a gigantic bulldozer that can destroy anything in its path. Think of the storm surge as a moving wall of water weighing millions of tons. The storm surge itself is caused by the wind and pressure 'pushing' the water into the continental shelf and onto the coastline caused by a hurricane. The height of the storm surge is the difference between the observed level of sea surface and its level in the absence of the storm. In other words, the storm surge is estimated by subtracting the normal or astronomical tide from the observed or estimated storm tide.

The astronomical tide is the results from the gravitational interactions between the Earth, moon, and sun, generally producing two high and two low oceanic tides per day. Should the storm surge coincide with the high astronomical tide, several additional feet could be added to the water level, especially when the sun and moon are aligned, which produces the highest oceanic tides (known as syzygy).

Hurricanes have a vacuum effect on the ocean. The water is pulled toward the hurricane, causing it to 'pile up' like a small mountain. A mound of water forms under the center of a hurricane as the intensely low pressure draws water up. The shape of the shoreline and the ocean bottom has a great deal to do with a storm surge's magnitude. Over the ocean, this mound of water is barely noticeable, but it builds up as the storm approaches land. The surge's height as it reaches land depends upon the slope of the ocean floor at the coast. The more gradual the slope, the less volume of sea there is in which the surge can dissipate and further inland the water is displaced. This is why Hurricane Katrina did so much damage in 2005 and why areas like New Orleans in the United States will continue to remain vulnerable to future hurricanes. This dome of water can be up to 40 to 60 miles long as it moves onto the shoreline near the landfall point of the eye. A cubic yard of sea water weighs approximately 1,700 pounds and this water is constantly slamming into shoreline structures, even well-built structures get quickly demolished because this water acts like a battering ram on these vulnerable shoreline structures.

The highest storm surge ever recorded was produced by the 1899 Cyclone Mahina, which caused a storm surge of over 13 meters (43 feet) at Bathurst Bay, Australia. This value was derived from reanalysis of debris sightings and eyewitness reports, as a result it is controversial within the meteorological community, but clearly a phenomenal storm surge occurred. In the United States, the greatest recorded storm surge was generated by 2005's Hurricane Katrina, which produced a massive storm surge of approximately 9 meters (30 feet) high in the town of Bay St. Louis, Mississippi, and in the surrounding coastal counties, while Hurricane Camille came in second with 24 feet in 1969. The worst storm surge, in terms of loss of life, was the 1970 Bhola cyclone and in general the Bay of Bengal is particularly prone to tidal surges. In the Bay of Bengal area, often referred to as the "storm surge capital of the world", 142 moderate to severe storm surge events are on record from 1582 to 1991. These surges, some in excess of eight meters (26 feet), have killed hundreds of thousands of people, primarily in Bangladesh. The Caribbean Islands have endured many devastating surges as well. These powerful hurricanes listed above caused very high storm surge. However, worldwide storm surge data is sparse. Hurricanes and the accompanying storm surge they produce can even affect the very depths of the ocean. In 1975 some meteorological and oceanographic instruments were dropped from a research reconnaissance airplane in the Gulf of Mexico showed that Hurricane Eloise disturbed the ocean hundreds of feet down and created underwater waves that persisted for weeks.

Tropical Wave:

This is an inverted trough of low pressure that moves generally westward along with the trade winds. A trough is defined as a region of relative low pressure. Tropical waves occasionally intensify into tropical cyclones. They are also called *easterly waves*. The majority of the world's tropical cyclones form from easterly waves.

Tropical Disturbance:

A discrete tropical weather system of apparently organized thunderstorms or convection - generally 100 to 300 miles in diameter - originating in the tropics or subtropics, having a non-frontal migratory character, and maintaining its identity for 24 hours or more. Disturbances associated with perturbations in the wind field and progressing through the tropics from east to west are also known as *easterly or tropical waves*.

Tropical Depression:

An organized system of clouds and thunderstorms with a well defined circulation and maximum sustained winds of 20 to 33 knots. The tropical disturbance becomes classified as a tropical depression when a closed circulation is first observed and sustained winds are less than 33 knots or 39 mph.

Tropical storm:

An organized system of strong thunderstorms with a well defined circulation and maximum sustained winds of 34 to 63 knots. At this point the storm is given an assigned name.

Hurricane:

This the term used in North Atlantic basin to describe a severe tropical cyclone with a well defined circulation and having winds in excess of 64 knots (74mph) and capable of producing widespread wind damage and heavy flooding.

Hurricane season:

This is the part of the year having a relatively high incidence of hurricanes. The hurricane season in the North Atlantic runs from June 1 to November 30 each year.

Hurricane Alert:

A hurricane alert indicates that a hurricane poses a threat to a specific area or region within 60 hours and residents of the specified area should start to make any necessary preparations.

Hurricane Warning:

A warning is given when it is likely that a hurricane will strike a specific area within 36 hours. At this point residents should have completed the necessary preparations for the storm.

Hurricane Watch:

A hurricane watch indicates that a hurricane poses a threat to a specific area within 48 hours and residents of the area should be well into the process of preparation for the hurricane.

All Clear:

'All Clear' simply means that the hurricane or tropical storm has left the specific area and all the Alerts, Warnings, and Watches are lifted but the residents in that area should exercise extreme caution for downed power lines, debris, fallen trees, flooding etc.

Other Hurricane effects

Tornadoes:

Tornadoes are not normally a tropical phenomenon but are frequently spawned by hurricanes on crossing coastlines and islands. Tornadoes may form especially in the spiral rainbands of a hurricane as it moves onshore. The changing wind speeds with height acts like a huge twisting mechanism, thus allowing the possibility of tornado formation. Since tornadoes form in conjunction with strong convection, they are more likely to occur near the outer edge of the eyewall cloud or in the outer rainbands.

Lightning and Hail:

Lightning and hail are less frequent occurrences during hurricanes than other severe weather events like thunderstorms. Lightning is more frequent during a typical afternoon thunderstorm because there are more factors present that promote lightning development. The same reason generally holds true concerning hail during a hurricane. There will be some lightning during a hurricane but some of the 'flashes' will actually be electric transformers exploding or power lines sparking; sending an eerie glow in the sky.

Economic Impact:

How many persons died and what was the damage? These are the two most frequently asked questions about tropical cyclones and rightly so. The approximately 80 tropical cyclones that occur throughout the globe each year cause billions of dollars in damage and kill many thousands of persons. However, in addition to the cost, there may be some economic benefits to be derived from tropical cyclones. The direct or indirect costs from a tropical cyclone can be divided into a number of broad categories, some of which include, cost of damage, cost of preparedness, cost of the warning service, cost of relief, loss in business revenue and losses to fisheries and agriculture. Although we tend to focus on the losses due to a tropical cyclone, a complete economic study must also consider the benefits. In many arid regions in the tropics, a large portion of the annual rainfall comes from tropical cyclones. These rains often fill water reservoirs, save crops from drought and the economic agricultural gains more than offset the coastal losses. Another possible economic benefit of a tropical cyclone is the increase in some businesses during the recovery. In fact, outside aid may prompt a local economic boom in the affected community. However, the net economic impact on the country is still negative.

CHAPTER FOUR

The Classification of Hurricanes

THE SAFFIR-SIMPSON HURRICANE DAMAGE-POTENTIAL SCALE

Saffir-Simpson Hurricane Damage-Potential Scale

Scale Number (Category)	Central Pressure		Winds		Storm Surge		Damage
	Millibar	Inches	Miles per hour	Knots	Feet	Meters	
1	>=980	>=28.94	74-95	64-82	4-5	~1.5	Damage mainly to trees, shrubbery, and unanchored mobile homes
2	965-979	28.50-28.91	96-110	83-95	6-8	~2.0-2.5	Some trees blown down; major damage to exposed mobile homes; some damage to roofs of building
3	945-964	17.91-28.47	111-130	96-113	9-12	~2.5-4.0	Foliage removed from trees; large trees blown down; mobile homes destroyed; some structural damage to small building
4	920-944	27.17-27.88	131-155	114-135	13-18	~4.0-5.5	All signs blown down; extensive damage to roofs, windows, and doors; complete destruction of mobile homes; flooding inland as far as 10 kilometers (6 miles); major damage to lower floors of structures near shore
5	<920	<27.17	>155	>135	>18	>5.5	Severe damage to windows and doors; extensive damage to roofs of homes and industrial buildings; small buildings overturned and blown away; major damage to lower floors of all structures less than 4.5 meters (15 feet) above sea level within 500 meters of shore

Courtesy of the Department of Meteorology-Nassau, Bahamas. It must be noted that the Classification by central pressure came to an end in the 1990s, and wind speed alone is now used. These estimates of the central pressure that accompany each category are for reference only. Also, these surge values are for reference only. The actual storm surge experienced will depend on offshore bathymetry and onshore terrain and construction.

The Saffir-Simpson Hurricane Damage Potential Scale is a classification used for most western hemisphere tropical cyclones which exceed the intensities of "tropical depressions" and "tropical storms," and thereby become hurricanes. The scale divides hurricanes into five categories distinguished by the intensities of their sustained winds. Hurricanes are ranked according to strength and by the amount of damage they cause. The weakest hurricane is designated a Category 1 status with maximum sustained winds from 74 mph to 95 mph and an average storm surge of 4 to 5 feet above sea level. In contrast, a Category 5 hurricane has maximum sustained winds of greater than 155 mph and a storm surge of greater than 18 feet. Storm surge depends on many factors such as, the shape of the continental shelf just offshore, whether the hurricane makes landfall at high or low tide, and the location of the offshore and onshore winds relative to the eye of the hurricane.

As a result of the difficulty in relating the different and varying factors or characteristics of a hurricane to the destruction potential, the Saffir-Simpson Damage Potential Scale was developed in 1969 and completed in 1971. The scale was introduced to the general public in 1973, and saw widespread use after Neil Frank replaced Simpson at the helm of the National Hurricane Center in 1974. This scale was named for Herbert Saffir a civil engineer in Coral Gables, Florida and Robert Simpson, a meteorologist and the then Director of the National Hurricane Center in Miami, Florida. It has been used for well over 37 years to estimate the relative damage potential of a hurricane due to wind and storm surge. The initial scale was developed by Mr. Herbert Saffir (who at the time was well known as the father of the Miami's building codes) while working on commission from the United Nations to study low-cost housing in hurricane-prone areas. While performing the study, Saffir realized that there was no simple scale for describing the likely effects of a hurricane. Knowing the usefulness of the Richter Magnitude Scale in describing earthquakes, he devised a similar 1-5 scale based on wind speed that showed expected damage to structures. Saffir looked at the scale from an engineering point of view because he was well-versed in Miami's Building Codes. Saffir then gave the scale to the National Hurricane Center, and Simpson added in the likely effects of storm surge and flooding. Simpson became the Director of the National Hurricane Center in 1968 and he was already one of the world's leading authorities on tropical cyclones and a veteran of numerous Air Force and Navy flights into these hurricanes. Simpson later recalled that the National Hurricane Center at the time was having difficulty telling disaster agencies how much damage to expect from particular storms.

Using a mixture of structural engineering and meteorology, they constructed the Saffir-Simpson Damage Potential Scale because both men had first-hand experiences with hurricanes. It does not take into account rainfall or location, which means that a Category 3 hurricane which hits a major city will likely do far more damage than a Category 5 hurricane which hits a rural area. The Saffir-Simpson Scale classifies hurricanes into Categories 1,2,3,4, and 5, depending on the barometric pressure, wind speed, and storm surge and destruction. A Category 1 hurricane, for example, would inflict minimal damage, mainly to shrubbery, trees, foliage, unanchored structures, mobile homes, small craft, and low-lying areas that could become flooded. Whereas, a Category 5 hurricane would cause catastrophic damage, such as blown down trees, power lines, and poles; overturned vehicles; torn down or blown away buildings; complete destruction of mobile or manufactured homes and massive flooding. According to Robert Simpson, there is no reason for a Category 6 on the Saffir-Simpson Scale because it is designed to measure the potential damage of a hurricane to man-made structures. If the speed of the hurricane is above 156 mph, then the damage to a building will be "serious no matter how well it's engineered." However, the result of new technologies in construction leads some to suggest that an increase in the number of categories is necessary. This suggestion was emphasized after the devastating effects of the 2005 Atlantic hurricane season. During that record year Hurricane Emily, Hurricane Katrina, Hurricane Rita, and Hurricane Wilma all became Category 5 hurricanes. A few newspaper columnists and scientists have brought up the idea of introducing a Category 6 and amending the scale to include the risk of flooding but in most cases it is often rebuffed.

The practical usefulness of the Saffir-Simpson Scale is that it relates properties of the hurricane to previously observed damage. Until the Saffir-Simpson Damage Potential Scale was developed, hurricanes were referred to as, *Great (or Extreme) Hurricanes, Severe Hurricanes, or Minor, Minimal or Major Hurricanes.* A Minor Hurricane had maximum winds of 74 mph and a minimum central pressure of 29.40 inches. A Minimal hurricane had maximum winds of between 75 to 100 mph and a minimum central pressure of between 29.03 to 29.39 inches. A Major hurricane had winds between 101 to 135 mph and a minimal central pressure of 28.01 to 29.02 inches. An Extreme or Great hurricane had winds of 136 mph or over and a minimum central pressure of 28.00 inches or less. However, these terms are no longer used but may appear in historical materials now and then. It is important to note that when dealing with narrative descriptions of historical events, these determinations must be somewhat subjective. For the purposes of this book, these categories will be any storm causing devastating damage through either wind action or storm surge. Some authors over the years have used the word or terminology 'extreme' very loosely to describe the worst of these events but I will refrain from using that terminology. The word 'extreme' in my opinion would imply the 'peak' or 'maximum' of a very powerful and destructive storm. For this book, I prefer to use the more acceptable and more appropriate word of 'Great' to label these very destructive and powerful storms but I will mention it when it is only necessary. It is important to note that tropical storms are named but are not assigned a Saffir-Simpson category number.

Only a few Atlantic hurricanes have made landfall with winds estimated to have reached the rarefied extreme of 200 mph, at least in gusts. These includes, the Great Labour Day Hurricane of 1935 which passed over the Florida Keys (inspiring the classic Humphrey Bogart movie *Key Largo*); Hurricane Camille, which came ashore at Pass Christian, Mississippi in 1969, and Hurricane Andrew in 1992, which struck the lower Florida Peninsula. Some top wind speeds from some of these powerful Atlantic storms will never ever be known because in most cases the instruments were destroyed before they measured the worst of their respective winds. This is because very few anemometers are capable of accurately measuring the winds of a Category 5 hurricane. The list of Category 5 Atlantic hurricanes encompasses 32 tropical cyclones that reached the extremely rare Category 5 intensity on the Saffir-Simpson Hurricane Scale within the Atlantic Ocean (north of the equator), the Caribbean Sea and Gulf of Mexico. They are the most catastrophic hurricanes that can form on planet Earth. They are relatively rare in the North Atlantic Ocean, and generally occur only about once every three years on average in the North Atlantic basin. Only four times-in the 1960, 1961, 2005 and 2007 hurricane seasons-have multiple Category 5 hurricanes formed. Only in 2005 have more than two Category 5 storms formed, and only in 2007 has more than one made landfall at Category 5 strength.

The Classification of Tropical Cyclones Around the World

TERM:	DEFINITION:	REGION USED:	Season:
Tropical Cyclone	A non-frontal synoptic-scale low-pressure system originating over tropical or subtropical waters with organized convection (i.e., rain shower or thunderstorm activity) and definite cyclonic surface wind circulation.	Global	
Tropical Depression	A tropical cyclone with *maximum sustained surface winds* of less than 39 mph.	Global	
Tropical Storm	A tropical cyclone with *maximum sustained surface winds* of at least 39 mph but less than 74 mph.	Global	
Hurricane	A tropical cyclone with *maximum sustained surface winds* of at least 74 mph.	North Atlantic Ocean, Northeast Pacific Ocean east of the International Dateline, and the South Pacific Ocean east of 160°E.	June-November
Typhoon	A tropical cyclone with *maximum sustained surface winds* of at least 74 mph.	Northwest Pacific Ocean west of the International Dateline.	April-January
Severe Tropical Cyclone	A tropical cyclone with *maximum sustained surface winds* of at least 74 mph.	Southwest Pacific Ocean west of 160°E and Southeast Indian Ocean east of 90°E.	October-May
Severe Cyclonic Storm	A tropical cyclone with *maximum sustained surface winds* of at least 74 mph.	North Indian Ocean.	April-December

*Unfortunately, there are at least two definitions of this term in widespread use. Most countries (including us here in the Bahamas) use the World Meteorological Organization's definition, which is a ten-minute average wind at an elevation of ten meters. But the United States uses a one-minute average, which is almost always higher.

Tropical cyclones are ranked according to their maximum winds using several scales and methods depending on which area of the world they are located. These scales are provided by several bodies, including the World Meteorological Organization, the U.S. Joint Typhoon Warning Center, the National Hurricane Center in Miami, and the Bureau of Meteorology in Australia. The National Hurricane Center uses the Saffir-Simpson Scale for hurricanes in the eastern Pacific and Atlantic Basins. Australia uses a different set of tropical cyclone categories for their region. Many basins have different names of hurricane/typhoon/cyclone strength. The United States National Hurricane Center, the main governing body for hurricanes in the North Atlantic region classifies hurricanes of Category 3 and above as *Major Hurricanes*. Whereas, the U.S. Joint Typhoon Warning Center classifies typhoons with wind speeds of at least 150 mph (67 m/s or 241 km/h, equivalent to a strong Category 4 storm) as *Super Typhoons*. The term 'major hurricane' supplants the previously used term of *Great Hurricane* which was used throughout the 1950's and the 1960's.

The use of different definitions for maximum sustained winds creates additional confusion into the definitions of cyclone categories worldwide. The Saffir-Simpson Hurricane Scale is used only to describe hurricanes forming in the Atlantic Ocean and Northern Pacific Ocean east of the International Date Line. Other areas use their own classification schemes to label these storms, which are called 'cyclones' or 'typhoons' depending on the area where they occur around the world. The Australian Bureau of Meteorology uses a 1-5 scale called *Tropical Cyclone Severity Categories*. Unlike the Saffir-Simpson Scale, severity categories are based on the strongest wind gusts and not sustained winds. Severity categories are scaled somewhat lower than the Saffir-Simpson Scale. A Category 1 storm features gusts less than 126 km/h (78 mph), with a severity Category 2 tropical cyclone, being roughly equivalent to a Saffir-Simpson Category 1 hurricane, while gusts in a Category 5 cyclone are at least 280 km/h (174 mph).

The U.S. Joint Typhoon Warning Center classifies West Pacific typhoons as tropical cyclones with wind speeds greater than 73 mph (118 km/h). Typhoons with wind speeds of at least 150 mph (67 m/s or 241 km/h, equivalent to a strong Category 4 hurricane) are dubbed *Super Typhoons*. In the Southwestern Indian Ocean: (1) a "tropical depression" is a tropical disturbance in which the maximum of the average wind speed is 28 to 33 knots (51 to 62 km/h); (2) a "moderate tropical storm" is a tropical disturbance in which the maximum of the average wind speed is 34 to 47 knots (63 to 88 km/h); (3) a "severe tropical storm" is a tropical disturbance in which the maximum of the average wind speed is 48 to 63 knots (89 to 117 km/h); (4) a "tropical cyclone" is a tropical disturbance in which the maximum of the average wind speed is 64 to 89 knots (118 to 165 km/h); (5) an "intense tropical cyclone" is a tropical disturbance in which the maximum of the average wind speed is 90 to 115 knots (166 to 212 km/h); and (6) a "very intense tropical cyclone" is a tropical disturbance in which the maximum of the average wind speed is greater than 115 knots (greater than 212 km/h).

The Beaufort Wind Scale

Force	Wind (Knots)	WMO Classification	Appearance of Wind Effects On the Water	On Land
0	Less than 1	Calm	Sea surface smooth and mirror-like	Calm, smoke rises vertically
1	1-3	Light Air	Scaly ripples, no foam crests	Smoke drift indicates wind direction, still wind vanes
2	4-6	Light Breeze	Small wavelets, crests glassy, no breaking	Wind felt on face, leaves rustle, vanes begin to move
3	7-10	Gentle Breeze	Large wavelets, crests begin to break, scattered whitecaps	Leaves and small twigs constantly moving, light flags extended
4	11-16	Moderate Breeze	Small waves 1-4 ft, becoming longer, numerous whitecaps	Dust, leaves, and loose paper lifted, small tree branches move
5	17-21	Fresh Breeze	Moderate waves 4-8 ft taking longer form, many whitecaps, some spray	Small trees in leaf begin to sway
6	22-27	Strong Breeze	Larger waves 8-13 ft, whitecaps common, more spray	Larger tree branches moving, whistling in wires
7	28-33	Near Gale	Sea heaps up, waves 13-20 ft, white foam streaks off breakers	Whole trees in motion, resistance felt walking against wind
8	34-40	Gale	Moderately high (13-20 ft) waves of greater length, edges of crests begin to break into spindrift, foam blown in streaks	Whole trees in motion, resistance felt walking against wind
9	41-47	Strong Gale	High waves (20 ft), sea begins to roll, dense streaks of foam, spray may reduce visibility	Slight structural damage occurs, slate blows off roofs
10	48-55	Storm	Very high waves (20-30 ft) with overhanging crests, sea white with densely blown foam, heavy rolling, lowered visibility	Seldom experienced on land, trees broken or uprooted, "considerable structural damage"
11	56-63	Violent Storm	Exceptionally high (30-45 ft) waves, foam patches cover sea, visibility more reduced	
12	64+	Hurricane	Air filled with foam, waves over 45 ft, sea completely white with driving spray, visibility greatly reduced	

Information Courtesy of the Department Of Meteorology, Nassau, Bahamas.

This was a scale that was developed by Sir Francis Beaufort in 1805 of the British Navy and was based solely on human observation. The Beaufort Wind Scale is now universally used around the world by seamen and lay persons alike. In 1805-06 Commander Francis Beaufort (Later Admiral Sir Francis Beaufort) devised a descriptive wind scale in an effort to standardize wind reports in ship's logs. As a result of this scale we have hurricane winds starting at 64 knots. His scale divided wind speeds into 14 Forces (later reduced to thirteen) with each Force assigned a number, a common name, and a description of the effects such a wind would have on a sailing ship. Since the worst storm an Atlantic sailor was likely to run into was a hurricane that name was applied to the top Force on the scale. During the 19th century, with the manufacture of accurate anemometers, actual numerical values were assigned to each Force Level, but it wasn't until 1926 (with revisions in 1939 and 1946) that the International Meteorological Committee (predecessor of the World Meteorological Organization) adopted a universal scale of wind speed values. It was a progressive scale with the range of speed for Forces increasing as you go higher. Thus, Force 1 is only 3 knots in range, while the Force 11 is 8 knots in range and Force 12 starts out at 64 knots (74 mph). There is nothing magical in this number, and since hurricane force winds are a rare experience, chances are the committee which decided on this number didn't do so because of any real observations during a hurricane.

Indeed the Smeaton-Rouse wind scale in 1759 pegged hurricane force winds at 70 knots (80 mph). Just the same, when a tropical cyclone has maximum winds of approximately these speeds we do see the mature structure (eye, eyewall, spiral rainbands) begin to form, so there is some unity with setting hurricane force winds in this neighbourhood. For example, if whole trees moved and resistance was felt while walking against the wind and the waves produced white foam with streaks on it then the observer would categorize it as a gale. In the 1800's and early 1900's Bahamian fishermen used this Beaufort Wind Scale almost exclusively to gauge the intensity of a storm. If a tropical storm or hurricane was in the vicinity of the Bahamas, many Bahamians (especially the older ones) would say that 'gale was travelling.' Even in historical records in the Bahamas, many of these storms were simply referred to as 'gales' or 'severe gales' rather than hurricanes or tropical storms. This often resulted in many of these storms going unreported or under-reported because a gale in meteorological terms simply meant that these storms had sustained wind speeds of between 34 to 47 knots (39 to 54 mph) as opposed to 64 knots (74 mph) or greater for a hurricane. Although the traditional definition of a hurricane is Beaufort Force 12 winds ('air filled with foam, sea completely white with driving spray, visibility greatly reduced'), nowadays the Saffir-Simpson Scale is used, especially in this region of the world. It is a scale which is used as a quick means of informing not only meteorologists, but also the public, of the relative intensity of an approaching storm.

In Meteorology as in nature, the elements always try to achieve a perfect balance but thankfully they never do. For example, a hurricane's main objective is a simple one, to take heat from the equator to the poles and likewise, the cold front's objective is similarly to take cold air from the poles to the equator but thankfully none of them ever gets to achieve their objectives so they continue trying in this never ending cycle and the result is life here on Earth as we know it today. The sun is our only source of heat on a global scale. Around 70% of the Earth's surface is covered in water-mostly the oceans. Since water holds heat energy better than the land, our tropical oceans are extremely efficient in storing energy transmitted by the sun. So the heat generated by the sun and stored in the oceans is the first major ingredient for fueling hurricanes. Hurricanes form over tropical waters where the winds are light, the humidity is high in a deep layer, and the surface water temperature is warm, typically 26.5 degrees Celsius or greater over a vast area, often between latitudes 5 degrees to 25 degrees north or south of the equator. Over the tropical and subtropical North Atlantic and North Pacific oceans these conditions prevail in the summer and early fall; hence, the hurricane season normally runs from June through November. At this time the water is hot enough to create atmospheric convection that casts moisture 10 miles up into the atmosphere.

These extremely hazardous weather systems occur most commonly across the low-latitude Northwest Pacific and its 'downstream' land areas, where on average just over a third of the global total of such storms develop. In an average year there are approximately 80 of these Tropical Cyclones which form over warm tropical oceans with 48 of them becoming hurricanes and 20 of them becoming intense hurricanes. Many residents within this region perceive the North Atlantic Ocean basin a prolific producer of hurricanes because of the worldwide publicity these storms generate. In reality, the North Atlantic is generally only a marginal basin in terms of hurricane activity. Every tropical ocean except the South Atlantic and Southeast Pacific contains hurricanes; several of these tropical oceans produce more hurricanes annually than the North Atlantic. Hurricanes are generally a summer phenomenon, but the length of the hurricane season varies in each basin, as does the peak of activity. The Northeast Pacific averages 17%, the Northwest Pacific averages just over 33%, while the North Atlantic typically sees about 12% of the world's total of tropical cyclones, while the other regions accounts for the remaining 38%(the percentages may vary from year to year and basin to basin but these are just conservative averages) of the world total of hurricanes. Additionally, most basins use a 10-minute average of sustained wind speeds to determine intensity, as recommended by the WMO, but this is not the case in the North Atlantic and Northeastern Pacific regions, where 1-minute averages, almost always higher, are used.

Tropical Cyclone Map

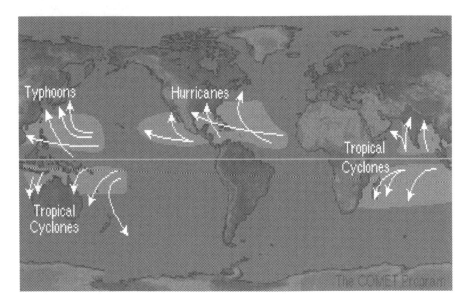

(Courtesy of www.comet.ucar.edu)

- **Northern Atlantic Ocean:** The most-studied of all tropical basins and accounts for approximately 12% of the world's total tropical cyclones. Tropical cyclone formation here varies widely from year to year, ranging from twenty eight to one per year with an average of around ten. The United States Atlantic and Gulf Coasts, Mexico, Central America, the Caribbean Islands, and Bermuda are frequently affected by storms in this basin. Venezuela, the south-east of Canada and Atlantic "Macaronesian" islands are also occasionally affected. Many of the more intense Atlantic storms are Cape Verde-Type hurricanes, which forms off the west coast of Africa near the Cape Verde Islands. On rare occasions, a hurricane can reach the European mainland such as, Hurricane Lili, which dissipated over the British Isles in October of 1996 and Tropical Storm Vince in September 2005, which made landfall on the southwestern coast of Spain in the record breaking 2005 North Atlantic hurricane season. In an average year, about 10 storms form in this basin with 6 of them becoming hurricanes and of that total 2 of them becoming intense hurricanes. In this basin, the hurricane season runs from June 1 to November 30 with the peak of the season occurring around September 10.
- **Northeastern Pacific Ocean:** This is the second most active basin in the world accounting for approximately 17% of the world's total tropical cyclones, and the most compact (a large number of storms for such a small area of ocean). Storms that form here can affect western Mexico, Hawaii, northern Central America, and on extremely rare occasions, California and Arizona. There is no record of a hurricane ever reaching California; however, to some meteorologists, historical records in 1858 indicate that there was a storm which struck San Diego with winds of over 75 mph. In an average year, about 17 storms form in this basin with 10 of them becoming hurricanes and of that total 5 of them becoming intense hurricanes. In this basin, the hurricane season runs from May 15 to November 30 with the peak of the season occurring around August 25.

- **Northwestern Pacific Ocean:** Tropical cyclone activity in this region frequently affects China, Japan, Hong Kong, the Philippines, and Taiwan, but also many other countries in Southeast Asia, such as Vietnam, South Korea, and parts of Indonesia, plus numerous Oceanian islands. This is by far the most active basin, accounting for over 33% of all tropical cyclone activity in the world. The coast of China sees the most land falling tropical cyclones worldwide. The Philippines receives an average 18 typhoon landings per year. Rarely does a typhoon or an extratropical storm reach northward to Siberia, Russia. In an average year, about 27 storms form in this basin with 17 of them becoming hurricanes and of that total 8 of them becoming intense hurricanes. It is interesting to note that in this basin, the hurricane season occurs year-round with the peak of the season occurring around September 1 and the minimum occurring in February.

- **Northern Indian Ocean:** This basin is sub-divided into two areas, the Bay of Bengal and the Arabian Sea, with the Bay of Bengal dominating (5 to 6 times more activity). This basin's season has an interesting and rare double peak season; one in April and May before the onset of the monsoons, and another in October and November just after the monsoons. Tropical cyclones which form in this basin has historically cost the most lives — most notably, the November, 1970 Bhola Cyclone killed approximately 300,000 to 500,000 persons mainly in Bangladesh and coastal India from drowning. Nations affected by this basin include India, Bangladesh, Sri Lanka, Thailand, Myanmar, and Pakistan. Rarely, a tropical cyclone formed in this basin will affect the Arabian Peninsula. This basin accounts for about 12% of the worlds' total of tropical cyclones. In an average year about 5 storms form in this basin with 2 of them becoming hurricanes and of that total 1 becoming an intense hurricane. In the North Indian basin, storms are most common from April to December 30, with peaks in May 15 and November 10.

- **Southwestern Pacific Ocean:** Tropical activity in this region largely affects Australia and Oceania. On rare occasions, tropical storms reach the vicinity of Brisbane, Australia and into New Zealand, usually during or after extratropical transition. This basin accounts for about 11% of the worlds' total of tropical cyclones. In an average year about 10 storms form in this basin with 5 of them becoming hurricanes and of that total 2 of them becoming intense hurricanes. In this basin, the hurricane season runs from October 15 to May 1 with the peak of the season occurring around March 1.

- **Southeastern Indian Ocean:** Tropical activity in this region affects Australia and Indonesia. According to the Australian Bureau of Meteorology, the most frequently hit portion of Australia is between Exmouth and Broome in Western Australia. This basin accounts for about 7% of the worlds' total of tropical cyclones. In an average year about 7 storms form in this basin with 3 of them becoming hurricanes and of that total 1 becoming an intense hurricane. In this basin, the hurricane season runs from October 15 to May 1 with the peak of the season occurring January 15 and February 25.

- **Southwestern Indian Ocean:** This basin is often the least understood, due to a lack of historical data. Cyclones forming here impact Madagascar, Mozambique, Mauritius, Reunion, Comoros, Tanzania, and Kenya. This basin accounts for about the remaining 8% of the worlds' total of tropical cyclones. In an average year about 10 storms form in this basin with 5 of them becoming hurricanes and of that total 2 of them becoming intense hurricanes. In this basin, the hurricane season runs from October 15 to May 15 with the peak of the season occurring January 15 and February 20.

A hurricane is a circular, cyclonic system with a diameter anywhere from 100 to 500 miles extending upwards to heights of 40,000 to 50,000 feet. They draw their energy from latent heat from the warm tropical seas and they are generally smaller than middle-latitude cyclones, which on the other hand depend on the tropics-to-pole temperature gradient for their energy. At the base of the hurricane, air is sucked in by the very low pressure at the center and then spirals inward. Once within the hurricane structure itself, air rises rapidly to the top and spirals outward. It is this rapid upward movement of great quantities of moisture rich air that produces the enormous amounts of rain during a hurricane. A hurricane consists of huge swirl of clouds rotating around a calm center-the eye-where warm air is sucked down. Clouds, mainly cumulonimbus clouds are arranged in bands around the eye, the tallest forming the wall of the eye. The eyewall as it is commonly called is the area of highest surface winds in the tropical cyclone. It is composed of many strong updrafts and downdrafts. The mechanisms by which the eyewall and the eye are formed are not very well understood but it is generally thought that the eye feature is a fundamental component of all rotating fluids.

Hurricanes have very strong pressure gradients with isobars that decrease in value toward the center of the very low pressure. The strong pressure gradients are the main reason behind the powerful winds of the hurricane. In addition, the resulting latent heat of condensation that is released provides the power to drive the storm. High pressure air in the upper atmosphere (above 30,000 feet/9,000m) over the storm's center also removes heat from the rising air, further driving the air cycle and the hurricane's growth. As high pressure air is sucked into the low-pressure center of the storm, wind speeds increase. At the center of the hurricane is the eye of the storm, which is an area of calm, usually warm and humid, but rainless air. Spiral rain bands and these bands of heavy convective showers that spiral inward toward the storm's center surround hurricanes. Cumulus and Cumulonimbus clouds ascend and lightning develop. Although a great deal of time, money and effort has been spent on studying the development, growth, maturity and tracks of hurricanes, much is still not known about these mysterious but powerful storms. For example, it is still not possible to predict the exact track of a hurricane with pinpoint accuracy, even though it can be tracked with weather radars and studied through reconnaissance aircrafts, computer models and weather satellites. Furthermore, meteorologists can list factors that are favorable for development of a hurricane or list pre-conditions that are necessary for the formation of a hurricane but they can't say with a degree of certainty or pin-point accuracy that in a certain situation or scenario that a hurricane will definitely develop and travel along a particular path. However numerical weather predictions models are becoming more accurate and precise in trying to predict the movement and strength of these storms. In actual fact, meteorologists from all around the world have come to rely on the accuracy of these models to help predict the movement and strength of these storms thereby improving the hurricane forecast of these dangerous storms.

CHAPTER FIVE

FORECASTING THE WEATHER IN EARLIER TIMES AND HOW BAHAMIANS TRACKED AND MONITORED HURRICANES IN THE LATE 1800S AND EARLY 1900S.

Today, meteorologists have an impressive array of technological devices and scientific techniques at their disposal, in order to forecast or predict changing patterns of weather and climate. However, for thousands of years, man has relied upon a combination of superstitions and observations to predict the weather. Over time ideas that particular gods controlled various aspects of the weather were gradually complemented and superseded. They did this by looking at natural indicators such as, wind speed and direction, cloud formations, the colour of the sky, certain optical effects and the behaviour of animals and plants. Weather folklore is indebted to oral tradition, since most ancient peoples enjoyed minimal literacy. Predicting the weather accurately ensured their very survival. 'Old wives tales' and popular sayings underwent many changes as they were passed from one generation to the next, travelling widely and enjoying multiple distortions along the way. Many sayings simply relied on close observations of the skies and common sense. Clouds, for example, were called by various names depending on their changing appearance.

The ability to predict the weather was of great importance to many Bahamians such as, sailors, fishermen and farmers, as well as others who also lived off the land and the sea. Their very livelihoods, and even lives, often depended upon weather conditions. Across the Bahamas, and particularly on the Family Islands, where conditions were most variable, almost every island developed its own weather lore. These weather lores often found expressions in many proverbs and sayings over the years.

Some of these have no scientific groundings at all and rarely prove to be accurate. However, many of those relating to the short term, which was based on observations, still hold true to this day. Longer range forecasts, particularly those that are centered on particular days of the year and based on superstitious beliefs also tend to be inaccurate. On the other hand, there are those that developed from long-term observations of seasonal weather patterns and other natural cycles, which continue to hold some truth.

Meteorology is a young science and it is only in the last two centuries that we have learned how the sun's energy acts on the Earth's atmospheric envelope to produce the planet's diverse weather episodes and climatic zones. Fortunately, we no longer believe, as primitive peoples did, that hurricanes, thunderstorms, rainbows and other atmospheric phenomena were omens sent by sky deities. We try to control the weather, to harness its extraordinary forces, yet we are still fascinated at nature's climatological handiwork. The tropics lie between the Tropic of Cancer and the Tropic of Capricorn (latitude 23.5°north and south). It is only in this zone that the sun is directly overhead which results in the temperatures always being high and the seasons are marked only by changes in wind and rainfall, thus providing the perfect breeding grounds for hurricanes to form and survive.

Today, weather forecasting uses the application of science and technology to predict the state of the atmosphere for a future time and a given location. Hurricanes can be difficult to forecast. Nowadays, even with our advanced technology and satellites, forecasters have difficulty predicting the path of a storm. The responsibility of predicting these sometimes very erratic tracks falls on the shoulder of the National Hurricane Center (NHC) in Coral Gables, Florida (near Miami). The NHC forecasters have many tools at their disposal, and receive data from many different sources. Some of the sources include station data, satellite information, aircraft reconnaissance reports, ship reports, and radar to name a few. One of the most useful tools forecasters have at their disposal is the use of 'super' computers. Several of these advanced computer programs have been created to simulate the atmospheric dynamics. The information that comes into the center is entered into these super computers, and an atmospheric model projection is produced. There are several computer models that are created. Some models are statistical while others are dynamic. Statistical models use the climatological data of past hurricanes movements to predict the movement of the current storm. Dynamic models use equations to simulate atmospheric conditions at different levels to predict a storm's future movement.

In the past, human beings have attempted to forecast the weather informally for millennia, and formally since at least the nineteenth century. Weather forecasts are made by collecting quantitative data about the current state of the atmosphere and using scientific understanding of atmospheric processes to project how the atmosphere will evolve. Our brief exploration into weather forecasting pretty much follows the techniques and methods developed by early weather wizards. From the earliest of times, hunters, farmers, warriors, shepherds, and sailors learned the importance of being able to tell what the weather might be up to next. Ancient civilizations appealed to the gods of the sky. The Egyptians looked to Ra, the sun god. The Greeks sought out the all-powerful Zeus. Then there was Thor, the god of thunder and lightning in ancient Nordic times. Hurrikán was the Mayan god of hurricanes. Such societies, such as the Aztecs, used human sacrifice to satisfy the rain god, Tlaloc. Native American and Australian aborigines performed rain dances. Those who were able to predict the weather and seemed to influence its production were held in highest esteem. After all, they appeared to be very well connected.

Even in the Bible times references to weather prediction are prevalent in both the Old and New Testaments. For the most part, they are instructive or cautionary, rather than serving as mere descriptions. The passages generally serve as reminders of God's power. One notable exception occurs in Matthew(KJV) 16:2-3, when Jesus instructs a group of fishermen: *"When it is evening, you say, 'It will be fair weather, for the sky is red.' And in the morning, 'It will be stormy today, for the sky is red and threatening.'"* More typical is the following verse from Psalm 107:25, 29: *"For He commandeth, and raiseth the stormy wind, which lifteth up the waves thereof…He maketh the storm a calm, so that the waves thereof are still."* Because winds are invisible yet powerful, they make for a convenient expression of God's will on Earth: Exodus 10:12-13: *"…And the Lord brought an east wind…(and) the east wind brought the locust."* Exodus 14:21: *"…And the Lord caused the sea to go back by a strong east* wind…" Genesis 8:1-2: *"…And God made a wind to pass over the Earth, and the waters assuaged…and the rain from the heaven was restrained."* But the Lord's wrath can also express itself through the weather, and it does so frequently: Psalm 78:47: *"He destroyed…their sycamore trees with frost…"* Psalm 18:12-14: *"…He shot out lightning, and discomfited them."* 1 Kings 8:35-36 (2 Chronicles 6:26-27): *"When heaven is shut up, and there is no rain, because they have sinned against thee; if they pray…and turn from their sin, when thou afflictest them: Then hear thou…and give rain…"* Psalm 78:47-48: *"He destroyed their vines with hail…He gave up their cattle also to the hail…"*

One of the earliest scientific approaches to weather prediction occurred around 300 B.C.E., documented in Aristotle's work, "Meteorologica." The ancient Greeks invented the term *meteorology*, which means the study of atmospheric disturbances or meteors. Aristotle tried to explain the weather through the interaction of Earth, fire, air, and water. His pupil Theophrastus really went to work and wrote the ultimate weather text 'The *Book of Signs*,' which contained a collection of weather lores and forecast signs. Amazingly it served as the definitive weather book for 2,000 years. Theophrastus's weather lore included colours of the sky, rings and halos, and even sound. Hippocrates—also known as "the Father of Medicine"—was also very much involved with the weather. His work *On Airs, Waters, and Places* became a medical classic, linking good health with favourable weather conditions. The opening of his work begins with the advice that those who wish to investigate medicine must first begin with an understanding of the seasons and weather. Weather forecasting advanced little from these ancient times to the Renaissance. Then beginning in the fifteenth century, Leonardo da Vinci designed an instrument for measuring humidity called a hygrometer. Later Galileo Galilei invented the thermometer and his student Evangelista Torricelli came up with the barometer for measuring air pressure. With these tools, people could monitor the atmosphere. Then Sir Isaac Newton derived the physics and mathematics that accurately described the atmosphere. Newton's work on motion remains *The Book of Signs* of modern meteorology. To this day, his principles form the foundation of all computer analyses and predictions.

Progress in understanding and predicting the weather is one of the great success stories of the twentieth century science. Advances in the basic understanding of weather dynamics and physics, the establishment of global observing system, and the advent of numerical weather prediction models have all put weather forecasting on a solid scientific foundation. The deployment of weather satellites and radar together with emergency preparedness programs have led to dramatic declines in deaths from severe weather phenomena, such as hurricanes and tornadoes. These days, once an all-human endeavor based mainly upon changes in barometric pressure, current weather conditions, and sky conditions, forecast models are now used to determine future conditions. Nowadays, there are a variety of end uses to weather forecasts. Weather warnings are important forecasts because they are used to protect life and property. Forecast based on temperature and precipitation are important to agriculture, and therefore to traders within the commodity markets. Temperature forecasts are used by utility companies to estimate demand over the upcoming days. On an everyday basis, people use weather forecasts to determine what to wear on a given day. Since outdoor activities are severely curtailed by heavy rain, strong winds and localized floods, forecast can be used to plan activities around these events, and to plan ahead and survive them.

Today, hurricanes kill or injure people and destroy property and cause millions of dollars in damages. Preparations for hurricane landfalls also disrupt schedules and plans across much wider areas than those affected by high winds, storm surge, or torrential rains. These preparations further impose substantial, but poorly quantified, economic costs. Contrary to initial expectations and popular belief, it is not the high winds but the moving water (the storm surge) that causes the most hurricane-related deaths. Historically, storm surge, where onshore hurricane winds push the sea or mound of water inland, has been the greatest cause of hurricane mortality. For example, *The Great Nassau Hurricane of 1926, The Great Bahamas Hurricane of 1929,* and *The Great Hurricane of 1866* killed hundreds of persons and many were washed out to sea from their sea-side homes by the storm surge and wind driven flooding. At present, most of the hurricane related deaths in the Bahamas have been caused simply by drowning in floods resulting from the torrential hurricane rainfall. Two recent examples of this are, Matario Pintard who died in the flood waters in Freeport, Grand Bahama in Hurricane Wilma of 2005, and Kevin Milford who died in Exuma in the flood waters from Hurricane Noel of 2007. However, this low death toll came about recently because of early evacuations and better and timelier hurricane forecast warnings for the impacted area.

In the past, a forecast was considered successful if it specified the position and intensity of the hurricane for times ranging from 24 through 72 hours after the initial time. However, today, the public at large has come to expect a great deal of specific details and pin-point accuracy from the local meteorologist, including spatial distribution of rainfall, winds, flooding and high seas, for times as long as 120 hours into the future. Meteorologists have over the recent year's maintained reliable, homogenous statistics on forecast accuracy for more than half a century. These 'verification' statistics provide reliable metrics of meteorological performance over these years. In terms of results, late twentieth century forecasting methods prevents 90% of the hurricane related deaths that would occur with techniques used in the late 1800s and early 1900s, but it is difficult to demonstrate any effect on property damage. What was poorly known back then were the economic and human impacts of the response to impending hurricanes. Hurricane forecasting is a successful enterprise with demonstrably favorable benefit-to-cost returns. Compared with the early 1900s, today, track forecasting accuracy is improving steadily, but intensity forecasting and prediction of local wind, rainfall, and sea state still remain problematic. Generally, because more accurate hurricane forecasts pose significant operational, technological, and scientific challenges, we should expect progress to be incremental, although cumulative.

Since the turn of the century, hurricane related deaths here in the Bahamas have dropped considerably while property damage has increased in the extreme. The reason is obvious: hurricane forecasting has improved tremendously with time so that watches and warnings are getting to people with plenty time to evacuate and prepare. We are getting out of harm's way when the hurricanes strike, but sadly, our property is getting ever closer to danger's edge. With the explosion of growth along our coastal regions, it is no wonder we have multi-million and billion dollar hurricanes. We have seen the grief, hardship and devastation that recent hurricanes such as, Andrew, Wilma, Jeanne and Frances caused. Even though Grand Bahama and North Eleuthera were the focus of much attention in the wake of Andrew, Frances, Jeanne and

Wilma, fortunately that has changed recently. There are other islands that are just as vulnerable to the effects of even minor hurricanes: Abaco, Long Island, Mayaguana, New Providence and many others in our chain of islands that now gather similar attention from the government and the private sector. Even our tourism industry is affected by these annual threats and a direct hit by a substantial hurricane in areas, such as in Nassau or Grand Bahama, would potentially harm our national economy and our number one industry of tourism in a significant way. Although, the Bahamas has suffered from massive floods, lightning strikes, tornado outbreaks, hurricanes pose a greater risk in any given year to our lives and our economy than all other natural disasters combined. Hurricanes have played a significant role in our nation's history both in present day as well as during the colonial times as this book will show. It's just a matter of time until the next 'big' one makes hurricane history.

Fortunately, man's prediction of the weather has come a long way in just the last century and a half. Today's meteorologists no longer look into crystal balls or observe animals and birds behaviors to predict the onset of a hurricane. Nowadays, he has far more sophisticated tools available to him, from satellite images to advanced Doppler radars. He can make fairly accurate predictions for the weather up to a week or more in advance. Yet even with all of these early warnings, the coast still sustains a lot of damage whenever a hurricane comes through because there is simply no time to fully prepare. A meteorologist can only make an educated guess and even with this guess he can be wrong. At the moment, there are two ways which meteorologists predict hurricanes and they are; 1) seasonal probabilities and 2) the track of a current hurricane. These two fields are very different in their methods and approaches.

A seasonal probability predicts the number of named storms and their breakdown by intensity (i.e. the number of hurricanes, tropical storms, intense hurricanes, etc.). They can also predict approximate wind speeds and intensity for these hurricanes. Named storms are typically predicted based on past occurrences and current measures of factors in the climate and in predicting them; they are only labeled as probabilities. On the other hand, once a hurricane has formed, it can be tracked. Scientists can usually accurately predict its path for 3-5 days in advance. A hurricane's possible trajectory is usually represented as a cone, which shrinks over time as the error in the prediction decreases. To predict the path of these storms, meteorologists can use many different weather models. In the North Atlantic, there have been great strides made in the science of forecasting hurricanes, but there is still a lot to do. One major problem is accuracy. The National Hurricane Center in Florida has been forecasting the paths of hurricanes since the early 1950's. They issue 120-hour, 96-hour, 72-hour, 48-hour, and 12-hour forecasts. The error decreases as the time before landfall decreases and the error has also decreased over the years as models become more accurate and advanced.

Today, the responsibility of forecasting the weather for the Bahamas rest on the shoulders of the Bahamas Department of Meteorology based in Nassau, but that was not always the case. In 1935 the Bahamas Telecommunications Department in conjunction with the United States Weather Bureau organized a network of weather observing stations. The Bureau provided the instrumentation and forms to record the information, along with the necessary instructions and annual tours were arranged to inspect and upkeep the instruments. The information was disseminated in accordance with international standards and practices. Aviation forecast began in 1943 during the Second World War when the Royal Air Force established an Aviation Forecast Office at Oakes Field. At that time only a few Bahamian weather observers aided the Air Force but the number increased in 1945 when the Aviation Forecast Office was transformed into a civilian Air Ministry Office.

Formation of the British Caribbean Meteorological Service in 1951 resulted in the transfer of the Bahamian weather observers from the Air Ministry. The comprehensive functions of the Service were:- (a) collection and dissemination of meteorological information (b) provide services for aviation, the general public and research (c) provision of hurricane warnings, (d) provide advice to the Government and its agencies for planning purposes, and (e) participation in the activities of the World Meteorological Organization (WMO) and the International Civil Aviation Organization (ICAO). Reconstitution of the Caribbean Meteorological Service in 1962 prompted the Bahamas Government not to be associated with it anymore. In turn, the Bahamas Government established its own Meteorological Office as an autonomous section of the Department of Civil Aviation. This lasted from 1963 to 1972. The Bahamas Meteorological Service was created as a separate Department of Government in 1973 while under the Ministry of Tourism. Since 1973 the Department of Meteorology has been under various Ministries but its mandate remained the same. The Department of Meteorology is committed to providing high quality meteorological and climatological information on a timely basis, to be used by special interests and the public at large for research, education and the protection of lives and property.

In 1866, many Bahamians depended heavily on weather lore and other natural signs to forecast the weather. Many of these weather traditions were simply passed down from generation to generation. The purpose of these weather lores was to instruct early farmers, sailors, fishermen, and others on how to predict the weather. Bahamians who made their living outdoors depended heavily on the weather and that has always been the case during these times. Today, meteorologists make use of satellites, weather balloons, super computers, Doppler radars, and a complex communications network to produce reasonably accurate daily weather forecasts. However, in 1866, Bahamians had to rely on other weather indicators to advise them on what kind of plans to make. Some of these indicators have a true correlation with factors that do affect the weather. Others have no relationship at all to the weather.

During the late 1800s up until the mid 1930s there were several ways in which residents knew that a storm was approaching the Bahamas. Many of these methods were often weather folklores or simple deductions of the weather based on past experiences. Unfortunately, the warning system back then was not as effective or efficient as the warning system nowadays. Typically coastal residents may have had less than a day or even hours to prepare or evacuate from their homes to escape from an approaching hurricane. For this reason and because of more substandard housing, the damages sustained and the death toll back then were much higher than that of today.

Watching the sea rise or storm surge just before the onset of the hurricane.

Before the onset of an approaching storm, the sea-level often rose to above normal positions. By watching this rise in the sea-level, the locals could tell whether there was an approaching storm. Today this rise in the sea-level just before the onset of the storm and during the storm is referred to as the storm surge. Just before the onset of an approaching hurricane, the seas would give these residents a small window of opportunity to prepare for a hurricane or to evacuate to a hurricane shelter.

Watching the changes in the clouds and other weather elements

The weather lore that follow have been derived from several sources including, older Bahamian fishermen and older persons within the Bahamian community and the sayings are very old and have been passed on from generation to generation. One of the first signs of an approaching hurricane is the movement and elemental changes of the various clouds according to these local fishermen. They said that these clouds often appeared in distinct stages. They would first notice the cirrus-form clouds followed by the alto-stratus or nimbostratus clouds as the storm approached the Bahamas. This was then followed by stratus-form clouds and finally to cumulus and cumulonimbus type clouds as the storm arrived over that particular island. These residents especially on the Family Islands might not have known the types of clouds or names of the clouds but they definitely knew the process by which these storm clouds appeared during a storm arrival. They used this process as an indicator to prepare for the approaching storm. They also had the clouds in combination with the increasing winds and the rainfall which over time became stronger and heavier as the hurricane approached the islands.

According to other Bahamian fishermen, atmospheric pressure also helped them determine the weather. They said that knowing from which way the wind was blowing helped them to locate where highs and lows were relative to their position. For example, if they stood with their backs to the wind, a high pressure cell will probably be to their right. If their right was west, then they predicted fair or improving weather, because weather systems usually move from west to east. Furthermore, the ways in which the wind direction changed also helped them to predict the weather. If the wind was out of the south, then it changes to the southwest, then west, then northwest, it is changing in a clockwise direction and they deduced that the wind was veering. If it changes in a clockwise direction, such as first blowing out of the west then southwest, then south, then southeast, the wind was said to be backing. Sometimes a backing wind is a sign of an approaching storm front they speculated. The speed of the wind was also an indicator of the changing weather. A strong wind usually means a big differential in the air pressure over a small space. This meant that a low pressure system was approaching and it would in all likelihood be intense. Many of the sayings of weather lore made use of the correlation between these weather indicators and the affects they may have on observable phenomena. For example, as the humidity becomes higher, human hair becomes longer. It follows, then, that if your hair seems to curl up at the end and seems more unmanageable, it could be a sign of rain. They also said another good sign of high humidity is salt. Salt tends to become sticky and clog the holes in the salt shaker if the humidity is high.

Signal flag-in Nassau and on The Family Island lighthouses

All British Imperial Lighthouse Service light stations were issued a set of signal flags, which were kept ready once there was an approaching storm to warn incoming or outgoing ships and residents of an approaching hurricane. For centuries before the introduction of radios, sharing of information between ships, from shore to shore and from sea to shore posed communications problems. The only way for mariners to pass a message from one ship to another or from ship to land was by visual signals. For many years preceding the invention of the telegraph(and during its invention), some type of semaphore signaling from high places, towers or forts were used to send messages between distant points. To this day, we still signal ships at sea with flags flown from shore-based towers and from other ships displaying storm warning flags. On Hog Island (now called Paradise Island), there was a lighthouse and to the right of this lighthouse was a flag and a flagpole which displayed the Union Jack of Great Britain. If there was a hurricane travelling, that flag would be removed and be replaced with a specialty hurricane flag. This flag consisted of a red coloured flag with a black square in the middle. Similarly, if there were any gale conditions being experienced, the gale flag would be used (two red triangle flags indicated gale warnings with winds between 34 to 47 knots). These flags were only taken down after the dangers associated with the hurricane or the gale conditions had dissipated. There were also hurricane flags placed on Fort Charlotte and Fort Fincastle to warn residents of an impending storm. Similar events would also take place on the Family Island lighthouses if they had knowledge of an approaching hurricane. These signal flags also gave residents on Nassau and the Family Islands a small grace period to prepare for a storm. In this day and age of satellite communications, radios, televisions, computers and instant information everywhere, these flags are rarely used. Actually, there is a famous painting by the world famous artist Winslow Homer showing some pastel coloured Bahamian houses on Paradise Island. Along with these houses, there are some coconut trees and a hurricane signal flag and flagpole swaying in the winds near the lighthouse on Paradise Island during a hurricane in 1899. This world famous water colour painting is now on display in the Metropolitan Museum of Art in New York.

The Parameter or Barometer Shell

One of the ways local residents on some Family Islands tried to forecast the weather was by the use of a local shell called the '*Parameter or Barometer Shell*.' The shell got its name from the barometer instrument used for measuring atmospheric pressure. The content of the shell was allowed to dry out and then the shell was painted in a blue dye called 'Iniqua Blue.' According to some local residents, they swore that this method of weather forecasting was indeed very accurate and quite reliable. The shell would be hanged up in most of the homes at the time and if it was going to rain the shell turned speckled white. For heavy rain, the dots would turn significantly bigger and the colour of the blue ink would turn to a deeper shade of blue. If the rain was light, the dots would become much smaller in size, and if it was calm or fair weather, the shell turned ashy white, as you can guess this was an unreliable method to forecast the weather as compared with the modern methods and instruments of today. Today meteorologists still use an instrument called a barometer to measure air pressure.

Watching the birds and other animals

According to some residents especially on the Family Islands, they would watch the birds especially the sea birds making preparations for

95

an approaching storm. They said that if there was a storm approaching the island, the sea birds would fly back onto the mainland in large flocks from the various islands and cays to seek shelter from the storm. Numerous Family Island residents said that these birds had a 'sixth sense' when it came to hurricanes, because they would not return seaward until the hurricane had passed over that particular island. Others said that the caged and farm animals like the chickens, pigs and goats would start behaving differently just before the onset of a hurricane by trying to get out of their cages or simply making much louder noises than usual. This off course was a very unreliable method as compared to the methods of today and perhaps was one of the reasons why the death toll was so high on many of the Family Islands. Before giant hurricane waves slammed into the Bahamian coastline in the 1800s and 1900s, many Bahamian residents swore that, wild and domestic animals seemed to know what was about to happen and fled to safety. According to several eyewitness accounts, they said that the following events happened just before the onset of a hurricane. First, wild and domestic hogs, chickens, goats, sheep and other animals screamed and ran for higher ground or away from the coast. Second, dogs and cats would refuse to go outdoors or leave the yard. Egrets, seagulls, frigate or hurricane birds, flamingos and other seabirds would abandon their low-lying breeding areas near or on the coast and would proceed to move to higher grounds.

The belief that wild and domestic animals possess a sixth sense and that they knew in advance when the hurricane would strike has been around for centuries. Wildlife experts believe that animals' more acute hearing and other senses might enable them to hear or feel the Earth's pressure changes, tipping them off to an approaching hurricane disaster long before humans realize what's going on. In most cases, after a hurricane passage over that particular island, many of these residents reported that relatively few animals had been reported dead, reviving speculation that those animals can somehow sense an impending disaster. On the beach, some Bahamians were washed away by the storm surge but some of these residents reported seeing very few, if any animals washed ashore in the storm. The Bahamian coast in 1866 was home to a variety of animals including, crabs, iguanas, lizards, shore birds and seagulls, flamingos and other land animals. Quite a number of these residents reported that they did not see any animal carcasses nor did they know of any, other than one or two fish caught up on the shore in the wake of the storm. Along the shore many persons perished from the storm surge, however, many Family Islanders reported that the majority of the goats, sheep, cattle and dogs were found unharmed after the storm passage.

Flamingos, White Crown Pigeons and other birds that breed during the summer months on many of the Bahamian Islands, including, Andros, Abaco, Eleuthera, Inagua, and quite a few other islands as well flew to higher ground ahead of time and away from the hurricane prone coastal areas. Many of these residents said that they watched this movement and made preparations for an impending storm after they noticed these birds migrating. South Androsian native the late Mr. Daniel Rahming recalled White Crown Pigeons and other seabirds frantically flying away just before the onset of the Great Bahamian Hurricanes of 1926 and 1929. The late Mr. Illford Forbes, another South Androsian resident, who lived on the coast in the settlement of High Rock, said his two dogs would not go for their daily run on the beach before this hurricane struck. "They are usually excited to go on this outing," he said. "But on this day of the hurricane, they refused to go and most probably saved my and their lives." Alan Rabinowitz, Director for science and exploration at the Bronx Zoo-based Wildlife Conservation Society in New York, says animals can sense impending danger by detecting subtle or abrupt shifts in the environment. "For example, Earthquakes bring vibrational changes on land and in water, while hurricanes cause electromagnetic changes in the atmosphere," he said. "Some animals have acute sense of hearing, touch and smell that allows them to determine something coming towards them long before humans might know that something is there." Did humans lose their sixth sense? At one time humans also had this sixth sense, Rabinowitz said, but they lost this ability when it was no longer needed or used.

Radio, Telegraph and Telephone

News about an impending storm was broadcast over the radio but at this time radio was considered a luxury item and out of the reach of the masses. The much needed radio service provided by ZNS never really began to operate as a broadcast medium until 26th May of 1936. The telegraph was also another method of hurricane warning which came in handy for the Family Island residents. During the time of rapid change in the telegraph industry, the telephone was patented by Alexander Graham Bell in 1876. Although the telephone was originally expected to replace the telegraph completely, this turned out not to be the case: both industries thrived side by side for many decades. On some of the major islands, there was a local telegraph station and this station provided a valuable link between the islands and New Providence and indeed the rest of the world. The phone was also available initially but not to the masses and at the time it was considered a luxury item that only the rich in the society could afford. Eventually, with ZNS coming on stream, it provided a much needed and a very valuable tool as a hurricane warning service. At the time, officials in the Bahamas Government were concerned that residents on the Family Islands were not getting timely weather reports and hurricane warnings. As a result, ZNS Radio Bahamas was born to fill this void. Many Family Island residents complained to the government that they were not being alerted to the presence of these powerful storms as they passed through the Bahamas. The end result of this was that, many lives were lost in the process to these storms. Actually, one of ZNS Bahamas's first mandate was to provide a hurricane warning service to the major Family Islands around the Bahamas. As a result of this important mandate, many lives were saved.

Newspapers

Often news about an impending storm would be featured in the local newspapers of *The Nassau Guardian, The Tribune* and *The Gazette*. Many times if some other island in the Caribbean experienced this storm and it was headed in the general direction of the Bahamas it was given prominent front page coverage in these newspapers.

Barometer

The instrument used to measure air pressure is called a barometer. The change in the pressure, and how fast it is changing, is more indicative of the weather than the pressure itself. Pressure differences are caused by the uneven heating of the surface of the Earth by the sun. Rapidly falling pressure or low pressure areas almost always means an approaching storm system. Rapidly rising pressure or high pressure areas almost always means clearing and cooler weather ahead. High pressure areas are produced by heavy sinking air. They are characterized by clear weather and little or no precipitation. An area of high pressure is sometimes called a high pressure cell, or simply, a 'high.' Low pressure cells are usually called 'lows.' As air rises, it cools and cooler air can hold less moisture. So if the rising air reaches an altitude where it is too cool to hold the amount of moisture it had on the ground, that moisture condenses out as clouds and precipitation. Thus, low pressure areas produce cloudy and rainy weather. A hurricane is low pressure system characterized by heavy precipitation and strong winds.

Although Evangalista Torricelli, a student of Galileo, invented the mercury barometer in 1643, however, it was the discovery of the Aneroid Barometer in 1843 by Lucien Vidie that the barometer came into common usage. This barometer was used in the Bahamas as early as 1854 and the following rules for its use were explained by an unnamed observer, an inhabitant of Harbour Island(Taken from the book '*The Harbour Island Story*' by Ann and Jim Lawlor-Used with permission):

1. *In the hurricane months if the barometer falls with a N or NE wind, it should awake attention, and if it falls below 29.90, it is almost certainly a gale approaching, even though it might be perhaps a 100 miles off.*
2. *During the approach, the barometer falls from noon until morning and then rises to noon again; every day falling lower than the previous day.*
3. *From sunrise to noon, any rise less than 0.05 is unimportant, but the smallest fall during that period, certainly indicates bad weather.*
4. *On the contrary, from noon to morning, its fall is not conclusive of bad weather, but its rise certainly indicates improved weather.*
5. *Though the weather is ever so threatening at sunset, the rise of 0.05 or upward assures you that there will be no gale before morning.*
6. *Though the weather be ever so fair in the morning, the fall of 0.05 before noon, betokens a gale before night (provided it's already below 29.90).*

These rules and guidelines were strictly adhered to by most of the residents and observers on the various Family Islands to give them some kind of indicator of an approaching weather system.

The barometer of the days gone by was the Bahamian resident's version of the radio and television of today. Many residential homes had as a staple in their homes a local barometer to warn them about impending hurricanes. However, these barometers gradually faded out of these homes once radios and televisions were introduced to the masses as a hurricane warning system. The majority of the fishing boats and schooners going out at sea on sponging and fishing trips often had a barometer on their boats especially during the hurricane months of June through November when the hurricanes were known to strike. Whenever there was a steep drop in the barometric pressure that would be one of the first signs of an approaching storm. They would turn the ship around and then immediately make their way back to the mainland. Some of the fishermen would move their boats out of the water and onto the mainland or into the mangrove swamps where they would be safe and protected from the storm. The local Family Island Commissioner also had a barometer stationed at his residence or in his office. If he noticed that the barometer readings indicating that a storm was approaching that island, he would then go about informing the residents in the community to start making the necessary preparations for the impending storm. In addition, those private residents who had a household barometer often took it upon themselves to warn other residents who didn't have a barometer. That would mean battening down the family house and staying indoors or move to one of the nearest hurricane shelters, which at the time were comprised of mostly churches and schools on the various islands.

Word of mouth

This was a very effective form of warning system for the residents on the various Family Islands. If there was a steep drop in pressure indicated by the barometer, an usual rise in the sea level, or if a resident by any other means found out that there was a hurricane travelling. That person would immediately take it upon himself to go around and warn other residents that they needed to take the necessary precautions before the storm passed near to or over that island. This also meant that once the word was received in Nassau and on the Family Islands, this resident or the local Family Island Commissioner would proceed to warn other residents on this respective island about an approaching storm.

CHAPTER SIX

THE WRECKING INDUSTRY BEFORE AND DURING THE GREAT BAHAMAS HURRICANE OF 1866.

Bahamian wreckers were a godsend to shipwrecked mariners (From the collection of The Mariners' Museum, Newport News, Virginia-Used with permission).

Blockade running in the Bahamas during the American Civil War was extremely profitable and supplemented income made by the fairly lucrative wrecking and salvaging industry. As well travelled routes passed through or near the Bahamas, its waters, lurking with many dangers, became an ideal area for salvaging shipwrecks. The islands, cays and rocks of the Bahamas arise from two irregular platforms, 2 ½ miles above the Atlantic Ocean platform, known as the Little and Great Bahama Banks. It was no surprise that many unsuspecting vessels found themselves in deep trouble among the reefs and shoals of the Little and Great Bahama Banks, which had become, not surprisingly, a favourite meeting spot of the wreckers. In and around the islands, the hidden reefs and shoals, the changing sandbanks and the unpredictable winds and currents, especially in the hurricane months, all conspired to make Bahamian waters the terror of navigators and much to the delight of the Bahamian wreckers. Thus, an only slightly productive archipelago acquired another means of support well suited to a people long accustomed to roving and predatory ways. The occupation of salvaging was known as 'wrecking'; however, two other terms were also once in common use, namely 'raking' and 'wracking.' To 'go wracking' derived its meaning from 'wrack,' a foundered ship. The passage through the Bahamas was termed the most dangerous area of any country along the Atlantic coast. At the time of this great hurricane, many of these ships that were engaged in the wrecking and sponging trades were destroyed by this hurricane. Many of these vessels and schooners were simply destroyed at sea or in many of the harbours around the Bahamas. The losses of these vessels were significant because at this time the colony depended heavily on maritime commerce.

The term 'wreckers' referred to a group of daring seamen who sailed out in fair or foul weather and risked their lives, limbs and vessels to save men, ships, and cargoes dashed up on the Bahamian Reefs. Stories of Bahamian wreckers have long captured the interest and imagination of the Bahamian public. Books like *Reap the Wind*, which was made into a Hollywood movie starring John Wayne, short stories like John Hersey's *"God's Hint"* about the preacher who was also a wrecker, magazine articles, and newspaper accounts have portrayed wreckers in many roles from swashbuckling heroes to ruthless pirates. Abaconians and Harbour Island residents often told the story of the local minister who tricked his congregation in the race to a wreck by leaving them deep in prayer and while their eyes were closed he immediately rushed out at sea to be the first one on the wreck to claim the majority of the shares. This was because in the wrecking era, the race was to the swiftest, for the first man to 'speak' the wreck became the wreckmaster and was in charge of the rescue venture. The sight of 6 to 8 wrecking vessels with 14 to 15 men in each all racing to be the first one at the wreck was not uncommon in the heyday of the Bahamian wrecking industry. Unfortunately, most of these tales have showed these Bahamian wreckers in an unfavorable light. But what was the true scope and character of these Bahamian wreckers? Were they simply rogues or saviours? Were they unscrupulous men who thought only of the profit to be made through the misfortunes of others, or were they honest men who performed a humanitarian and vital service to men, ships, and property in distress? This chapter will attempt to answer many of these questions through the stories of these wreckers and the impact that they had on the Bahamian society.

Bounded by treacherous coral reefs, the archipelago of the Bahamas is made up of over 700 islands scattered over 100,000 square miles of breathtaking clear turquoise and cobalt seas. Most of the 23 inhabited islands are sparsely populated. Though frequently associated with the Caribbean, the Bahamas is separate, situated north of the Caribbean Sea in the Atlantic Ocean and more closely aligned with its northern neighbour, the United States. The Bahamas has easily recognizable appeal with dazzling and amazing treacherous coral reefs situated around these islands. These reefs can be an amazing asset but they can also pose significant danger to many sailors trying to traverse these dangerous seas. In the age of sail, these islands and its deep water channels became the favored passage for shipping traffic between ports in the western Caribbean, Central and North America, the Gulf of Mexico and ports along the Atlantic east coast and in Europe. Because of the swift flowing Gulf Stream Current, unpredictable countercurrents, calms in summer, hurricanes in summer and fall, gales in winter, and inaccurate charts, the passage through the Bahamas was considered one of the most dangerous shipping routes in this region and ideally suited for the wrecking and salvaging industry. As shipping traffic through the Bahamas gradually increased, so did the number of shipwrecks. By the 1850s, ships were piling up on the reef at the rate of nearly one per week. It was this harvest of wrecks that gave rise to the wrecking industry, which in turn led to the development of many of the settlements along the coast of the Bahamas.

A Storm driving a ship onto a Reef (From the collections of the Mariners' Museum, Newport News, Virginia-Used with permission).

During 1700s and 1800s Bahamians developed the commerce of wrecking, i.e. salvaging goods from wrecked ships. With pirating or piracy no longer an occupation without heavy risks, Bahamians took up wrecking and salvaging as the major trade of the post-pirate era. Shipping and trade had increased and numerous shipping vessels travelling from various countries using the Bahamas as a frequent trade route to and from Europe, the Caribbean and the Americas. At this time, "wrecking", or salvaging of shipwrecked boats, became a mainstay of the Bahamian economy and a very lucrative business. The system required that the salvaged cargo, considered to be imported goods, be shipped to Nassau where they were consigned to an agent for auction with the government taking 15%, the agents 15% and 40 to 60% going back the wreckers. The ship owners received the 10-30% that was left, which doesn't seem like much, but had it not been for the wreckers and the system, they would have received nothing.

By the mid-nineteenth century, the wrecking industry of the Bahamas had mushroomed into a thriving business, the chief wrecking centres being at Nassau, Abaco and Harbour Island. During the years between 1845 and 1870, 40% of Bahamian imports came from the salvaging accidental or induced wrecks. Wrecking was the mainstay of the Bahamian economy through most of the 19th century. For example, by 1845, wrecking was the main source of the income for the majority of the inhabitants of Harbour Island and three-quarters of the male population, approximately 300 men (of a total of 1745), earned some or their entire livelihood as wreckers. In 1858 there were 302 ships and 2,679 men (out of a total population of 27,000) licensed as wreckers in the Bahamas. In that year, salvaged wrecked cargo brought to Nassau was valued at £96,304, more than half of all imports to the Bahamas. More than two-thirds of the exports from the Bahamas were salvaged goods. Even so, the average annual income of an ordinary seaman on a wrecking ship was about £20.

The wrecking industry also created lucrative spin off industries such as, the Bahamian boat building industry. The wrecking industry enriched the shipbuilders by creating a demand for more vessels and providing wrecked rigging, barometers, steering wheels, anchors, lumber and other chandlery supplies at good prices. For example, in the heyday of wrecking, between the years 1855 to 1864, Harbour Island shipwrights built 26 vessels, totaling 1,227 tons, some of which were custom built for wrecking. Apart from this immediate division of the spoils, the wrecking industry provided employment for those who built the vessels and those who rigged them and kept them in repair. Food, clothing and almost every article of domestic and industrial use flooded the country at costs far less than if they had been regular imports. Lawyers benefited from the necessary legal work involved in drawing up papers, adjusting claims and appearing in court. But the merchants received the lion's share through the lucrative business of trading in salvaged goods. Without the Bahamian wreckers, hundreds of thousands of dollars worth of imperiled merchandise which was saved, would have been swallowed up forever by the sea. And this merchandise proved to be a great benefit for the Bahamian people and the society at large. There were many to say that far too little of the proceeds found its way to the rightful owners of the goods. But it must be remembered that if it were not for the effort of the wreckers, the owners would have received nothing.

Typically, hurricanes and coral reefs were the natural causes of these shipwrecks but for the natives these were often to infrequent to occur. So in fact, some historians suggested that various tricks were used to lure the ships onto the reefs, and this was quite popular on the islands of Abaco and Eleuthera (and some other islands as well). At a large reef off Spanish Wells, Eleuthera, a reef called *'Devil's Backbone,'* there are many ships that are wrecked there today from this era. This attested to the success of the following ruse; lanterns were placed on buildings and on donkeys at night, and moved to strategic areas, to fool the captains into thinking they were the lights of lighthouses. These misplaced lights caused many ships to sail off course and onto the rocks or coral reefs. In Bimini, it was reported that some residents would beckon the ships on land and while these residents would be busy distracting the ship's captain and crew, other residents would sneak in the back of the ship and drill a hole in the hull of the ship to force it to sink so that they can salvage the cargo from the ship.

Other noted historians, such as, Dr. Gail Saunders and John Viele opposed these stories as simply legends and folklore stories. John Viele, author of *'A history of wrecking in the Florida Keys,'* states that such tricks simply would not work. He points out that mariners interpret a light as indicating land, and so they avoid them if they cannot identify them. Furthermore, oil lanterns cannot be seen very far over water at night, unless they are large, fitted with mirrors or lenses, and mounted at a great height (i.e., in a lighthouse). In hundreds of admiralty court cases heard in Key West, Florida and the Bahamas, no captain of a wrecked ship ever charged that he had been led astray by a false light. A Bahamian wrecker, when asked if he and his crewmates made beacons on shore or showed their lights to warn ships away from the land at night, he is reported to have said, *"No, no(laughing); we always put them out for a better chance by night."* It was said that captains were bribed to run their ships aground, and after the lighthouses were erected, keepers were often bribed to darken them on occasion. This was especially popular in Spanish Wells, and Harbour Island. The local population even resisted the construction of lighthouses during the period 1845 to 1870. More than 300 vessels were shipwrecked over the years, so the wrecking industry provided a significant boost to the local economy. The wrecked and salvaged goods from these islands were taken to Nassau for auction but some of the goods were kept for personal use. Actually, many of the resident's homes on these islands were noted for the unusually high concentration of fine furniture, barometers, clocks and fine chandeliers which the locals used for their personal use after salvaging them from the wrecks.

These Bahamian wreckers were intense at their work and nothing stood between them and their fortune, often not even surviving crew members. Infact, the construction of these lighthouses were often impeded by locals who cut off supplies and did everything imaginable to halt construction of these valuable navigation aides. As such, the lighthouse was a direct threat to the wrecker's livelihood and its construction was vehemently opposed by the locals. After all, they reasoned, the Lord put the reef there and he made the winds to blow and the seas to rage. Lighthouses were the works of men and, all things considered, they preferred to be on the side of the Lord. A few years after the lighthouse at Hope Town, Abaco began to function, lightning struck the tower one night and the inhabitants were convinced that the Almighty God had intervened on their behalf. The next night, however, the light shone forth as bright as ever much to their dismay and bitter disappointment. There were reports by the supervisors of the construction of the lighthouses that some local residents sank supply ships bringing in building materials for the construction of these lighthouses, while others withheld fresh water and food from the construction workers. Once the lighthouse in Abaco was completed, several families of the wreckers took their houses apart, stick by stick and brick by brick and shipped them to Key West and reassembled them there, where the wreckage and salvaging trade was still viable and the pay was higher. In actual fact, many Key West, Florida residents today can trace their roots back to the Bahamas and the wreckage and salvaging era was one of the reasons for this migration to Key West.

With wrecking on the increase on numerous islands throughout the Bahamas, a number of strategically placed permanent lighthouses were built on several of these islands. One of them was in Hope Town, Abaco, and this lighthouse still stands to this day and is a very important tourist attraction on this island and is a great reminder of this island's vivid historical past. The familiar white lighthouse at the entrance to Nassau Harbour had been erected as early as 1817. The first really powerful lights on the important shipping lanes were those placed on the Great Isaacs Rock (1859), Cay Lobos (1860), Stirrup's Cay (1863), Elbow Cay (1863), Abaco (1863), Castle Island (1868), Inagua (1868) and Bird Rock (1876). England's Imperial Board of Trade decided in 1863 to build a lighthouse at Hope Town to warn ships away from the extensive Elbow Reef, thus the original and correct name for the lighthouse in Abaco was the Elbow Reef Lighthouse. Today however, many people erroneously refer to the lighthouse as the Hope Town Lighthouse, but it was built to send sailors away from Hope Town, not to guide them in.

With the addition of more than thirty automatic acetylene lights, by the end of the century not only were the chief shipping lanes guarded by major beacons, but there was scarcely a stretch of regularly navigated waters in the many islands of the Bahamas out of range of at least one guiding light. The resident's animosity began in 1836 when the first two major lighthouses were built in the Bahamas by the British Imperial Board of Trade. One was located on the southern tip of Great Abaco at Hole-in-the-wall and the other at Gun Cay just south of Bimini. Concerned shipping interests had implored England to improve navigation aides in her colonies because of the increasing number of ships that were leaving their cargoes and bodies here in the Bahamas. Only by the late 1800s did the trade decline with the advent of numerous lighthouses throughout the Bahamas, better navigational charts and the introduction of steam and motorboats.

The history of wrecking in this region started with the natives of the Florida Keys, who, beginning in the early 1500s, paddled out to the reef to investigate and plunder shipwrecks. If there were any survivors, the natives usually killed or enslaved them. The next wreckers to arrive in the Keys were the members of the Spanish expeditions who came to recover treasure from sunken galleons. Among them were African slaves and Keys natives whom the Spanish employed as salvage divers. The Spanish were followed closely by the Bahamian "wrackers," as they called themselves, who came to hunt turtles and cut hardwood timber as well as to salvage wrecks. They operated in the Keys for nearly one hundred years before the Americans took possession and forced them to leave. The Bahamians then picked up on this trade because they began to realize the immense profits that could be gained from a wreck, so it became an important industry in the 1700s and 1800s. During the Great Bahamas Hurricane of 1866, the wrecking industry was at its heyday but there was a gradual decline in this industry after the American Civil War.

The story of Bahamian wrecking goes back as far as the Eleutheran Adventurers. The first wreckers in the Bahamas came from Bermuda in 1648 as members of a group of English Puritans seeking religious freedom. They called themselves the *Eleutheran Adventurers* and the island on which they settled on was called Eleuthera. It is perhaps ironic that the first Puritan settlement, on the north coast of Eleuthera was decided by the fateful shipwreck of Captain William Sayle on the Devil's Backbone. The first documented story of a wrecking adventure in the Bahamas was passed on to us by a young Bermudian wrecker named Richard Richardson. He was inspired by the tales of the treasure-laden Spanish galleons as they passed through the Bahamas and he came to Sayle's House at Governor's Bay. There he met the servants of Bermudian Captain William Jeames who were staying at Sayle's House and had contracted the use of his shallop for wrecking purposes. On August of 1657, Richardson and his company manned their shallop and sailed with Jeames' company to a wreck north of Jeames' Man Island. There this trip was met with great success and on the first journey they recovered £2600 sterling which was placed in £100 bags, and shared at Governor's Bay, according to the agreement of 'share and share alike'; one £100 bag went to Captain Sayle's shallop and £130 to each wrecker. After a second journey to the same wreck, they returned to 'Spanish Well' to make the share, and each wrecker received about £80 sterling plus a share of silver that comprised of about 1400 pieces of eight. Furthermore, the £68,000 troy of silver treasure, raised from the Spanish Galleon *Conception* at Silver Bank, north of the Old Bahama Channel, by Captain William Phips in 1687, stirred the imagination and wetted the appetites of every sailor to go out on the treacherous Bahamian waters to look for wrecked silver and gold treasure laden ships. In fact, when Governor Fitzwilliam arrived in 1733, he remarked on the wrecking exploits of the inhabitants who knew where every Spanish wreck was located except for the one on which there were 3 million pieces of eight.

With blockade running a thing of the past, the Bahamian sailors reverted to wrecking and salvaging industry as their perennial standby. In 1865 Bishop Venables reported that the inhabitants of Bimini were entirely engaged in the dubious trade and seemed "nearly the most degraded people that I have yet visited." According to historian Michael Craton, in 1858 there had been 302 licensed wreckers, employing 2,679 men as crew, and those figures were equaled or surpassed in the first years after the Civil War. In an average pre- war year, some twenty-five vessels went aground in Bahamian waters, officially netting about £10,000 in salvage and an unknown additional amount that did not go through official channels. Wrecks were considered a regular, almost predictable, resource. In 1864, there were 48 ships wrecked and 19 damaged. In 1865, the figures were 30 and 31 respectively, and in the year of the Great Bahamas Hurricane of 1866, there were 63 and 31 respectively. Between 1855 and 1864, 37 ships were salvaged, valued at £59,988, an average of £1,620 each. In addition, 59 derelicts produced material worth £11,318. These were the official figures and doubtless there were many other ships picked off the rocks but not recorded. In 1866, for instance, of the 63 vessels wrecked, 34 were fully investigated but the fates of the others were officially cited as "mysterious."

Wreckers removing valuable cargo from inside of a wrecked ship (The Illustrated London News, Vol. 17, 1850. From the collections of The Mariners' Museum, Newport News, Virginia-Used with permission).

In 1866, when this hurricane struck the Bahamas, wrecking was at its peak and only £14,000 worth of sponges (the second industry) was harvested from the Bahamian sea-bed. This was less than one-tenth of the value of salvaged goods from wrecking. After the American Civil War and the resumption of normal trade, it appeared that the wrecking and salvaging industry would regain its former importance. In 1865 before the hurricane, the last year of blockade running, only £28,000 of wrecked goods were salvaged, but the following year after the hurricane, that figure jumped to £108,000. The American Civil War sharply decreased the volume of shipping around the Bahamas, and the wreckers suffered greatly with far fewer wrecks to salvage. The end of the Civil War brought back increased shipping and wrecks. In 1870 it soared to £154,000, an all-time high. Between 1845 and 1870, more than 300 ships were wrecked on the Bahamian reefs and shoals. The crew of these, totalling thousands of men, frequently had one hope of salvation and that was the Bahamian wreckers. The remark was made that 'so long as ships sailed the ocean and Bahama reefs stood in their way there would be wrecks.' But the very next year wrecking profits began to drastically decline and it was never reversed, and by the end of the century the wrecking industry was all but dead.

The underwriters from New York and Liverpool, the Hanseatic League, and the Board of Trade in London raised concerns about the high risks and loss of vessels engaged in commercial trade, fraudulent practices and collusive wrecking-the practice of willful wrecking through a prior agreement between a wrecker and a captain of a foreign vessel. This decline in the wrecking trade was attributed to many factors, among them was the fact that steam was taking over from sail. Second, better qualified captains and officers were employed and insurance companies were demanding greater seaworthiness of ships. Third, a network of lighthouses built by the Imperial Government, and the availability of more reliable charts also contributed to safer navigation and fewer wrecks. Fourth, with the advent of the electric telegraph, the captain and crew were better informed about the adverse weather conditions. In addition, the steamships from the eastern seaboard could take a more direct route south. They no longer travelled through the Northeast Providence Channel to get to Nassau or the Gulf but went directly south, hugging the eastern US coast. So Harbour Island and

Abaco two of the main wrecking centres in the Bahamas were no longer on the main sea-routes and wrecking opportunities were fewer. By 1868, it was reported that people of Harbour Island which at one time was the stronghold of wrecking were all gone and Eleuthera residents turned their attention to the more lucrative sponging industry and pineapple cultivation.

When the Great Bahamas Hurricane of 1866 struck the Bahamas, it provided a very rich and profitable harvest for the wreckers but sadly, their days of prosperity were numbered. This was because of the introduction of lighthouses throughout the Bahamas. Despite the most vicious opposition, the Imperial Lighthouse Service erected lighthouses and beacons and the Admiralty produced the first accurate charts of Bahamian waters significantly reducing the wrecks which occurred in these treacherous waters. When this hurricane struck the Bahamas, many Bahamian men were quite busy on the open waters either harvesting sponges or working in the wrecking industry trying to make a living for their families. Many of these native vessels or schooners were blown up on the reefs or were simply destroyed by this powerful hurricane. So even though this hurricane decimated the Bahamas, it provided some temporary employment for many of these unemployed Bahamian men.

For a period of nearly one hundred years before the Americans took possession, the Florida Keys were the providence of the Bahamian vessels that went there to hunt turtles, cut hardwood timber, and salvage wrecks. When farming failed to provide sufficient subsistence, the seamen, known as "wrackers," turned to salvaging wrecks to help make a living. The disposition of goods salvaged from wrecks was governed by strict rules set forth in the Adventurers' *Articles and Orders*. Any guns and ammunitions found in the wrecks became the property of the community for its defense. Wrecked ships and goods were sold at auction. The wreckers received one-third of the proceeds, the public treasury one-third, and the remaining third was divided among the original settlers or their heirs in equal shares.

Attracted by the news of the growing number of wrecks, more Bermudian seamen came to the Bahamas. The island of New Providence, which has a deep, protected harbour, was settled in 1656 and eventually became the capital of the Bahamas. It is not known when Bahamian wrecking vessels began coming to the Florida Keys, but the fact that the Spanish commander of the lost 1733 flota was concerned that Bahamians might attempt to salvage some of the treasure indicates they were already coming to the Florida Keys in the 1730s. Although the Florida Keys were Spanish territory, the authorities in Havana made no serious effort to keep the Bahamians away. In fact, when Spain ceded Florida to England in 1763, the departing Spanish took most, if not all, of the remaining Florida Keys natives with them to Havana. With the threat of attack by the natives eliminated, the number of Bahamian vessels coming to the Florida Keys began to grow. One year later, a Spanish official on his way from Havana to St. Augustine counted fourteen Bahamian vessels in the Florida Keys. The military governor of East Florida was upset that the Bahamians, despite the fact that they were fellow Englishmen, were trespassing on his territory and taking away valuable turtles, hardwood timber, and prized wrecked cargoes. He said, *"The people from Providence were certain unruly rascals, and that an order would soon have to be sent...to seize and punish them."* However, it was a known fact that the governor did not have the means to enforce his threat, and the Bahamian turtle hunters and wreckers continued to come to the Florida Keys in greater numbers as the main fertile grounds for wrecking and salvaging.

Wreckers at Work during a wrecking operation (Harper's New Monthly Magazine, Vol. 18, 1858/59, pg. 577. Courtesy of Florida State Archives-Used with permission).

In 1770, a British frigate, *HMS Carysfort*, went aground on the reef that still bears her name. Two days after their ship went up on their reef, the crew had the welcome sight of a Bahamian sloop and a Bahamian schooner coming to anchor nearby. The sloop carried out and planted the frigate's bower anchor as a means to haul the ship off, while the schooner carried provisions and other materials ashore to lighten the frigate. By jettisoning guns, cutting away masts, and other extraordinary measures, the frigate's crew finally heaved their vessel afloat the next day. George Gauld, an English cartographer, surveyed the Florida Keys between 1773 and 1775 to produce accurate charts. In his sailing directions for the Keys, he advised shipwrecked mariners to stand by their vessels after going aground to ensure their chances of being rescued by the Bahamian wreckers. He said, *"If we consider the activity with which the wreckers always exert themselves, we must look upon them as a set of very useful men."* Finally, the captain of the ship *Sophia Bailey*, which ran aground on a Florida Reef in 1785, had this to say of the Bahamian wrecking captains who got his ship afloat again: *"Captain Bell and the rest of the Captains have behaved with the greatest civility; and I shall make it my business to report their friendly conduct to all the underwriters at Lloyd's Coffee-house. You will be pleased to reward them for their trouble."*

Wrecking crew during a salvage operation. (Sketch by S.G. W. Benjamin in Harper's Weekly, Oct. 19, 1878, Courtesy of Florida State Archives-Used with permission).

The Bahamian wrecking vessels consisted of small sloops or schooners. Their crews were comprised mostly of whites, some free blacks, and some slaves and were men who had been seamen from their childhood days. As Governor Dunmore noted, some of them were descended from pirates who ruled Nassau in the early 1700s, and they retained a trace of outward appearance of their freebooter ancestors by carrying knives in their belts. One observer described them as *"hardy and adventurous Mariners whose power of diving is extraordinary."* In most cases, the turtling-wrecking vessels were owned by the merchants of Nassau. During the trip, they loaded the vessels with a few barrels of pork and biscuits. The crew members were expected to supplement their inadequate supply of provisions by fishing and hunting in the Florida Keys and the Bahamas. If there were a large number of wreckers operating from the same harbour, one or two of them would be assigned to fish for the entire fleet. However, they would receive a full share of the salvaged goods and income just like the others taking part in the salvage operations. The length of a voyage varied from several weeks to several months; depending on the success the boat captains had in filling their vessels with salvaged goods, turtles, or hardwood timber. Inaddition, they would salvage as much of the doomed ships' rigging, sails, and other valuable equipment of the wrecked ship as they could.

The captains favored the anchorage at Key Tavernier in the Florida Keys as a wrecking station because it commanded a view of Carysfort Reef, where the greatest number of wrecks occurred. The anchorage at Indian Key was also much used because of the availability of an abundant supply of fresh water from a large sinkhole at the eastern end of nearby Lower Matecumbe Key. The Bahamian vessels also made use of the natural harbours at Key Biscayne, Bahia Honda, Key Vaca, Big Pine Key, and Key West. In fact, it was the Bahamian wreckers which gave Newfound Harbour at Big Pine Key its name. According to the shipping news in the Bahama Gazette, during 1790 there were forty arrivals in Nassau of wrecking vessels from the Florida Keys. Some of these vessels made two, three, or four trips to the Keys during the year. The number of vessels operating in the Keys was not less than twenty-five, of which ten were sloops and fifteen were schooners. Arrival reports for the following year indicated that at least thirty-seven Bahamian vessels, twenty-three sloops, and fourteen schooners had been to the Keys.

The methods used by the Bahamians to get ships off the reef and to save their cargoes were much the same as those used by the American wreckers who succeeded them. However, the Bahamian wreckers developed and used a technique that was apparently not adopted by the Americans. The Bahamian salvage divers used an inverted cask with air trapped inside of it to prolong their working time underwater at the wreck. While condemnation of Bahamian wreckers in the 1600s as rascals, descendants of pirates, and members of a lawless race may have had some element of truth, by the end of the eighteenth century, such labels no longer applied. An article in a Bahamian newspaper shed a new light on their character. A writer who called himself *"A Friend to the Truth"* had this to say in the *Royal Gazette* on August 13, 1806: *"The Natives of the Bahamas have always as far as ever came to my knowledge, acted with Honor and Honesty to those unfortunate persons who wrecked among them; and the universal practice is, to appoint indifferent persons to say what they ought to be entitled to for their services; by which a number of lives and considerable property are saved..."*

As the years passed and the traffic through the Straits of Florida increased and wrecking became a more beneficial and profitable industry, the Bahamian vessels in the Keys turned more and more to wrecking and less and less to turtling and cutting timber. The wreckers brought their salvaged cargoes to Nassau, where the goods were sold at auction. Customs duties took fifteen percent, and the governor received a tithe. On goods not claimed by owners, the Vice Admiralty Court took thirty percent. As a matter of fact, after the end of the War of 1812, the annual revenue from duties, estimated at fifteen thousand pounds sterling, became the main source of income for the city of Nassau. Salvage awards to the wrecking vessels ranged from between forty to sixty percent of the net value of the cargo saved. Half of this went to the owner and half to the crew, divided into shares according to an agreement drawn up before the voyage. Although the wrecking and salvaging trade was generally viewed as a very lucrative occupation, this was not true for the crew of these vessels. In reality, a wrecking crewman's average take was less than the wage of a common labourer. Eventually, the Bahamian wreckers confined their trade strictly to the islands of the Bahamas when the Americans Congress in 1825 passed a law forbidding non-Americans from salvaging wrecks anywhere in the United States. This new legislation by the US Government made it illegal for these activities to continue and any wrecking ship engaged in the jurisdiction of the US on the Florida Coast was seized and forfeited and any wrecked goods salvaged on the Florida Keys belonged to the United States.

In the course of the salvage operations, particularly in rough weather, wrecking vessels suffered much damage (Chronicles of the Sea, No. 58, Dec.15, 1838, pg. 457. From the collections of The Mariners' Museum, Newport News, Virginia-Used with permission).

Because of its strategic position at the entrance to the Gulf of Mexico and gateway to the western Caribbean, the Bahamas became a major shipping lane in the 1800s. Many of these islands became major shipping ports and wrecking centers. Efforts were eventually made to make the passage through the Bahamas safer by erecting lighthouses and conducting surveys to develop accurate shipping charts and these were done to decrease the amount of wrecks happening within the Bahamas. As more and more lighthouses marked the reef (much to the disgust of the wreckers), as accurate charts of the Bahamas and the reef became available, and as steam replaced sail, the days of the sailing wreckers drew to an end and was replaced by the more lucrative sponging industry. By 1896, when wrecked goods were valued at only £2000, sponge products had climbed to £81,000. Sponging had taken the place of wrecking as the main maritime industry of the Bahamian people.

CHAPTER SEVEN

BLOCKADE RUNNING IN THE BAHAMAS JUST BEFORE THE GREAT BAHAMAS HURRICANE OF 1866.

Busy Nassau Harbour during the blockade years with bales of cotton from the Confederate States being unloaded at Nassau, 1864. (Courtesy of the Illustrated London News, April 18, 1864, Courtesy of the Department of Archives, Nassau, Bahamas).

The fledgling United States of America, which were united in their resolve to be independent from Great Britain, were sharply divided over the issue of slavery. This division led to a war between the North and the South, which began on the 12th April 1861. President Abraham Lincoln, a Northerner, ordered a blockade of all the Southern ports from Virginia to Texas, a distance of 4,000 miles. The major Southern ports covered by the President's order were Savannah, Charleston and Wilmington. The Confederate States of America badly needed manufactured goods, but could not produce them because there were only a few factories. There was also a need by the Confederacy for guns and ammunition. Where the Confederacy lacked manufactured goods, there was an abundance of cotton. A way had to be found to circumvent the blockade, and trade cotton for manufactured goods, guns and ammunition.

For most of the 19th century, the Bahamian Islands were tranquil, although not very prosperous owing to few trading opportunities. Most families lived on subsistence farming until blockade running came along and changed that. The Bahamas, particularly Nassau, became a very important trans-shipment point for the receipt of cotton from the South in exchange for manufactured goods, guns, ammunition, medicines and clothing from the factories of Europe. This illegal trade became known as blockade running and the ships that tried to evade the blockade were known as blockade runners. Special vessels were built to facilitate the running of the blockade.

*The Civil War Blockade Ship the Banshee on the open
waters (Sketch Courtesy of R.G. Stevens).*

Blockade-runners were the fastest ships available, and often lightly armed and armored. Ordinary ships were too slow and visible to escape the Navy. Most were operated by the British and concentrated on running between Confederate-controlled ports and the ports of Havana, Cuba; Nassau, Bahamas, and Bermuda, where British suppliers were receiving and offering trade but Nassau held the place of importance since it was nearer and less coal was required. Their operation was quite risky since the blockading fleets would not hesitate to fire on them. However, the potential profits (economically or militarily) from a successful blockade run were tremendous, so blockade-runners typically had excellent crews. Although having the modus operandi similar to that of smugglers, blockade-runners were often operated by private British citizens (using Royal Navy Officers on leave) and sometimes in partnerships with persons from the South as part of the regular fleet. As the Union tightened and strengthened the blockade of the Southern ports, it became necessary to build these faster vessels. These were, perhaps, the prototype for today's fast boats. Ordinary ships built in the United States and Europe were too slow and visible to escape the Navy so the blockade runners therefore relied mainly on new ships built in England with low profiles, shallow draft, camouflaged with grey paint, and high speeds. Their paddle-wheels, driven by steam engines burned smokeless anthracite coal and could make 17 knots or more, which was faster than nearly anything in the US Navy. The blockade runners preferred to run past the Union Navy on moonless nights or at least before the moon rose or after it set and in some cases the sailors were forbidden even to light their smoking pipes.

Private British investors spent perhaps £50 million on the runners ($250 million in U.S. dollars, equivalent to about $2.5 billion in today's currency). The pay was high: a Royal Navy officer on leave might earn several thousand dollars (in gold) in salary and bonus per round trip, with ordinary seamen earning several hundred dollars. In fact, a captain could get $5,000 in gold for a round trip, and a pilot $3,500. Even common sailors might get $250 for a trip, more than a year's pay in the Navy. On dark nights they ran the gauntlet to and from the British islands of Bermuda and the Bahamas, or Havana, Cuba, 500-700 miles away. In these neutral ports, cargo was transferred to southern blockade runners for the final dash past the union Navy. The ships carried several hundred tons of compact, high-value cargo such as, cotton, turpentine or tobacco outbound, and rifles, medicine, brandy, lingerie and coffee inbound. They charged from $300 to $1,000 per ton of cargo brought in; two round trips a month would generate perhaps $250,000 in revenue (and $80,000 in wages and expenses). Between 1861 and 1865 about 400 vessels entered Nassau from Confederate ports, 156 of these coming from Charleston and 164 from Wilmington. In most of these vessels there were usually two pilots, one a non-Bahamian and the other a Bahamian who was responsible for taking the ship in and out of Nassau Harbour and navigating through the treacherous Bahamian waters. During the period of the War, there were 88 ships which left Nassau for Southern ports, though 432 of these supposedly cleared for New Brunswick or ports in the West Indies.

Nassau Harbour, ordinarily quiet enough, was teeming with activity during these war years. *The Bahama Herald*, May 14, 1862, listed all the craft in the harbour on that particular date, conclusive evidence that the world had at last discovered the Bahamas. These craft included: eight steamers; *H.M.S.S. Bull Dog*, *Thomas L. Wagg* (also known as the *Nashville*, a famous Confederate privateer), *Stellin*, *Kate*, *Cecile*, *Nelly*, *Elizabeth*, and *Nassau*; as well as one British ship; two barques--one British and one French; six brigs--four of them American, one British, and one Spanish. There were six schooners-one American, one Brazilian and four others from various countries. There were five topsail schooners of which one was British. There were quite a number of smaller crafts, some of which were schooners and others steamers. The steamers *Minnow* and *Oreto* were located at Cochrane's Anchorage near the harbour. In Nassau, money flowed like water, labouring wages more than doubled in the urgent business of building warehouses, and moving goods. In Nassau, life was easy and free so Out Island people flocked into the capital to claim their share of this seemingly inexhaustible wealth. Often, there was no place to live, but that did not stop them from coming, so often times these workers slept on porches, in sheds, on the street and between bales of cotton. Their pockets were filled with money and that was the most important thing.

The excitement, extravagance and waste existing at Nassau during the days of blockade-running exceeded belief. Nassau, long the obscurest of British colonial capitals, and with an ordinary poor and indifferent population, became overnight the host to a reckless, wealthy and extravagant crowd of men from many nations and many ranks. English and American businessmen took over Bay Street and the harbour front. The new Royal Victoria Hotel, built at a cost of £26,000, was the centre of business and social activities. There, on the cool verandahs and patios, daring captains and pilots, eager buyers and sellers, Confederate officers and agents, and Federal spies, would talk over the news, arrange deals, throw dice, eat their sumptuous meals and drink champagne. Shops and warehouses sprouted up as fast as they could be built and they were filled to capacity with supplies to cater to this wealthy crowd.

After the introduction of steam communications between New York and Nassau began in 1859, and the blockade running era, it became necessary to build a hotel to accommodate this large influx of visitors. The Royal Victoria Hotel was built by the Bahamas Government to fill this need. An Act to erect the hotel was passed in April 1859 and the building of the Royal Victoria Hotel soon commenced. It was completed during the prosperous days of the American Civil War and the unprecedented influx of visitors necessitated an expansion of the original plans for the hotel. A period of great prosperity followed and the Royal Victoria Hotel became the scene of great excitement being patronized by members of the Confederate army and daring blockade runners.

There were newspaper correspondents, English Navy officers on leave with half pay, underwriters, entertainers, adventurers, spies, crooks and bums. Fortunes, which ordinarily could not be accumulated in a lifetime, were made in a few weeks. Quinine, which could be bought in Nassau for $10 was worth $400 in Charleston. An investor who bought $100 worth of cotton in Wilmington would receive $1000 for the same weight in England. Captains, pilots and sailors of the blockade runners found it impossible to spend, or even squander, all of the money they made here in Nassau. Out Islanders flocked to the little city to grab a share of gold which flowed like water. One visitor reported that there were traders of so many nationalities in Nassau that the languages on the streets reminded one of the tongues of Babel. *"The wharves of Nassau,"* wrote one commentator, *"were piled high with cotton...the harbour was crowded with lead-coloured, shortmasted, rakish looking steamers; the streets...swarmed with drunken revelers at night."* The city of Nassau enjoyed a booming trade from the blockade runners. England tried to maintain neutrality during the War but the Bahamas made their own interpretation of British neutrality. They construed the laws of neutrality vigorously against the United States and as laxly as possible toward the South. In other words, the Bahamians were pro-confederate because of the many economic benefits derived from being sympathizing to them.

As a result of the American Civil War and the subsequent trade in blockade running, the Bahamian economy benefited tremendously. There was a building boom; government revenues increased, as did employment for Bahamians. It was during this period that the Royal Victoria Hotel, which was named in honour of Queen Victoria, was built in 1861. There were improvements in public works and the police force was increased. Unfortunately for the Bahamas, the American Civil War ended on the 8th April, 1865 with the surrender of the Confederacy, resulting in the cessation of blockade running. Nassau and the entire Bahamas, which had prospered from the calamity of the Civil War, were destined to share the fate of the defeated Confederacy. Wharves, warehouses, hotels, and boarding houses were quickly emptied, the 'dancing saloons in Grants Town' closed, employment and extravagant expenditure and lifestyles were also suddenly ended, and government projects were cancelled before completion. So demoralizing was the sudden cutback to merchants, professionals, and workers alike and so great the fears among the ruling social class of crime and popular discontent that many expressed the wish that the bonanza of the blockade running had never happened. In fact, this pronouncement was stressed by a middle-class black writing in *The Nassau Guardian* in 1868, under the nom-de-plume Africus: *"In our present state it can be truly said that labourers are plenteous, but there is very little field and scarcely any harvest…There is not a glance of any more brighter days, or a prospect of pecuniary prosperity here. Previous to the late American War we were better off, I may say, in many things."* The tremendous boom that the Bahamas had experienced ceased as abruptly as it began. During the period of prosperity brought on by the blockade running, many persons-among them sea captains, smugglers, spies and merchants came to the Bahamas. Many of these persons remained in the Bahamas, thus influencing its culture and the course of Bahamian history.

Individuals may have profited largely, but the Bahamas probably benefited little. The Bahamas Government managed to pay its debt amounting to £43,786, but crime increased and sickness became prevalent. The cessation of the trade was marked, however, by hardly any disturbance; there were no local failures, and in a few months the steamers and their crews departed, and New Providence subsided into its usual state of quietude. This, however, was not fated to last long, for in October 1866 a most violent and powerful hurricane passed over the island, devastating orchards, destroying fruit-trees, and damaging the sponges, which had proved hitherto a source of profit. The hurricane, too, was followed by repeated droughts, and the inhabitants of the Out Islands were reduced to indigence and wanting for more.

When the Great Hurricane of 1866 struck the Bahamas, the last of the blockade runners, a boat called *The General Clinch* was in the Nassau Harbour. Even though the blockade had ended for well over a year prior to the storm passage, this ship was smashed to pieces by this powerful hurricane. Certainly there was a dreadful fate in store for the city of Nassau after the blockade. In 1866 the worst hurricane of the century hit the Bahamas. The ocean rolled completely over Hog Island (now called Paradise Island) and into the harbour with crests of waves over sixty feet high. Boats were dashed to pieces, houses and forests went down like reeds. Nassau was like a city that had been sacked and burned by the enemy. Many of the new buildings and other significant improvements acquired during the war and the blockade simply disappeared or was destroyed by this hurricane. So great and so complete was the tragedy that many saw in it the hands of a vengeful God punishing a wicked and disobedient people for their over-indulgence and recklessness. No building escaped damage and some, such as John S. George's brand-new warehouse, were totally destroyed. Rebuilding and repairs completely drained Nassau's resources, private and public. By 1869, the very credit of the Bahamas Government was threatened, and despite an official inquiry into expenditure, officers' salaries fell three months into arrears. Repeated droughts followed the hurricane and most of the Bahamians were reduced to a state of poverty. For many years afterwards, Bahamians were accustomed to speak of the year of 1866, as the 'year of the great hurricane.' Prior to this year, individual hurricanes which struck the Bahamas normally only affected only a particular section of the archipelago, leaving the rest of the islands relatively unscathed. But this particular storm swept and devastated the entire chain of islands as you will see later.

CHAPTER EIGHT

THE GREAT BAHAMAS HURRICANE OF 1866 IMPACT ON THE ISLANDS OF THE BAHAMAS.

Natural disasters are nothing new to the Caribbean region and the Bahamas is no exception. However, the *Great Bahamas Hurricane of 1866*(sometimes also referred to as *'The Great Bahama Hurricane of 1866' or 'The Gale of 1866'[in those days hurricanes were simply referred to as 'Gales' rather than hurricanes]*) was definitely one of the most dangerous, destructive and enduring hurricanes to ever make its trek across these archipelagic islands. The exact death toll is unknown but it was estimated that as much as 387 persons died in this deadly hurricane. In 1866 the colony of the Bahamas was heavily dependent on sponging, fishing, farming and wrecking and salvaging for their livelihood. The Great Bahamas Hurricane of 1866 was uniquely different than many of the more recent destructive Bahamian hurricanes like Andrew, Floyd, Frances and Jeanne. Simply because it occurred in the late 1800's at a time when the technology that we have today was not available for storm tracking. There were no satellites, radars, radios, televisions, or computers to give the residents of these islands any kind of advanced notice that a storm was approaching. This storm sneaked up on these islands like a thief in the night, causing widespread chaos and significant damage to many homes and businesses. The collapse of blockade running had produced an awful slump, and then the hurricane came along and destroyed what was left of the Bahamian economic way of life.

Meteorological History

This storm was a classical Cape Verde-type hurricane and was first observed on September 24 off the coast of Africa. This well-known intense hurricane was well documented around the region and in the

Bahamas. The *New York Times*, October 25, 1866 reported that the ship *'Jarien'* from Rio de Janeiro encountered this hurricane in the central Atlantic. This is the earliest and easternmost report of an encounter with this storm. It headed west-northwestward, reaching major hurricane strength north of the Lesser Antilles on the 29th. As it neared the Bahamas it strengthened to a powerful 140 mph Category 4 hurricane, causing widespread damage across the islands and leaving behind a significant death toll. This storm left St. Thomas, the Virgin Islands, on the morning of September 28, 1866 where several ships were blown ashore and a pier demolished.

By the early hours of September 30th it was affecting the Turks and Caicos Islands where 75% of the entire population was left destitute and homeless because the storm destroyed hundreds of homes, resulting in 63 deaths. This storm then entered the islands of the Southeast Bahamas where Mayaguana recorded gale force winds coming from the northeast. By eight o' clock that morning the hurricane had progressed as far as Matthew Town, Inagua, and a 'light wind' was reported at Fortune Island(now Long Cay), just northwest of Crooked Island. San Salvador (then Watlings Island) received the outer fringes of the hurricane at three in the afternoon, and by eight o'clock in the evening of Sunday, September 30th, Cat Island and Long Island were being battered by the storm. It was at that time that the first evidence of the storm was felt in Nassau.

The day had passed as usual; the people had attended the usual evening church services, spending the hours after on their verandahs socializing. The air was still and as one writer in the Nassau Guardian noted, *"all was calm and tranquil...there was, however, a peculiar reddish hue in the heavens...and an unusual warmth in the atmosphere."* At eight o' clock that evening, the winds were blowing from the north and it grew stronger as the night progressed and the barometer reading was 30.16 inches on the day of the 30th to 29.80 inches at 11:00am the following morning. The hurricane remained over Nassau for the rest of the day, the twenty three diameter eye passed over the town in the early evening. There was a lull then for as long as an hour and a half; then the winds increased in intensity from the opposite direction and continued to blow violently until 2:00am (on October 2nd) when it gradually subsided. The barometric pressure, taken during the lull, was as low as 27.70 inches, and was recorded about half an hour before the winds began to blow again. Sea surges swamped the harbour, disregarding the islands which normally acted as a buffer against these storms.

A writer who talked with eye witnesses a few years later recalled, *"The Ocean rolled completely over Hog Island in surges so enormous that the crest was even with the gallery of the lighthouse, sixty feet above the sea. Houses and forests went down before the wind like reeds; many which withstood its force when it blew from the north-east collapsed when it shifted to the south-west. In twenty-four hours the city was like a town sacked and burned by the enemy..."* The hurricane moved away from New Providence quickly; by the morning of October 3, it had left the waters of the Bahamas. It then recurved out to sea without affecting any other landmasses. The last report on the system was on October 5, after resulting in massive casualties in the Bahamas, it caused an additional 250 deaths from the steamer *Evening Star* (from Sinking of the Titanic). It is very possible that the hurricane was stronger while over open waters in the Atlantic, but the meteorological records from the 1800s and early 20th century were very sparse and also contributed to the reduced number of tropical cyclones in the hurricane season archives of 1866.

Meteorological Track of The Great Bahamas Hurricane of 1866

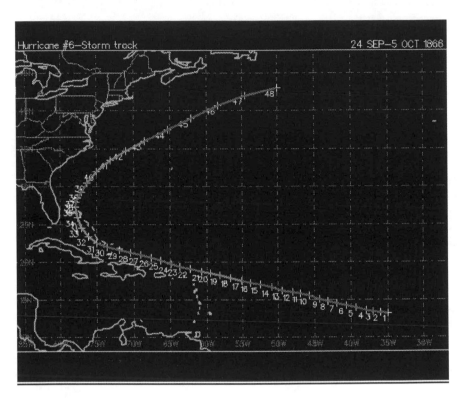

This map shows the track of the Great Bahamas Hurricane of 1866 as it moved through the Bahamas (Information courtesy Of Unisys's Weather Inc.).

Date: 24 SEP-5 OCT 1866
Hurricane #6

ADV	LAT	LON	TIME	WIND Kt(mph)	STAT
1	13.20	35.00	09/24/00Z	80 (92 mph)	- HURRICANE-1
2	13.30	36.00	09/24/06Z	80 (92 mph)	- HURRICANE-1
3	13.40	37.00	09/24/12Z	80 (92 mph)	- HURRICANE-1
4	13.60	38.00	09/24/18Z	80 (92 mph)	- HURRICANE-1
5	13.90	39.40	09/25/00Z	80 (92 mph)	- HURRICANE-1
6	14.20	40.70	09/25/06Z	80 (92 mph)	- HURRICANE-1
7	14.50	42.00	09/25/12Z	80 (92 mph)	- HURRICANE-1

ADV	LAT	LON	TIME	WIND Kt(mph)	STAT
8	14.80	43.20	09/25/18Z	80 (92 mph)	- HURRICANE-1
9	15.10	44.30	09/26/00Z	80 (92 mph)	- HURRICANE-1
10	15.50	45.70	09/26/06Z	80 (92 mph)	- HURRICANE-1
11	15.80	47.00	09/26/12Z	80 (92 mph)	- HURRICANE-1
12	16.00	48.00	09/26/18Z	80 (92 mph)	- HURRICANE-1
13	16.20	49.50	09/27/00Z	80 (92 mph)	- HURRICANE-1
14	16.60	50.90	09/27/06Z	80 (92 mph)	- HURRICANE-1
15	17.00	52.50	09/27/12Z	80 (92 mph)	- HURRICANE-1
16	17.20	53.90	09/27/18Z	80 (92 mph)	- HURRICANE-1
17	17.50	55.10	09/28/00Z	90 (104 mph)	- HURRICANE-2
18	17.90	56.70	09/28/06Z	90 (104 mph)	- HURRICANE-2
19	18.20	58.20	09/28/12Z	90 (104 mph)	- HURRICANE-2
20	18.50	59.50	09/28/18Z	90 (104 mph)	- HURRICANE-2
21	18.70	60.70	09/29/00Z	100 (115 mph)	- HURRICANE-3
22	19.10	62.30	09/29/06Z	100 (115 mph)	- HURRICANE-3
23	19.40	63.70	09/29/12Z	100 (115 mph)	- HURRICANE-3
24	19.70	64.90	09/29/18Z	100 (115 mph)	- HURRICANE-3
25	20.20	66.30	09/30/00Z	100 (115 mph)	- HURRICANE-3
26	20.60	67.60	09/30/06Z	100 (115 mph)	- HURRICANE-3
27	20.90	69.00	09/30/12Z	100 (115 mph)	- HURRICANE-3
28	21.20	70.40	09/30/18Z	100 (115 mph)	- HURRICANE-3
29	21.60	71.90	10/01/00Z	110 (127 mph)	- HURRICANE-3
30	22.00	73.60	10/01/06Z	110 (127 mph)	- HURRICANE-3
31	22.50	75.00	10/01/12Z	120 (138 mph)	- HURRICANE-4
32	23.40	76.10	10/01/18Z	120 (138 mph)	- HURRICANE-4
33	24.50	77.10	10/02/00Z	120 (138 mph)	- HURRICANE-4
34	25.90	77.60	10/02/06Z	120 (138 mph)	- HURRICANE-4
35	27.30	77.90	10/02/12Z	110 (127 mph)	- HURRICANE-3
36	28.00	77.80	10/02/18Z	110 (127 mph)	- HURRICANE-3
37	28.50	77.60	10/03/00Z	100 (115 mph)	- HURRICANE-3
38	29.30	77.10	10/03/06Z	100 (115 mph)	- HURRICANE-3
39	30.50	76.30	10/03/12Z	90 (104 mph)	- HURRICANE-2
40	32.00	75.00	10/03/18Z	90 (104 mph)	- HURRICANE-2
41	33.50	73.10	10/04/00Z	90 (104 mph)	- HURRICANE-2

ADV	LAT	LON	TIME	WIND Kt(mph)	STAT
42	34.70	71.00	10/04/06Z	90 (104 mph)	- HURRICANE-2
43	36.00	68.50	10/04/12Z	80 (92 mph)	- HURRICANE-1
44	37.50	65.30	10/04/18Z	80 (92 mph)	- HURRICANE-1
45	39.00	62.10	10/05/00Z	80 (92 mph)	- HURRICANE-1
46	40.70	58.40	10/05/06Z	80 (92 mph)	- HURRICANE-1
47	42.00	54.50	10/05/12Z	70 (81 mph)	- HURRICANE-1
48	43.00	50.00	10/05/18Z	70 (81 mph)	- HURRICANE-1

Information Courtesy of National Climatic Data Center and National Hurricane Center (NOAA), and Unisys's Weather.

According to observations, the Great Hurricane of 1866 entered the Bahamas by the Southeast Bahamas somewhere between the islands of Mayaguana and Inagua on a northwesterly track with the sustained winds of approximately 130 mph. It then passed just due southwest of the island of San Salvador and made a direct passage over the island of Crooked Island. After making a passage over the Island of Crooked Island it then crossed over the islands of Long Island and Exuma. After passing over the Exuma Cays, its direction changed to a more northwesterly track. It was during this time that its intensity increased and was packing sustained winds of over 140 mph. After leaving Exuma, its forward speed increased and its movement changed to a more north northwesterly direction. It then went on to devastate with a direct hit, the island of New Providence as a strong Category 4 or perhaps borderline Category 5 storm. The hurricane then crossed over central Grand Bahama on a now more northerly track and it then exited the Bahamas into the open waters of the Atlantic.

DAMAGES

Nassau

THE HURRICANE ON THE BAHAMAS—SCENE AT NASSAU, NEW PROVIDENCE ISLAND, OCTOBER 1, 1866.

The Illustrated view of Nassau Harbour during the Great Bahamas Hurricane of 1866 (Courtesy of Jonathon Ramsey, Balmain Antiques and Harper's Weekly).

In 1861, the official population of the city of Nassau was estimated to be approximately 11,503 persons and of that total approximately 3,713 persons lived in the suburbs of Grants Town, Bain Town and Delancy Town. By 1866, the unofficial population was estimated to be somewhere in the vicinity of 12,000 to 13,000 persons. In the harbour, every vessel and boat, with one single exception, was driven ashore or badly damaged and wrecked. The southern shore was strewn with wrecked boats and in some places was piled on top of one another. An engraving published by Day & Son in London, from a sketch made by Lieut. Bale, of H.M. 1st West India Regiment, gives a view of part of the harbour and of the stranded shipping after the storm. The road along the coast to the east of the island was blocked up with colonial vessels pilled on top of one another making the road impassable. One ocean steamer was found miles away from its original mooring and another '*The General Clinch*' the last of the blockade runners remaining in the harbour had been smashed into countless pieces against the public wharf, after having crushed and inflicted a similar fate upon a colonial schooner. Proximity to the U.S. continued to provide opportunity for illegal shipping activity. In the course of the American Civil War (1861 to 1865), the Bahamas prospered as a center of Confederate blockade-running. During the Prohibition era, these islands served as a base for American rumrunners. Nassau was a place of no special importance before the war. Its inhabitants lived chiefly by fishing, sponging and wrecking. But with the demands of the blockade, it suddenly became a commercial emporium. Its harbour was crowded with ships of many countries. Its wharves were covered with cotton-bales awaiting transportation to Europe, and with merchandise ready to be shipped for the blockaded country. Confederate agents were established here, and took charge of the interests of their Government in connection with the contraband trade. Money was quickly earned and was freely spent, and the war, at least while it lasted, enriched the community.

The number of foreign vessels in the harbour at the time was small but of the colonial vessels and boats the number was great. Of the crafts in the harbour, 92 were totally destroyed, 97 were badly damaged and 43 were slightly damaged. With these vessels a greater part of the population depended heavily on maritime commerce for their survival. As stated earlier, the Bahamas in 1866 relied heavily on wrecking and salvaging, sponging and fishing for their livelihood and with all of these industries they depended heavily on these vessels for daily survival. Many of the streets of New Providence were filled with debris from fallen trees, damaged houses and in most cases roofs were torn off, sometimes in whole and at other times in pieces. Many trees were uprooted and their branches were torn off and thrown about like match sticks. No building escaped damage and some, such as John S. George's brand-new warehouse, was totally destroyed. At Fort Charlotte, the Artillery Barracks were unroofed-the Esplanade wall was destroyed and the terrace washed away. The two beacons, one on the terrace and the other on the top of the hill, used as leading landmarks for entering the Nassau Harbour, were blown down. The sea had broken through the Esplanade and shore barrier, and washed hundreds of tons of sand and wreckage into the road. Further on down the street, it was washed away in several places, so that it was rendered impassable for quite a while after the storm. Furthermore, communications with the west of the island was halted for carts and carriages for a considerable time. Between the Fort and Fleming Square many of the houses were badly damaged, blown down or totally destroyed and the road was rendered impassable. In some cases wooden houses were displaced and found several hundred feet away from where they were originally located.

After the Great Bahamas Hurricane of 1866, the town of Nassau was totally devastated. This is an extremely rare photo of Fredrick Street after the hurricane. The house in the foreground, to the right, a landmark to this day, was known during part of the 1900s as the Damianos House. In 1866, it was a Commissary for the West India Regiment and quarters for some of its officers. The far corner of its roof points at the house on the north corner of Shirley Street and Frederick, now known as the Rees Building. Below Damianos House is a horse and dray (Taken from the book 'Reminiscing II- Photographs of Old Nassau' by Ronald Lightbourn, used with permission).

In the Navy and Ordnance yards, which were adjoined to each other and the piers were washed away and the wooden stores, bathing-houses, boat-sheds and parts of the surrounding walls were blown down. The eastern wing of the Barracks was unroofed and part of the officers' quarters was unroofed and the other sides escaped with only slight damage. The Military Hospital, just repaired and improved, was unroofed, and some parts of its walls were blown down. One portion of the Commandant's quarters was blown down and the remainder unroofed and badly damaged and the other officer's detached quarters and Mess House were unroofed and flooded. The Government House and all the public buildings were badly damaged and the entire upper story was rendered uninhabitable and the Governor and his family were relocated to a private resident's house until the repair could be done to the building itself. The main public building, accommodating the courthouse and council member quarters was unroofed and badly damaged. The dome of the Nassau Prison was partly stripped and the main building of the New Providence Asylum was partly unroofed.

This illustrated picture shows the damaged ruins of the Trinity Methodist Church after the Great Bahamas Hurricane of 1866, taken from photographs by Mr. W. Davenport. (Courtesy of the Nassau Department of Archives/Illustrated London News-Used with permission).

Trinity Church, which had been finished just a few months before the hurricane at considerable expense, was blown down and was not reopened until 1869. This building was built for the Wesleyan Methodists, at a cost of nearly £8000, one fourth of which was contributed by a grant from the local Government. It was opened for public worship in April, 1865. The Great Hurricane of 1866 destroyed it. It was rebuilt and reopened in 1869 and again destroyed in 1886 by another hurricane. Being rebuilt in its original Gothic Style of architecture (the plan was originally drawn in England by Mr. Pocock), it was rebuilt with the present roof being about ten feet lower than the former one. The cost of the building and its re-erection cost nearly £14,000, about £4,250 being granted by the Legislature. In 1928 and 1929 it was again badly damaged by these two great hurricanes. However, the insurance claims were sufficient to put back the church as it is today. There has been no significant change to the fabric of the church since then.

Bethel Baptist Church was also blown down but was rebuilt by the congregation and aided by a grant of £200 by the Legislature. The Church at St. Anne's and Dunmore Chapel, to the east were totally destroyed. The Cathedral, St. Mathew's Church, the Missionary Hall, St. Andrew's Presbyterian Church and Ebenezer Church were all badly damaged in some way or the other. The Girl's Western School, the principal school house on the Woodcock property and Mr. Watkins School-House Chapel were among those that were blown down. The Theatre was also unroofed and badly damaged. The extensive buildings at the Quarantine Station on Athol Island, which was only recently completed a few months before the hurricane, were all blown down. On Bay Street, a large number of stores were totally destroyed and many others suffered tremendous damage to both the buildings and the supplies within them. In the Downtown area, a total of 27 shops and several warehouses were totally destroyed, 46 were badly damaged and 19 were unroofed. Even the dead bodies were affected by the disaster. An old cemetery on the western seashore was washed out and bones and skulls littered the beach. Almost all of the street lamps were totally destroyed or damaged. The lantern at Hog Island (now Paradise Island) was broken, and most of the lamps and reflectors were either destroyed or badly damaged. The reports of the summary of damages sustained to the city of Nassau were as follows: -

	Eastern District	Grants Town	Western District	Total
Houses Destroyed	231	269	112	612
Houses Damaged	287	277	49	613
Warehouses Destroyed	3	14	-	17
Warehouses Damaged	5	13	-	18
Shops Destroyed	9	1	3	13
Shops Damaged	17	4	-	21
Out Buildings Destroyed	319	228	85	632
Out Buildings Damaged	48	77	5	130
Churches and Chapels Destroyed	3	2	-	5
Churches and Chapels Damaged	1	1	-	2
Schoolhouses Destroyed	4	1	1	6
Schoolhouses Damaged	-	2	-	2
Theatre Destroyed	-	1	-	1
Persons Rendered Homeless	487	339	208	1034

The summary of damages sustained to the city of Nassau after the Great Bahamas Hurricane of 1866 (Taken from Governor Rawson's Report).

The Illustrated view of the wreckage at Nassau Harbour after the Great Bahamas Hurricane of 1866. This illustration shows the effects of the hurricane at Nassau, from photographs by Mr. W. Davenport where it shows the sea wall or as it was called then The Public Abutment, broken and bestrewed with fragments of the wreck of The General Clinch and other vessels driven against it (Courtesy of The Illustrated London News and Mr. Jonathon Ramsey, Balmain Antiques).

Inagua

The storm first made its impact in the Bahamas on the island of Inagua on the 30th September 1866. The first sign of an approaching storm was felt sometime around 11am and the storm reached its peak sometime around 9pm to 12 midnight. The damage to this island was said to be minimal with the exception of three lost fishing vessels and two others slightly damaged. Fortunately, the life-blood of Inagua-the salt ponds were not badly damaged or disrupted. Inagua therefore escaped and the price of salt rose considerably, one-third or more, in consequence of the destruction of harvested salt in the Turks and Caicos Islands, and in other islands of the Bahamas group. From the report received from Cay Lobos lighthouse, on the southern edge of the Great Bahama Bank, some 250 miles due west of the island of Inagua, the greatest force of the hurricane was felt there about the same time as at Inagua.

Mayaguana

The centre of the hurricane passed over this island sometime just before midnight on the 30th September. At Betsy Bay, the main settlement, on the northwestern shore, ten out of the thirteen houses were totally destroyed.

Long Cay

The canal of the salt pond was seriously damaged. Between 50,000 to 60,000 bushels of salt or about one-third of the year's crop, were destroyed. Masonry buildings which had withstood the sea and floods for more and 50 years and many previous hurricanes disappeared in this hurricane. This island had one notable advantage and that was the fact that there were two to three rich resident proprietors with significant means who provided the destitute residents with employment. The population was almost exclusively engaged in the production of salt, and fortunately, the remaining two thirds of the crop were able to keep the island residents employed after the storm. Furthermore, the supplies sent down from Nassau were used to keep remaining residents from starving and employed after the storm. Houses to the leeward side of the salt heaps had salt showered on them like hail, and all the tanks were filled with salt or salt water. Here is the list of damages sustained to Long Cay: -

Totally Destroyed:

1 church (Episcopal)
1 chapel (native Baptist)
28 dwelling houses
41 other buildings
4 fishing vessels
12 boats

Damaged, Unroofed or Otherwise Affected by the Storm:

6 vessels
5 boats

1 Jailhouse
39 dwelling houses

East Bay Street totally devastated after the Great Bahamas Hurricane of 1866. The Harbour at right was not reclaimed until 1937-38, when Roland Symonette(later Sir Roland) moved his Hog Island shipyard to the Nassau side, and called it Symonette's Shipyard(Taken from the book 'Reminiscing II- Photographs of Old Nassau' by Ronald Lightbourn, used with permission).

Crooked and Acklins Islands

Three fourths of the dwelling homes were totally destroyed and the entire population of this island was left in a deplorable state without food or shelter. In many areas, the sea overflowed the fields, destroying all the vegetation, while the high lands were devastated by the violence of the wind and the rain. At Crooked Island, two native Baptist chapels were destroyed, and at Acklins there were three chapels destroyed. After the hurricane, the residents were able to survive of farm produce not destroyed in the storm and the money gained from the profitable wrecking and salvaging industry.

Ragged Island

From this island, it was reported that the public school house was blown down, but none of the private dwellings were seriously impacted. However, about 50,000 bushels of salt were lost by the rise of the storm surge during the hurricane. One schooner was driven ashore, and ten boats and schooners were more or less destroyed or otherwise badly damaged. The farming grounds were flooded and contaminated with salt water from the storm surge making them unusable for farming. The majority of the farm animals on this island were killed during the storm.

Long Island

The entire island of Long Island was said to be totally devastated and almost every building was swept to the ground. Ten days after the storm, the residents were said to be living in caves and suffering severely from starvation and only barely surviving of land crabs and fish. During the hurricane, 62 residents had to seek shelter in the prison and 23 residents had to seek shelter in the police office because their private residents were all destroyed by the hurricane. On one of the most flourishing estates at the north end, all of the buildings of the proprietor were blown down, except the kitchen, in which 47 persons had to seek refuge. The owner of the estate sent to Clarence Town, the seat of magistracy, for food but there was none to spare. In the settlement of Clarence Town, there were only five houses which remained standing. The Government schooner *Sarah E. Douglas* was blown from her anchorage at Long Cay and drifted out to sea and was later discovered demasted and destroyed on the shores of Long Island. The cotton plantations throughout the island were totally destroyed or otherwise badly damaged.

The damages to Long Island were as follows: -
3 churches (Episcopal)
2 churches (Baptist)
1 schoolhouse
5 stores
230 dwelling houses
5 schooners

2 sloops
16 boats

The three public buildings, showing significant roof damage from the Great Bahamas Hurricane of 1866. Bay Street, in front of them, would have been flooded with salt water by waves rolling in from the Nassau Harbour (Taken from the book 'Reminiscing II-Photographs of Old Nassau' by Ronald Lightbourn, used with permission).

Rum Cay

This island was said to be totally devastated by this hurricane. All of the local crops were totally destroyed and starvation was said to be widespread. The majority of the residents on this island, were left homeless or in a deplorable state as most of their homes were completely destroyed. The population of Rum Cay was mainly employed in raking salt and sadly about 130,000 bushels, the greater part of an unusually large crop, was destroyed by this hurricane. The damage to the salt-pond was estimated at £1,000. A resident of Rum Cay offered to repair the salt-pond for half that amount if he was allowed to be paid in corn for him and his labourers. Unfortunately, the proposal was met with some opposition so the offer was eventually refused.

1 church (Episcopal) destroyed
2 chapels (Baptist) destroyed
2 chapels (Baptist) severely damaged
1 police office and prison, unroofed
1 schoolhouse destroyed
3 canals of salt pond destroyed
2 stores destroyed
2 wharves destroyed
22 dwellings destroyed
18 dwellings, severely damaged

Watling's Island

On this island there was an old school house which was blown down and several dwelling houses were damaged and a schooner was lost on the coast with all persons onboard perishing. One witness remarked that the sea was stated to have, *"made fearful inroads upon the coast, and the spray to have blighted all vegetation, as if fire had passed over the island, burning off leaves and young shoots."*

Exuma

This island suffered tremendously, as all of the boats and means of transportation were destroyed in this hurricane. Fortunately, the people survived of the cotton and corn crops, which were to some extent left not too badly damaged by the hurricane. When Governor Rawson first arrived on Exuma, the local *Justice of the Peace* first informed him that relief supplies were not needed nor wanted. However, about 200 residents, who had come to the ship to procure the supplies and distribute them found this quite unacceptable. After hearing this news, they immediately threatened to lynch the local *Justice of the Peace* and tear down his office and home if he did not make haste and distribute the supplies.

The damages sustained to the island of Exuma were as follows: -
2 chapels (Episcopal) damaged

4 chapels (Baptist) destroyed
1 chapel (Baptist) damaged
2 lock-up houses unroofed
1 public school unroofed
2 salt stores destroyed
112 dwelling houses destroyed
97 out-houses destroyed
8 vessels (Exuma) destroyed
5 vessels (Nassau) destroyed
12 boats (Exuma) destroyed

San Salvador

On this island, two Episcopal churches and several private dwellings were totally destroyed. In addition, seven Baptist churches were totally destroyed and three others badly damaged. Many of the private resident's homes were totally destroyed. They were able to survive of salvaging a wreck on the western shore of the island. As for food, they were able to live of a few undamaged crops mainly, corn, peas and sweet potatoes. The resident *Justice of the Peace* did not require any supplies because the damages sustained to this island was not great as compared to the other islands. Actually, Reverend Sullivan, the clergyman recently appointed to this parish, even collected a few shillings and a small quantity of corn, and sent them to Nassau. He requested that this donation be forwarded to some of the suffering settlements in some of the adjoining islands. The boat 'American Eagle,' of Boston, sunk near the islands of Cat Island and San Salvador. After the storm, many dead bodies were picked up along the shore; and it was loaded with a shipment of brandy and fine wine. It was reported that over 100 dead bodies floated along the shore on this island and Cat Island. By looking at the bodies, the local residents were able to deduce that this boat originated from some European port and had migrant passengers on board.

Eleuthera

The damages sustained to the island of Eleuthera were as follows: -
19 churches and chapels destroyed
2 Episcopal churches destroyed
13 Wesleyan churches destroyed

4 Baptist churches destroyed
2 schoolhouses
240 dwellings destroyed
56 dwellings badly damaged
831 persons left homeless
8 vessels and boats destroyed
16 vessels and boats badly damaged

The Brig *Baltic* was an American general merchant ship, a wooden two masted vessel with brigantine rig. Her weight was 281 tons and she was built in Camden, Maine in 1854. Her owner was William H. Hooper of Camden, Maine. On September 17th, 1866 she was headed for the number one port in the United States at the time, Galveston, Texas. While en route from Europe with a large shipment of porcelain, English, Scottish, French and German China, medical and pharmaceutical supplies and food stuffs she had to pass through the Bahamas to get to Galveston. *The Great Bahamas Hurricane of 1866* caught the *Baltic*, she floundered and sank on a reef off Eleuthera and many persons drowned. Part of the cargo was recovered by Bahamian wreckers after the storm. The remainder of the cargo was just recently recovered from Bahamian waters by Bahamian and American salvagers in 1995 perfectly preserved under a protective layer of sand.

After the storm, approximately half of the pineapple crop was destroyed. Unemployment was said to be widespread and the people were almost near starvation and had to rely on the goodwill of the Bahamas Government for its survival after the storm. In the early nineteenth century, Rock Sound was visited by some Methodist Missionaries who built a large house (Manse) on the Sound in the centre of the settlement. This Manse was to be the focus for their teachings and mentoring the inhabitants of South Eleuthera. In this hurricane, it went on record as the forerunner of today's hurricane shelters when it housed a number of Rock Sound families whose homes were subsequently destroyed in the storm. In the settlement of Harbour Island (the main settlement on the island of Eleuthera at the time) not a house was left standing and the deputation of three, including the Methodist Minister, were sent to Nassau to plead for help. The Governor told them they had to rely on themselves for assistance. He replied in this manner, because he was preoccupied with his own ravaged capital of Nassau, where well over 612 houses were destroyed and an equal number badly damaged. Furthermore, more than a thousand people were left homeless in Nassau. The damages sustained in the settlement of Harbour Island were as follows: -

1 church (Episcopal) destroyed
1 police office and prison partially destroyed
2 schoolhouses destroyed
26 dwellings destroyed
21 dwellings badly damaged
4 schooners lost
12 schooners considerably damaged
2 sloops badly damaged

This is what the new John S. George building looked like before it was destroyed by the Great Bahamas Hurricane of 1866(Courtesy of Andrew McKinney).

The Great Bahamas Hurricane of 1866 devastated the upper storey of the new John S. George building. The upper floor was used occasionally as a dance hall and to house the United States Special Representative or the US Consul (today's version of the US Ambassador) who at the time was Mr. Kirkpatrick. It was never rebuilt after this storm, but the ground floor with its five distinctive arched openings was restored and has been used throughout the years by many shops-even a bank. Today, it is the T-Shirt Factory Outlet (Courtesy of Andrew McKinney and taken from the book 'Reminiscing II-Photographs of Old Nassau' by Ronald Lightbourn, used with permission).

Abaco

Damages sustained on this island was said to be widespread and quite devastating. The schoolhouse was blown down, many houses were totally destroyed and many others badly damaged. Two Wesleyan and one native Baptist chapels were totally destroyed. In terms of farming, the fields were totally destroyed and the salt water contaminated the soil and rendered it unusable for quite some time. Many of the islanders had to rely on the relief aid brought in from Nassau for their survival. In addition, most of them survived from the wrecking and salvaging industry on the southern shore of the island.

Andros

In the settlement of Red Bays, two churches were destroyed and most of the homes were washed away by the storm. The original Red Bays settlement was located three miles north of the contemporary Red Bays. This hurricane forced the evacuation of this low-lying original community to higher ground. Many of the survivors relocated to Lewis Coppitt, named for the family who owned most of the land there. Years later, Lewis Coppitt was renamed Red Bays to honour their heritage. Red Bays remained an isolated community, accessible only by boat or footpath through dense pine yards until 1968 when a logging company cut a road through the bush in order to remove fallen trees. Quite a number of persons lost their lives when the storm surge came in and washed away many of the houses with the inhabitants still trapped on the inside. At Fresh Creek, a church, the schoolhouse and several dwelling homes were been blown down and destroyed. At Calabash Bay, Staniard Creek, Bowen Sound, and Man-of-War Sound, several chapels and many dwelling homes were destroyed or badly damaged.

The Berry Islands

The population of the Berry Islands was very limited in size and scattered throughout the island in small numbers. Their dwelling homes suffered significant damage in some way or the other and the church, which was also used as a schoolhouse was also blown down by the hurricane.

Bimini

North Bimini's tiny population of 210 persons was nearly wiped out by this devastating hurricane. This storm took several lives and left behind much destruction and misery. The storm surge and rising floodwaters washed away several graves and unearthed many bodies in the process at the public cemetery on the southern end of the island of North Bimini. An endemic of the cholera disease caused by people drinking contaminated water swept through this small island community and left behind many deaths on this island. There are no exact figures available for the total number of deaths on this island but the count is believed to have been extremely high. All of the victims of the cholera disease were buried in a pit dug by the inhabitants just south of the Public

Cemetery in Alice Town. There were several severe injuries inflicted to persons on this island both onshore and at sea. There were two churches blown down from the hurricane along with several dwelling homes. However, like the people in Abaco, they were able to survive and live of the wrecking and salvaging industry after the hurricane.

Grand Bahama

Grand Bahama at the time was considered to be one of the poorest islands in the Bahamas. They had very little cotton crop and very little agriculture to rely on. Most of the dwellings homes and churches on this island were destroyed. The little crops which they had were wiped out by this hurricane because the hurricane passed directly over this island.

Turks and Caicos Islands

On this island some 800 homes were completely destroyed and 3,000 persons were rendered homeless and penniless. The natives were left only with the clothes on their backs because the hurricane destroyed everything else, including all of the food, clothing and living accommodations. Approximately 1,200,000 Bushels of salt were destroyed and 18 vessels were wrecked and totally destroyed. There were 20 persons (15 from Grand Turk and 5 from Salt Cay) who drowned in this storm and in total at least 63 persons died as a direct result of this hurricane. This does not include those that were lost at sea and those who sustained significant injuries such as, broken bones and severe internal injuries and would have in all likelihood died from those injuries.

After The Hurricane

After the hurricane, there was a reported steep rise in the price of building materials. Carpenters were said to be in such a great demand that they often had to be hired weeks in advance to help with relief work and rebuilding efforts of the many homes and businesses destroyed. It was estimated that the repair work for all of the public buildings was in the vicinity of £18,900. Most of the schools, both in Nassau and on the Out Islands were so badly damaged or simply destroyed, that they were rendered unusable. As a result, there was no school for quite a few weeks after the hurricane. When they finally got the schools re-opened,

17 of them had to be transferred to other buildings to accommodate the children. The available vessels that were left undamaged after the storm were dispatched to some of the islands and cays to rescue persons who were left stranded from the storm. On the first trip, 29 men, the crew members of six vessels were picked up on several of the cays stranded, naked and starving as a result of the storm.

Members of the Legislative Council and the House of Assembly met and held an Extraordinary Session of the Legislature on November 6th 1866. This was done to assess the damage sustained from the storm and to provide the Government's response and to assist the people affected by the storm. One of the notable measures they enacted was the appointing of a 'Central Relief Committee.' This committee was comprised of members of the two Houses of Legislature, leading public officers, the Receiver General and the Police Commissioner. Their job was to report back to the House of Assembly on the damages incurred as a result of the storm. In addition, they had to help with the distribution of relief aid and to render assistance to the entire population of the Bahamas when and where possible.

Cuba provided donations of much needed corn and cotton seeds. These seeds were freely distributed to many of the residents in Nassau and on the Family Islands to replace the ones that were lost as a direct result of the hurricane. Loans of a considerable amount were made available by England to help the local residents return to some degree of normalcy. In November, the Extraordinary Session of the Colonial Legislature also authorized an additional loan in the amount of £15,000 for the re-construction and repair of certain public buildings deemed important to the well being of the colony. The other public buildings which were not important to the running of the government were deferred to the following year to be repaired or rebuilt.

Every industry, with one notable exception was adversely affected by the devastation left by this hurricane. The major cash and food crops on many of the islands were destroyed, the fishing industry was crippled and the commerce-based capital was left even more impoverished than before. However, the wrecking and salvaging industry flourished and provided a valuable source of income for many Bahamians after the storm. Brought by the first settlers to the northern islands, the practice had spread to every section of the colony. Wrecked ships were visited by the locals of the nearest island and the goods on board salvaged for personal use or for sale. They also provided any necessary rescue operations to the crew at the same time. There were off course, the occasional corrupt group of wreckers who would place false lights upon the shoals in the hopes that a ship would run aground; but in 1866 there was no need for such underhanded ploys. After the hurricane, wrecks were bountiful, and the industry at the end of the year totaled £108,000, having increased 375% from £28,000 the year before. Although the hurricane caused much damage, it left as a legacy an industry which would help lift the colony out of depression of the following years. In 1870, wrecking was to bring over £150,000 into the colony, to send the Bahamas well on its way up to prosperity again.

CHAPTER NINE

SUMMARY OF GOVERNOR RAWSON W. RAWSON'S REPORT ON THE GREAT BAHAMAS HURRICANE OF 1866

"I have had two objects in preparing and printing the present Report; first, to put on record the history of that calamitous visitation which swept the greater part of the Bahamas Islands, and inflicted so much injury on the City of Nassau, in October, 1866; and secondly, to make public, in the most useful form, the data which I was able to obtain as to the track and rate of progress of the Hurricane. I doubt whether any opportunity has ever been offered, or rather taken, of obtaining similar data from so many detached points, and this is confirmed by the interest which Mr. John H. Redfield,-the son of the eminent American Meteorologist, W.C. Redfield,-and himself no mean proficient in the same science,-has taken in working out the results of the observations collected on this storm.

As my motto is SUUM CUIQUE, I desire to record that I am greatly indebted to Captain Stuart, the Deputy Inspector of Lighthouses, for his assistance in collating and arranging the Abstract of the Observations received....The description of the City of Nassau is a further contribution, which I offer to the people of the Bahamas, towards a correct knowledge of the Islands and of their capital city."

Rawson W. Rawson.

REPORT ON THE BAHAMAS' HURRICANE OF OCTOBER, 1866, With a Description of the City of Nassau.

Forming an Appendix to the Report of Governor Rawson, C.B., upon the Blue Book for the Year 1866.

The City of Nassau, the principal, or rather the only, town in the Bahamas, is situated on the northern side of New Providence, and extends for about three miles and a quarter along the shore, from Fort Charlotte almost to the northeastern point of the Island.

New Providence is one of the smallest islands of the group, having an area of only 85 square miles. It is located in the middle of the northern edge of the Great Bahama Bank, at the eastern entrance of a remarkable deep Sound, which is sufficiently described by its name, the "Tongue of the Ocean," and which penetrates the centre a distance of 110 miles. Besides Nassau and its suburbs, the island contains only four settlements, occupied exclusively by a coloured population, of which only one, called Sandilands, or Fox Hill, is at present entitled to the name of a village.

Nassau lies at the foot, and on the northern slope, of a low range of hills, not exceeding 70 feet in height above the sea, and at a distance of less than a quarter of a mile from the shore. Its Harbour is formed by a low narrow cay, or islet, called Hog Island which runs from the western extremity of the city, parallel to the shore, to the distance of rather more than a mile beyond the north-eastern end of New Providence. Here it is separated by a narrow channel from another similar islet, called Athol Island, at the eastern end which is the Quarantine Station. Southeast of Athol Island is Cochrane's Anchorage, which affords good shelter from the north for ships of large draft, and on the north are Hanover Sound, and the Salt Cay Anchorage, under the lee of the Salt Cay Rocks.

The hurricane was felt, more or less severely, at all the Lighthouses within the Bahamas. At Elbow Cay and the Hole-in-the-Wall, both on the coast of Abaco, and Great Stirrup's Cay, one of the Berry Islands, great damage was done to the towers on the first and last, and to the keepers dwellings. At Great Isaacs, Gun Cay, and Cay Lobos the injuries were less; at Cay Sal the damage done was insignificant, however, none escaped undamaged. The estimate of repair or damages was £4,500.

The estimate for repair of public buildings was £18,900 of places of worship belonging to the Church of England, an independent of the Colonial Government, £2,600, and of those belonging to the Wesleyans, £6,315.

For a week after the hurricane every school ceased work almost all the school-houses having been more or less damaged. Seventeen schools had to be transferred to other buildings.

"I employ the only available vessel in the harbour which arrived on the day after the storm, having been out of range of its greatest fury, to visit several of the uninhabited Cays in the neighbourhood upon which it was expected that some of the sponging vessels would be wrecked. On its first trip it brought in 29 men, the crews of six vessels, whom it had picked up on the Cays naked and starving."

"I invited the members of the Legislative Council and House of Assembly, most of who reside in Nassau, to meet me for the purpose of consulting with them as to the most convenient measures to be taken, and to apprise them of my intention of holding an Extraordinary Session of the Legislature on the earliest possible day, the 6th November, to which date the meeting of the House stood prorogued. I am happy to say that the members entered into my views, and indicated their readiness to support the measures founded upon them."

"I had appointed a Relief Committee for the city, comprised of leading public officers. I then added to it branch committees for the several districts of the city and island, consisting chiefly of members of the two houses, having for their special duties the objects described in the enclosed copy of the notice appointing them."

"The Police and Receiver-General were charged with the duty of ascertaining the nature and extent of the damage done to dwellings and shipping."

Damages Sustained to Ships after the Great Bahamas Hurricane of 1866

Ship's Name:	Type of Vessel:	Owner:	Type of Damage:
Adeline	Smack	WM Pritchard	Severely Damaged
Comet	Schooner	R. Stirrup	Severely Damaged
Industry	Sloop	W.A. Hall	Totally Destroyed
Surprise	Sloop	W.A. Hall	Totally Destroyed
Whym	Sloop	W.A. Hall	Totally Destroyed
White Squall	Sloop	Alexander Elden	Severely Damaged
Flying Cloud	Sloop	WM Elden	Slightly Damaged
Sarah	Sloop	WM. H. Bethel	Severely Damaged
Ernest	Sloop	James Fernandez	Totally Destroyed
Lady Slipper	Sloop	Joseph Fernandez	Badly Damaged
Lady Bannerman	Sloop	Mathew Hall	Badly Damaged
Firefly	Sloop	James Fernandez	Badly Damaged
Lelia	Smack	Thomas Finlay	Slightly Damaged
Willow	Smack	Christopher Brown	Slightly Damaged
Pilot Boat	-------	-----	Slightly Damaged
Union	Smack	WM. Moxey	Slightly Damaged
Dolphin	Smack	WM. Moxey	Slightly Damaged
Charles	Schooner	W.D. Albury	Badly Damaged
Ark	Sloop	Christopher Brown	Slightly Damaged
Defiance	Smack	WM Moxey	Very Badly Damaged
Handith	Sloop	Joseph C. Stirrup	Very Badly Damaged
Kate	Schooner	George Preston	Slightly Damaged
Ellen	Sloop	John Neely	Totally Destroyed
Surprise	Sloop	Salv. Green	Totally Destroyed
Star of the East	Schooner	Dennis Evans	Slightly Damaged
Trent	Sloop	Ben Bethel	Slightly Damaged
Lion	Smack	John Moran	Totally Destroyed
Margaret	Sloop	James Farrington	Totally Destroyed
Elizabeth	Sloop	James Neely	Totally Destroyed
William	Sloop	Joseph W. Pinder	Slightly Damaged
Mary	Sloop	-----	Slightly Damaged
Maria	Sloop	P. Sands	Slightly Damaged
Squirrel	Sloop	John W. Thompson	Slightly Damaged
Rose of Sharon	Sloop	WM. Moxey	Slightly Damaged
John	Sloop	Benj. Thompson	Slightly Damaged
Edwin	Sloop	John Russell	Slightly Damaged
Proceed	Sloop	John Evans	Severely Damaged
Jeff Davis	Sloop	John T. Thompson	Severely Damaged
Ella	Sloop	John A. Simms	Severely Damaged
Lily	Schooner	Charles Thompson	Slightly Damaged
Confidence	Schooner	Robert Sturrup	Slightly Damaged
Pinta	Sloop	Joseph W. Pinder	Severely Damaged
Lauretta	Smack	Joseph Moxey	Badly Damaged

Damages sustained to ships after the Great Bahamas Hurricane of 1866. Taken from Governor Rawson's Report on the Great Bahamas Hurricane of 1866-Courtesy of the Bahamas Department of Archives.

Yellow Tail	Smack	WM. Thompson	Slightly Damaged
Henrietta	Smack	Alexander Hart	Totally Destroyed
Nassau	Boat	John W. Thompson	Totally Destroyed
James Powers	Boat	John T. Thompson	Totally Destroyed
Susan Drew	Smack	John Pearce, Jr.	Totally Destroyed
Smoothing Iron	Smack	John Pearce, Sr.	Totally Destroyed
Fancy	Sloop	J. Wells	Badly Damaged
Arrow	Sloop	Ben Bethel	Badly Damaged
John W. Pinder	Sloop	J.W. Pinder	Badly/Dismasted
Confederate	Sloop	Henry Pinder	Totally Destroyed
Sparrow	Schooner	Thomas Pinder	Totally Destroyed
Lucy	Sloop	Clement Pinder	Severely Damaged
Louisa	Sloop	B.V. Hall	Severely Damaged
Elector	Schooner	John Pinder	Severely Damaged
Independent	Schooner	C. Pinder	Slightly Damaged
Fairplay	Schooner	John W. Pinder	Slightly Damaged
Cecelia	Sloop	James Price	Badly Damaged
Guide	Sloop	Theo Sturrup	Badly Damaged
G.L. Blond	Sloop	John Swain	Badly Damaged
Wanting	Sloop	WM. Swain	Badly Damaged
Fish Hawk	Sloop	Joseph B. Kemp	Badly Damaged
Diana	Sloop	Robert Pearce	Totally Destroyed
Emulous	Sloop	Robert Pearce	Badly Damaged
May Flower	Sloop	Robert Pearce	Slightly Damaged
Julia	Smack	WM. Pearce	Slightly Damaged
Dis Ting	Sloop	John Swain	Slightly Damaged
Triumph	Schooner	Theo Stirrup	Slightly Damaged
Arabella	Sloop	Thomas Kemp	Severely Damaged
Star	Sloop	Coffee Thrift	Totally Destroyed
Mary Hooper	Sloop	Symonette	Severely Damaged
Unknown	Schooner	Unknown	Totally Destroyed
Unknown	4 Smacks	Unknown	Badly Damaged
Isabella	Schooner	Benjamin V. Hall	Severely Damaged
Maria	Sloop(Sponger)	Thomas Brown	Severely Damaged
Grace	Smack	Edward Brown	Totally Destroyed
Unknown	Smack	Unknown	Totally Destroyed
Unknown	Smack	Sweeting	Totally Destroyed
Ocean Monarch	Schooner	W.S. Whitehead	Severely Damaged
Hattie	Schooner	W.E. Ambrister	Severely Damaged
Valiant	Sloop	January Rolle	Severely Damaged
United Force	Schooner	Catto	Totally Destroyed
Trial	Schooner	H. C. Lightbourn	Totally Destroyed
Priscilla	Schooner	Benjamin V. Hall	Severely Damaged
Unknown	Schooner	Unknown	Totally Destroyed
Unknown	Sloop	Unknown	Totally Destroyed

Damages sustained to ships(continued from previous page) after the Great Bahamas Hurricane of 1866. Taken from Governor Rawson's Report on the Great Bahamas Hurricane of 1866-Courtesy of the Bahamas Department of Archives.

None	Smack	Charles Minns	Severely Damaged
Lion	Schooner	Hepburn and Deal	Totally Destroyed
Unknown	Sloop	J. Demeritt	Totally Destroyed
Ellen	Sloop	Byron Bode	Slightly Damaged
Zebra	Schooner	P. Coakley	Severely Damaged
New year	Sloop	Henry McBride	Slightly Damaged
Express	Sloop	Boyd	Severely Damaged
Eureka	Sloop	WM. Simmons	Slightly Damaged
Hornet	Sloop	Cargill	Severely Damaged
Unknown	Sloop	Unknown	Totally Destroyed
Blooming Youth	Sloop	Evans	Split Open
Trial	Sloop	S. Sweeting	Foundered
Newton	Sloop	G. Renouard & Co.	Slightly Damaged
Olivia	Schooner	G. Renouard & Co.	Severely Damaged
Unknown	Sloop	Eppes Sargent	Severely Damaged
Mary Jane	Sloop	John Demeritt	Severely Damaged
Pearl	Schooner	John Demeritt	Slightly Damaged
Telfair	Schooner	WM. Eneas	Severely Damaged
Water Boat	Sloop	H.C. Lightbourn	Severely Damaged
No Name	2 Boats	H.C. Lightbourn	Severely Damaged
Little Emily	Sloop	H.C. Lightbourn	Severely Damaged
Arabella	Sloop	R.G. Sawyer	Totally Destroyed
Lauretta	Schooner	----	Severely Damaged
Golden Eagle	Schooner	J. Saunders	Severely Damaged
Charley	Sloop-Boat	C.J. Marshall	Slightly Damaged
Dat Ting	Sloop-Boat	B.L. Burnside	Totally Destroyed
Alice Flora	Schooner	Knowles, Sands	Severely Damaged
Reform	Schooner	H.E. Johnson	Slightly Damaged
John G.	Brigantine	Sawyer & Menendez	Slightly Damaged
Jane	Sloop	B.V. Hall	Totally Damaged
No Name	3 Boats	Saunders & Son	Totally Destroyed
No name	2 Lighters	----	Foundered
Mary	Schooner	J.W. Pinder	Dismasted
Tweed	Schooner	Fanning & Hasgill	Severely Damaged
Unknown	17 Boats	Unknown	Totally Destroyed
Unknown	8 Boats	Unknown	Severely Damaged
Unknown	2 Boats	W.S. Whitehead	Totally Destroyed
Unknown	1 Boat	Culmer	Totally Destroyed
None	2 Lighters	Sawyer & Menendez	Severely Damaged
None	1 Lighter	H. Adderley	Severely Damaged
None	1 Iron Lighter	George Preston	Severely Damaged
None	1 Boat	John S. Howell	Severely Damaged
None	1 Boat	McKinney	Severely Damaged

Damages sustained to ships (continued from previous page) after the Great Bahamas Hurricane of 1866. Taken from Governor Rawson's Report on the Great Bahamas Hurricane of 1866-Courtesy of the Bahamas Department of Archives.

Unknown	Sloop	R. Simons	Severely Damaged
Unknown	Sloop	C. Cooper	Severely Damaged
Unknown	Sloop	A. Williams	Severely Damaged
Unknown	Sloop	G Stuart	Severely Damaged
Relief	Steamer	John S. Howell	Severely Damaged
Teviot	Schooner	Unknown	Totally Destroyed
Sylvia	Schooner	Barlow & Armbrister	Totally Destroyed
No Name	2 Boats	M. Lowe	Totally Destroyed
Unknown	Smack	Unknown	Slightly Damaged
No Name	3 Boats	J.C. Rahming & Co.	Totally Destroyed
No Name	9 Boats	Unknown	Severely Damaged
No Name	1 Boat	H.M. Customs	Totally Destroyed
No Name	1 Gig	H.M. Customs	Slightly Damaged
Nimble	H.M.S. Ship	----	Slightly Damaged
None	1 Boat	Commissariat	Totally Destroyed
None	2 Boats	Garrison	Severely Damaged
Evelina	Schooner & Boats	Squires Brothers	Totally Destroyed
Union	Schooner & Boats	Rich	Slightly Damaged
Nelia Covert	Schooner	M. Lowe	Totally Destroyed
Oreto	Schooner	H. Thurston	Severely Damaged
Lily	Schooner	----	Totally Destroyed
W. Fletcher	Sloop	W.D. Albury	Totally Destroyed
Charles	Schooner	W.D. Albury	Severely Damaged
Sunbeam	Schooner	W.D. Albury	Severely Damaged
Evelina	Sloop	H. Bannister	Totally Destroyed
Madeline	Schooner	Deveaux	Slightly Damaged
Resolute	Sloop	Alexander Pratt	Slightly Damaged
Telfair	Sloop	Pearce	Slightly Damaged
Miriam	Schooner	H. Thurston	Severely Damaged
Home	Sloop	B.R. Shariff	Severely damaged
General Clinch	Steamship	Unknown Agent	Totally Destroyed-- This ship had just entered the Court of Vice-Admiralty
No Name	1 Boat	R.W.H. Weech & Co. Schooner Union	Totally Destroyed
Number of Vessels Totally Destroyed:	**93**		

Damages sustained to ships (continued from previous page) after the Great Bahamas Hurricane of 1866. Taken from Governor Rawson's Report on the Great Bahamas Hurricane of 1866-Courtesy of the Bahamas Department of Archives.

Number of vessels Severely Damaged:	97		
Number of Vessels Slightly Damaged:	41		
Total:	**231**		

Type of Vessel:	Nature of Damage:	Total:
Vessels ashore	Total Loss.	15
Vessels ashore	Got off and towed to Nassau.	1
Vessels ashore	Repaired and proceeded on voyage.	1
Vessel	Dismasted at sea.	4
Vessel	Dismasted and towed into Nassau.	1
Vessel	Damaged at sea.	2
Vessel	Totally destroyed at anchor and condemned.	2
Vessel	Abandoned.	1
TOTAL:		**30**

Top:
Damages sustained to ships (continued from previous page) after the Great Bahamas Hurricane of 1866. Taken from Governor Rawson's Report on the Great Bahamas Hurricane of 1866-Courtesy of the Bahamas Department of Archives.
Bottom:
Foreign Vessels Destroyed in the Bahamas during the Great Bahamas Hurricane of 1866. The captain and crew of three of the above vessels were totally lost, numbers unknown, and four seamen in another vessel were drowned in the storm. Taken from Governor Rawson's Report on the Great Bahamas Hurricane of 1866-Courtesy of the Bahamas Department of Archives.

Foreign Vessels Destroyed in the Bahamas during The Great Bahamas Hurricane of 1866

Of the Foreign vessels, thirty were cast ashore, while others were lost or badly damaged. Of the latter number, the largest portions were brought into Nassau for repairs, as well as their cargo which were saved from several boats that were stranded. The following two tables show the nature of the several disasters, and the district in which they occurred.

Islands where the Wrecks occurred

Island:	Number:
Abaco	7
Harbour Island	1
Eleuthera	4
New Providence	1
Andros	3
Great Stirrup's Cay	1
Grand Bahama	1
San Salvador	1
Fortune Island	1
Mayaguana	1
Inagua	2
Bimini	1
Sheep Cay Shoal, Grand Bahama Bank	1
Dismasted at sea	5
TOTAL:	30

Name:	Damage:
	Bay Street:
J.R. Hall	Warehouse and Stable destroyed.
C.W. Weech	One House and two warehouses damaged.
Thomas Williams	Roof of house partly blown off.
H.R. Saunders	House damaged, and the roofs of three Warehouses partly blown off.
J.J. Boyd	Warehouse and Out-buildings destroyed.
Sawyer & Mendez	Warehouse destroyed.
H. Gomez	Roof of house blown off.
G. Renouard	Roof of house blown off.
G. Renouard	House damaged.
W. Farrington	Roof of store blown off.
Sawyer & Menendez	Part of roof blown off.
Sawyer & Menendez	Roof and upper storey of store destroyed.
Sawyer & Menendez	Roof blown off house.
G.D. Harris	Roof of store blown off.
G.D. Harris	Roof and upper storey of store destroyed.
G.D. Harris	Store damaged.
G.D. Harris	Store destroyed.
G.D. Harris	House damaged.
H. Adderley	Roof of store Damaged.

Top:
The Islands where the wrecks occurred. Taken from Governor Rawson's Report of the Great Bahamas Hurricane of 1866-Courtesy of the Bahamas Department of Archives.
Bottom:
Damage sustained to houses and businesses after the Great Bahamas Hurricane of 1866. Taken from Governor Rawson's Report on the Great Bahamas Hurricane of 1866-Courtesy of the Bahamas Department of Archives.

Damage Sustained to Houses and Businesses in the City of Nassau

J.H. Rahming	Tin roof of store blown off.
Kemp & Albury	House damaged, and Coach-house destroyed.
H. Adderley	Roof of house damaged.
H. Adderley	House damaged and Out-buildings and Stables destroyed.
Mrs. G. Adderley	House Damaged.
Mrs. M.C. Johnson	Roof of house damaged and Piazza blown away.
Mrs. Goodman	Roof of house damaged and Piazza blown away.
W.J. Weech	Roof and piazza damaged.
H. Adderley	Roof of house destroyed
Mrs. Wall	Piazza and Gate damaged.
Squiers Brothers	Roof of store damaged.
R.W.H. Weech	Roof and upper storey of store blown down.
R.W.H. Weech	Roof and upper storey of store blown down.
J.S. George	House damaged.
J.S. George	Roofs and upper stories of two large stores destroyed.
Mrs. G. Adderley	Store destroyed.
W.J. Weech	Roof blown off store.
W. Albury & Sons	Roof and upper story of store blown down.
Alexander Johnson	Warehouse damaged.
J.C. Rahming	Warehouse destroyed and Stable damaged.
Mrs. Advenson	House destroyed.
Mrs. Smith	House destroyed.
R.E. Rigby	House destroyed.
Dowdeswell Street:	
Mrs. Easton	House destroyed.
A. Wallace	One house destroyed.
A. Wallace	One house destroyed.
E. Royley	One house destroyed.
E. Royley	One house destroyed.
Mrs. Knowles	One house destroyed.
R. Sumner	One house destroyed.
Shirley Street:	
W. Higgs	House destroyed.
Mrs. Sweeting	House destroyed.
A. Punchbar	House destroyed.
A. Wallace	House destroyed.
Mrs. Hill	House damaged.
Ebenezer Chapel	Damaged and three classrooms destroyed.
J.J. Corlett	School house destroyed.
C. Burnside	House significantly damaged.
Zion Chapel	Significantly damaged.

Damage sustained to houses and businesses (continued) in the city of Nassau after the Great Bahamas Hurricane of 1866. Taken from Governor Rawson's Report on the Great Bahamas Hurricane of 1866-Courtesy of the Bahamas Department of Archives.

Mrs. Mathews	House damaged.
T.B. Tynes	House destroyed.
B.L. Burnside	Roof of house damaged.
Bishop of Nassau	House damaged, kitchen and a small Bedroom destroyed.
N. Webb	House damaged.
Duke Street:	
A. Johnson	House destroyed.
Missionary Hall	Damaged.
East Hill Street:	
H.R. Saunders	Part of roof blown off house; Carriage-house damaged.
S.O. Johnson	House destroyed.
S.O. Johnson	House very badly damaged.
F. Duncombe	Stable blown down.
E.C. Moseley	Piazza and Pantry blown down, and servant's room destroyed.
E.C. Moseley	Iron roof of house blown off.
West Hill Street:	
T.C. Harvey	Roof partly blown off house.
J.A. Brook	House damaged.
J.H. Webb	House damaged, and Out-buildings destroyed.
Judge Doyle	Piazza.
Woodcock Trustees	House damaged.
Dillet Street:	
Bethel Chapel	Destroyed.
Bain's Town:	
Woodcock Schools	One destroyed and two damaged.
East Street:	
Dr. Kirkwood	House and Outbuildings damaged.
Judge Doyle	Roof and upper storey of house blown down.
Judge Doyle	Roof of Piazza blown off.
Mrs. Butler	House damaged.
Mrs. Farrington	House damaged.
A. Bain	House destroyed.
Parliament Street:	
G.C. Anderson	Gates damaged.
J. Pinder	Out-buildings destroyed.

Damage sustained to houses and businesses (continued) in the city of Nassau after the Great Bahamas Hurricane of 1866. Taken from Governor Rawson's Report on the Great Bahamas Hurricane of 1866-Courtesy of the Bahamas Department of Archives.

A. Johnson	Roof of house partly blown off.
Charlotte Street:	
G.W.G. Robins	Piazza damaged and Out-houses blown down.
G.D.Harris	Iron roof of Warehouse blown off.
Theatre	Destroyed.
Fredrick Street:	
W. Maura	Roof of house partly blown off.
A.T. Holmes	Out-buildings damaged.
Wesleyan Chapel	Destroyed, and Out-buildings damaged.
Mrs. Butler	House damaged.
W.H. Curry	Upper storey of new building blown down.
Market Street:	
A.T. Holmes	Roof blown off warehouse.
R. Sweeting	Roof of house blown off and store damaged.
T.K. Moore	Piazza damaged.
M. Menendez	Roof of house damaged.
E.B.A. Taylor	House and Out-buildings destroyed.
George Street:	
A. Johnson	Roof, Piazza and Gates damaged.
H. Adderley	Roof of house damaged.
A. Johnson	Piazza damaged.
B. Bode	Roof of house damaged.
Cumberland Street:	
W.E. Armbrister	House partly damaged, and Out-buildings destroyed.
G.P. Wood	House damaged and Coach-house destroyed.
T.K. Moore	Roof of Coach-house blown off.
B. Bode	House and Out-buildings damaged.
Queen Street:	
J. Roker	House destroyed.
Mrs. Jones	House destroyed.
E.A.J. Bethel	Roof of house blown off and Outbuildings destroyed.
J. Roker	House destroyed.
W. Sweeting	House damaged.
West Street:	
Baptist Mission	Five Out-buildings destroyed.
H.J. McCartney	House damaged.
H.J. McCartney	House damaged.

Damage sustained to houses and businesses (continued) in the city of Nassau after the Great Bahamas Hurricane of 1866. Taken from Governor Rawson's Report on the Great Bahamas Hurricane of 1866-Courtesy of the Bahamas Department of Archives.

Nassau Street:	
Mrs. G. Adderley	Roof and Piazza partly blown away.
King Street:	
T.K. Moore	New buildings partly destroyed.
Mrs. Farrington	House destroyed.
Marlbrough Street:	
G. Preston	Roof of house damaged and Kitchen destroyed.

Damage sustained to houses and businesses (continued) in the city of Nassau after the Great Bahamas Hurricane of 1866. Taken from Governor Rawson's Report on the Great Bahamas Hurricane of 1866- Courtesy of the Bahamas Department of Archives.

CHAPTER TEN

PERSONAL RECOLLECTIONS OF THE GREAT BAHAMAS HURRICANE OF 1866'S IMPACT ON THE BAHAMAS.

This account describes the great impact this hurricane had on the city of Nassau and on the islands of Eleuthera and Abaco:

Hurricane in the Bahamas-Nassau Half Destroyed

A terrible hurricane commenced in the Bahamas on the 30th ultimo, and lasted two days. Almost half of the town of Nassau was destroyed by the storm. Houses were blown down, roofs carried away, and trees uprooted. Trinity Church was demolished, the Government House lost part of its roof, and the roof of the Marine Hospital was entirely blown off. Vessels were driven ashore and knocked to pieces, and wharves were demolished. The neighbouring islands suffered in the same degree, and a large number of vessels have been lost or damaged. The hurricane is the severest which has been experienced since 1813.

The Nassau Guardian of the 3rd says the hurricane commenced on Sunday night, the 30th at 8 o'clock, blowing all night from the north. On Monday morning, the barometer went down, and later the gale became stronger.

A part of the town of Nassau was destroyed. Trinity Church was completely demolished. The Government House suffered considerably and lost a great part of the roofing. The entire roofing of the Military Hospital was carried away. From the Arsenal, West Bay Street, to the Eastward, no one could pass, on account of the obstruction in the way caused by the ruins of houses, boats, fragments of vessels and of the wharves. The Arsenal wharf completely disappeared. Many of the houses and stores that were thrown down were swept away by the hurricane, including the beef and fish markets. The catalogue of the property destroyed is very long.

The gunboat 'Nimble' was thrown on the bank in front of the Arsenal, notwithstanding the great efforts of her commander and officers. She does not appear to have suffered, however, and it is hoped she will be set afloat shortly.

The Canal Company's steamer 'Relief' is now hard and fast near the tower of the lighthouse; and the steamer 'General Clinch' went to pieces near the public abutment. The only vessel that rode out the hurricane was the 'Minnie Gordon,' as her spars and rigging were down.

The like weather has not been experienced since 1813. The most doleful accounts were being received daily of the effects of the hurricane in the adjacent islands.

The church at St. John, and thirty-six houses in Harbour Island, had been completely destroyed, and the establishments upon Spanish Wells, Current, Governor's Harbour, and Eleuthina have been completely swept away; Green Turtle Cay, Hope Town, and North Harbour are in ruins.

A correspondent at Great Harbour writes that the hurricane has ruined all the estates, destroyed the cisterns of water, public schools, and that the poorer classes were exposed to starvation. The schooner 'Victory,' schooner 'President,' and barque 'Ticker,' of New York, were lost here.

Courtesy of the National Library of New Zealand.

Nicolette Bethel's account of the Great Bahamas Hurricane of 1866.

In October of 1981 *The Journal of the Bahamas Historical Society* published in its magazine an excellent report on the Great Bahamas Hurricane of 1866 as researched and written by Bahamian Historian and author Nicolette Bethel, below is an excerpt of that report:

The Hurricane of 1866 by Nicolette Bethel
The Bahamas in 1866:

First settled over two hundred years before, the colony of the Bahamas had progressed little by 1850, and then in fits and starts rather than continuously. In 1866, it was working its way out of a depression which followed the prosperous years of the American Civil War. Blockade running, the act of slipping into the Union guarded ports of the South in order

Wayne Neely

to supply the Confederate States with manufactured goods they needed, brought quick, easy money into the country. But the era, though great, was also short-lived, and in 1865, three years after the beginning of the blockade running, the industry closed when the Confederation was defeated by the North. The colony suffered a sudden economic collapse....The Bahamas was not prepared for a disaster which would stir up the sea and flood the land, which would sink ships, wreck mansions and sweep away the flimsy shacks of the Valley. Nevertheless, the colony was visited by one. For in October 1866, a Hurricane the likes of which had never been seen by Bahamians living then swept the archipelago.

The Hurricane of 1866:

The hurricane later to be known as the "Great Bahama Hurricane" left St. Thomas, the Virgin Islands, on the morning of September 28, 1866. By the early hours of September 30 it was affecting the Bahamas; Mayaguana recorded gale force winds coming from the north-east. By eight o' clock that morning the hurricane had progressed as far as Matthew Town Inagua, and a "light wind" was reported at Fortune Island (now Long Cay), just northwest of Crooked Island. San Salvador (then Watlings Island) received the fringe winds of the cyclone at three in the afternoon, and by eight o' clock in the evening of Sunday September 30, Great Harbour Cay, Long Island, was being struck.

It was at that time that the first evidence of the storm was felt in Nassau. The day had passed as usual; the people had attended evening church services, spending the hours after on their verandahs socializing. The air was still; "all was calm and tranquil...there was, however, a peculiar reddish hue in the heavens...and an unusual warmth in the atmosphere." At eight o'clock, "a northerly breeze sprung up, which grew stronger throughout the night, and the barometer fell from 30.16 inches on the day of the 30th to 29.80 inches at 11:00am the following morning. The hurricane remained over Nassau for the rest of the day, the eye passing over the town in early evening. There was a lull then for as long as an hour and a half; then the wind "sprang up from the opposite quarter and continued to blow violently till 2:00am (on October 2) when it gradually subsided." The barometric pressure, taken during the lull, was as low as 27.70 inches, and was recorded about half an hour before the winds began to blow again.

168

Seas of tidal wave proportions swamped the harbour, disregarding the islands which normally acted as a buff against storms....The hurricane moved away from New Providence quickly; by the morning of October 3 it had left Bahamian waters, entering the mid-Atlantic where presumably it dissipated. As there are no records of the hurricane having hit any of the eastern states of the U.S.A., it is reasonable to assume that the storm simply died upon reaching cooler water.

Effects of The Hurricane:

Nassau suffered in the sunshine which followed the storm. No level of society had been left unscathed; the houses on the ridge, affected worst by the gales, lost roofs, and those still standing stood askew. Trees felled by the winds had caused much damage, crashing into houses and across streets. Along the harbourside, the warehouses which were the shelters of the unemployed were for the most part demolished; in the low-lying Valley, swamp water which had overflowed covered the land, stagnant, and breeding place for bacteria and flies. The few houses which had survived the hurricane stood like towers above the debris, and the fruit and vegetables which were the sole means of survival for the people of the Valley lay strewn across the lanes and alleys of the settlement. In total 601 houses were destroyed, and at least that number damaged; one thousand people were estimated to have been made homeless by the hurricane.

On the Out Islands; the results were much the same as those of New Providence. At Harbour Island, then the largest Out Island settlement, the year's vegetable crop was ruined; "hardly a house" was left undamaged. Upon appealing to the capital for assistance, the settlement was denied it; all the money possible was to be spent in rebuilding Nassau. At Rum Cay, fast developing due to a growing salt industry, the entire salt harvest was reclaimed by the ocean and every house was flattened.

If damage done on land was extensive, that at sea was worse. In Nassau Harbour, sheltered from most blows by its barrier islands "of more than 200 vessels...only one remained intact." Harbour Island lost every one of its boats to the hurricane and other settlements on other islands suffered the same fate....Wrecks were plentiful, and the income from the industry at the end of the year totaled 108 thousand pounds, having increased 375% from 28 thousand pounds the year before.

Although the hurricane caused much damage, it left as a legacy an industry which would help lift the colony out of depression of the following years. In 1870, wrecking was to bring over 150 thousand pounds into the colony, to send the Bahamas on its way up to prosperity again.

<u>The Hurricane of 1866</u>-The Journal of the Bahamas Historical Society, Volume III, No 1 pgs13-14 (October 1981) by Nicolette Bethel-used with permission.

Rev John Davey's account of the Great Bahamas Hurricane of 1866.

This account was taken from *'The History of Religion in the Bahamas'* series by Author and Historian Jim Lawlor in The Tribune dated Thursday, December 10th & 17th, 2009-used with permission.

The Baptist Magazine of 1866 contains a letter from Rev John Davey as follows:

The arrival of the Rev John Davey enables us to furnish our readers with more particulars of the effects of the Great Bahamas Hurricane of 1866 on the Mission property in Nassau. Through the good providence of God, Mr. Davey and his family reached their destination in safety, but not without experiencing very severe weather along the way. Under the date of November 17, he writes:-

"Our voyage across the Atlantic was a long and Dangerous one, and we were detained in New York a month, which was a great disappointment both to ourselves and the people.

The 'Corsica' reached the bar of Nassau early on the morning of the 7th, but found that the passengers would not be landed in boats the usual way on account of the heavy sea that was running. She gave signals respecting passengers and freight, and then proceeded in the direction of Cochrane's anchorage, in the hope that schooners would soon be dispatched to us, no schooner came alongside till the following morning.

Though the people were looking and waiting for us all day, and there was great uncertainty as to the time the schooner would arrive the morrow, yet when we got to the landing about noon, we found the shore lined with the members of the church, waiting to welcome us.

Their congratulations were very hearty, and two or three days after we arrived, we were fully employed in receiving visitors. But, though it was pleasant to see the people, it was distressing to hear their accounts of the desolating hurricane with which the colony had been visited.

I asked them in what light it was generally regarded and some said as a judgment from God. One aged African woman said to me, "Massa, God has punished we this year, nothing left to pick a copper," referring to the destruction of the crops."

The Mission property has sustained considerable damage through the hurricane. The portico of our large chapel, which was put up last year, was blown down, stripping away the cornice and the gutter, and thus laying the chapel open to the rams. The chapel gates were blown down and broken, and great quantity of glass destroyed in the chapel. The roofs of the Mission-House and outbuildings were so damaged that they must be shingled immediately.

But the saddest part of the story remains to be told. Bethel, the original Baptist chapel in the Bahamas, in which Mr. Burton laid the foundation of this Mission, after he was driven from Morant Bay, is leveled with the ground. This is a great grief to the poor people, especially the aged, who have worshipped in it so many years. It is very desirable that it should be rebuilt as speedily as possible, as the bulk of the members live in the neighbourhood of that chapel.

But they cannot possibly rebuild themselves in their present distressed circumstances, and therefore, I hope, that when the news of this great calamity reaches England, the friends of the Mission will kindly help us to repair our damaged chapel, and rebuild those that have been blown down.

The Episcopalians and Wesleyans have suffered as badly as ourselves, and therefore, we cannot look to them for help, who need all the means they have got to rebuild their own places of worship.

The hurricane was very severe upon other islands but I believe that the two principal chapels of our Society, beyond New Providence, sustained but little damage. There was not much injury done to property in Inagua, and though there was much private property destroyed at Turk's Island, yet the place of worship were not much damaged. Many of the Out-Island chapels were destroyed, but as they were not very costly buildings, I think they may soon be rebuilt.

From the Nassau Guardian we take the following description of the tempest:-

"A fresh breeze blew on Sunday evening last, and those who walked on the Esplanade or elsewhere, congratulated themselves on the favourable change in the weather; but to those used to observe the weather, appearances decidedly bespoke a 'blow.'

The wind increased during the night, and about 7 o' clock on Monday morning had become a regular gale, accompanied with rain.

The bar of the harbour appeared a ridge of foam, and the harbour itself, formed by the long, low rocky land "Hog Island" though it kept off the main sea, yet left all exposed to the violence of the wind, which kept steadily increasing.

The short seas breaking in rapid succession upon the line of wharves along Bay Street, the abutment of the Barrack-Square, the Esplanade, and rocky shore to the westward sending dense wreaths of spray over everything. Rumour soon reported much damage among the shipping.

Small boats, lumber, various gear and fragments began to bestrew the Ordnance Wharf, etc.' and in Bay Street the scene was excitingly sad, most of the spacious stores and warehouses (on the north side next to the harbour), principally with roofs of corrugated iron or other metals, were unroofed; immense sheets of metal were whirled along in the wind, and torn up like sheets of paper, and the whole thoroughfare was covered with portions of shipping and houses.

The passage was not only difficult in the extreme, the few people seen about being frequently brought to a stand-still by the corner of a street, and obliged to cling to lampposts or pillars of the piazzas, till a partial lull in the wind enabled them to make a run forward to go on afresh. The public market and wharf exhibited a scene of wild excitement, a number of vessels jammed together against the abutment-fishermen and boatmen shouting to the crews of the vessels, who, like those on shore were equally unable to save their property-the larger vessels rolling against the smaller, and smashing them to fragments, and in their turn were broken up against the stone wall of the wharf. The other streets began to show the effects of the storm-parts of the verandahs, window shutters, and branches of trees, and occasionally a whole tree were blown down.

About 1:30pm or 2pm, it was impossible to remain abroad; it was dangerous to take shelter under walls or houses, and totally impossible to remain standing when exposed to the presence of the wind, which shook every building.

The sensation within doors was like the vibrations of a railway car attached to an express train; the noise of the wind, combining with the sound of the waves, kept up a loud bellowing roar, varied with thunder-like gusts, and were succeeded by a crashing sound which indicated destruction of some kind or other.

Green seas were now breaking upon the wharves of the town and government property, sending their spray over the tops of the houses, and together with the heavy falling of rain and hail, made the air as obscure as the thickest fog, which, as it now and again cleared partially for a few moments, shows some further damage, houses being dismantled in all directions, and the fragments, intermingled with branches of trees, swept along at an alarming pace.

The trees that remained standing were being rapidly stripped of their leaves. Every house was in a state of commotion, the wind and rain penetrated everywhere, doing every kind of damage, and causing indescribable inconvenience. A lull in the storm occurred about 7:30pm or 8pm, which fortunately enabled those who had some shelter remaining, to offer a share of it to their less fortunate neighbours.

About 9 o' clock it sprung up again in a south-easterly direction, but with far less violence, and altogether subsided by day-break. Next morning, the whole scene was indeed a desolation, the most familiar objects were scarcely to be recognized; some gone entirely. Distressing accounts of the effects of the hurricane on the Out Islands are being received.

We learn with sorrow that St. John's Church and thirty-eight houses at Harbour Island have been leveled with the dust, and that the settlements of Spanish Wells, the Current, Governor's Harbour, and other parts of Eleuthera are nearly swept away.

At Abaco, the work of destruction has been awful. Our correspondent at Great Harbour, in a letter dated the 4ᵗʰ instant says, "I am sorry to inform you that we had a severe hurricane on the 1ˢᵗ of October, ruining all the plantations, making all the water in the tanks unfit for use, blowing down all the kitchens, several dwelling-houses, the public school-house, the assistant-keeper's dwelling, belonging to Elbow Cay Lighthouse, and doing a great deal more damage than I can mention. The poorer classes were *trusting to their plantations, which are all destroyed, and I expect they will starve."*

But as we look back in history-after the 1866 hurricane, once again as so many times in the past, the faithful residents rebuilt their lives, homes and community with the assistance of many other generous people. And nature reached out her healing hand as the flora and fauna slowly regenerated to bring back the enchantment and beauty of the Bahamas.

Ivan Ray Tannehill's account of the Great Bahamas Hurricane of 1866 as documented in his book, 'Hurricanes-*Their Nature and History.*'

The "Great Bahama Hurricane" of September and October 1866 was of wide extent and great severity. At 8pm of October 1 the vortex was over Nassau, barometer 27.7 inches. The calm lasted from 7:20 to 8:50pm from which it was concluded that its diameter was 23 miles. At first the clouds in the zenith seemed to revolve rapidly, then the stars appeared but banks of clouds remained all around the horizon in dense masses. Alexander Buchan said of this storm that "the long black list of wrecks recorded, bears testimony only too emphatic to the devouring energy of the hurricane."

Bishop Addington Venables's account of the Great Bahamas Hurricane of 1866.

Here is a report written in 1877 which briefly mentions the *Great Bahamas Hurricane of 1866*. In this report on the Anglican Churches in the Bahamas by Addington Venables, Bishop of Nassau reporting to W. Francis Henry in London, he reported on the state of affairs of the churches in the Bahamas.

In earlier days the whole Bahama group had, as an archdeaconry, formed the vast and unwieldy appendage of the diocese of Jamaica, receiving occasional visits from that Bishop; but in 1861 the Governments of the Bahamas and Turk's Islands were erected into a separate see, under Dr. Caulfield, the first Bishop of Nassau. Dr. Caulfield, however, only survived his appointment a few months, and with the succession of Bishop Venables the active missionary work of the diocese may only be said to have in truth begun. The colony, too, at this time was enjoying a season of unwanted commercial prosperity in connection with the Confederate ports, and blockade-runners were entering or leaving the Nassau Harbour at all hours, and, as may be supposed, a pretty brisk trade was being carried on.

The Bishop was naturally eager to get afield, but a touch of yellow fever, taken not long after his arrival, necessitated an absence for change of air during convalescence, and obliged him to defer his first visitation till the latter part of the year. His first impressions were, however, far from discouraging.

"The prospects of the Church here," he writes in April 1864, "seem hopeful as far as Nassau itself is concerned. The cathedral cannot supply sittings to meet the demand; two churches, attended principally by the coloured people, require enlargement; and by the next mail I expect the arrival of a clergyman to open an upper-class school, from which I hope much good may result. Andros and some of the more accessible islands I purpose to visit at once, but my general visitation must be deferred till the end of the year. I fear, however, instead of the resources of our Out-Islands being developed by the commercial activity which prevails at Nassau, that they have rather suffered by the war, as their population has been attracted to the capital by the high price of labour, so that I cannot expect the people in these Out-Islands to do much towards the support of their own clergy."

Towards the close of the year (1864) the Bishop made his first trip to some of the Out Islands. "I found much both to dishearten and to encourage us. Dissent has eaten deep into the people in some of the parishes, and the consequence (I hope I am not uncharitable in thinking so) has been a loss of Christian love." Efforts were, however, speedily commenced with a view of recovering these lost children of the Church; and a mission of a hopeful character was launched amongst the Baptist population of Fortune Island, in the more southerly division of the colony. After a visit to inspect the progress of the undertaking, the Bishop writes:-

"Mr. Ward, the young American whom I ordained at Christmas to take charge of the Fortune Island district, promises to turn out a first-rate man. He will, I trust, by God's help, be enabled to build up the Church in that district. At Fortune Island the church fabric, after having been closed for so long--two years--is now, although a large one for the population, so crowded that application has been made to the Legislature for assistance to enlarge it. At Crooked Island the Baptists have placed their chapel at his disposal, and show a disposition to join the Church in a body, their leader applying to be

employed as a catechist. At Acklin's Island the principal person in the place has offered to convert a building belonging to himself into a chapel, and to serve it himself as the catechist; and lastly, during the two months that Mr. Ward has been at work, he has baptized over a hundred children, and this among a population of 'Baptists'! The black people are not to be depended on for steadfastness, but still I cannot but be hopeful about this mission."

But when, in one of these early trips, the Bishop's course brought him to the Biminis Islands, introducing him to the home of the Bahama "wreckers," and their unprincipled traffic, his tone changes. "I cannot say much that is hopeful of the Biminis; the inhabitants seem nearly the most degraded people that I have yet visited. These islands are the great 'wrecking' rendezvous, lying as they do on the edge of the Gulf Stream, where the force of the current, together with adverse winds, drives many a vessel ashore on the shoals which abound in the neighbourhood. This, and the baneful traffic which it fosters, may account for much of the debased condition of the people, but as long as the system prevails little advancement can be made either in material prosperity or morality.

For not only is it a most lazy occupation, as those engaged must cruise about in idleness for months on chance of a wreck, which, if met with, does not bring them in what might have been earned by honest labour in less time, but the way in which this wrecking is carried on is most demoralizing. Captains are bribed, or, as the phrase here is, their fingers are 'buttered,' to put their ships aground. Wrecked property is considered fair plunder; and as every hand engaged on a wreck has a share of the salvage, shares are created by taking out wrecking licenses in fictitious names. I am credibly informed of a case in which licenses were taken out for three unborn children, two of which, when born, turned out to be girls! And I know of another man, of whom it is said that he used to take out wreck licences for his horse and cow. The worst of it is, that, as with smuggling at home, there exists a conventional morality with respect to wrecking, and the people do not recognise the sin of it. Mr. Lightbourne told me that a man applied to him to be admitted to Holy Communion, who yet did not see the iniquity of a pilot putting on a reef a vessel that he had undertaken to bring into port. The Governor is trying to enforce our wrecking laws, and the Trinity House is about to erect some new lighthouses, which will, I trust, in some measure check the abominable system."

From wild and lawless Bimini it was a relief to pass on to Andros Island, and to note the orderly Christian homes of its people, showing what the exertions of a faithful native catechist may effect. "Mr. Sweeting," adds the Bishop, "himself a black man, has been for years catechist, schoolmaster, magistrate, and friend to the people of this settlement, and his influence has told. I should be glad indeed if every place in our [24/25] Out Islands presented so good a specimen of a Christian settlement. Last year I confirmed there twenty-eight persons, and this year eighteen. There would have been more, but that a vessel from a neighbouring settlement some fifteen miles distant, bringing some more candidates to meet me at Fresh Creek, had to turn back in consequence of a head wind. Mr. Sweeting himself has had several escapes in one way and another, and amongst other deliverances was one from premature burial. He had nearly died of cholera, which carried off all his children but one; and while himself in a state of collapse, he was conscious of all that was going on, but could not speak, even when they were measuring him for his coffin. Fortunately he recovered in time, and one of his sons was buried in the coffin which had been made for his father.

"There had been a good deal of distress at this place, caused by heavy rains and floods, and the Governor had sent by us some corn for distribution to such as would undertake to plant cotton on Government lands, on the understanding that all the profits over and above the value of the corn advanced, should be the planter's own. We had our doubts as to the success of our mission, as the people of these islands have very little idea of depending upon their own exertions under such circumstances. The inhabitants have, however, undertaken to plant a good large field. I hope the results will be satisfactory, as, if so, it may lead to the continuous cultivation of this staple in the islands. I shall be anxious for its success, for I am convinced that the future of these [25/26] islands depends upon the successful growth of cotton, for which our soil is admirably adapted, and which we are now attempting to introduce into the colony. There is but one difficulty--the unwillingness of the people to work."

In this way the Bishop was engaged during the first two years of his episcopate, visiting in detail all the scattered portions of his diocese, and quietly though actively pushing forward the moral and material well-being of his people. But a period of greater trial and difficulty was at hand, requiring all the resources at his command to cope with it; and after two years of comparative peace, the diocese, and indeed the colony itself, passed under a dark and troubled cloud, from which they are only now slowly emerging.

In 1865 the American War came to an end, and with it the speedy subsidence of the unnaturally inflated commerce of Nassau during its continuance. "Our, trade," writes the Bishop in the summer of that year, "since the capture of the Southern parts, has collapsed. The merchants who made so much money in the blockade business have left the colony, and we have not now even the legitimate trade that we had in former years.

I hope we may be in a transition state to terminate in the development of fresh branches of industry, but just now we are in the depths." But lower depths had to be reached before long; and the diocese itself began to experience a variety of misadventure and ill-fortune. In the following year (1866) a terrible hurricane swept away eleven churches and five schools in a single night! The Bishop gave up the whole of his yearly income to replace the loss. And these devastations had hardly been repaired before a second hurricane, happily not inflicting so much damage, followed a few years later.

But a danger of a more serious kind was now beginning to threaten the very existence of the Church in these islands by the withdrawal of its endowments. The reaction which succeeded the commercial activity of the last few years was producing a general depression in every quarter of the colony. Money became scarce, the finances of the colonial exchequer grew embarrassed, and a cry for retrenchment was seized upon by the political Nonconformists for an attack upon the Church.

United States Consul Mr. Kirkpatrick's account of the Great Bahamas Hurricane of 1866.

On Monday, November 12, 1866, the United States Consul, Mr. Kirkpatrick stationed at Nassau reported on some of the damages sustained in the Bahamas by the storm. This report was concentrated mainly to damages sustained to American interests in shipping to the State Department in Washington (Courtesy of the Department of Archives-Nassau). Below is his detailed report on this storm:

The Late Hurricane of 1866:

Its Terrible Effects of the Bahamas Islands-Report from the United States Consul at Nassau.

Washington, Monday, November 12, 1866

United States Consul Kirkpatrick, at Nassau, in a letter dated October 10, to the State Department, says: "I have the honor to inform you since my dispatch No. 170 was forwarded, via Havana, that I am able to give you more correctly the losses to shipping in this vicinity and to those who have arrived here. There are a great many of whom nothing will be known. The British schooner 'Elite,' from Teneriffe for Nassau, was totally wrecked at Andes Island; all hands saved. British bark 'Sickle, Friend, Master,' from New York to Havana with a general cargo, was totally wrecked at Eleuthera Sept. 30; all hands saved.

British brig 'Active WILLINGATE,' master, from St. John for Matanzas, with lumber, arrived at Nassau in distress, with loss of topmasts and part of deck load lost. The United States steamship 'Tahoma,' Gibson, commander, from Pensacola, in distress, coaled and proceeded on her voyage. The American brig 'John Hastings,' of New-York, was seen on the 5th, abandoned. The foremast was gone and the mainmast-head gone, the sails in ribbons and the boat on deck bottom up. The American schooner 'Sath Rich,' of New York, BANTROFF, master, at Nassau, broke from her anchorage at East Harbor, was blown out to sea on Sept. 30, and arrived here on the 8th with loss of anchors, chains and mainmast. The American bark 'John Curtis,' of Brunswick, Maine, has reached the harbor (she was from Havana and bound to Turks' Island,) with loss of mast, rudder-head and other material damage. She was brought in by a wrecker, who assisted in getting her off in Southwest Bay. The American bark 'Anna M. Palmer,' of New York, from Havana, bound to Turk's Island, arrived here on the 13th inst. She was off here on the 7th, but could not enter; mainmast gone and other material damages.

A French bark was wrecked at Great Stirrup Cay. It capsized and went to pieces. All hands were lost. Five bodies were picked up nearly naked. An American bark of Searsport, Me., J.B. NICHOLS master, was brought here by wreckers on the 14th inst. She was from Wilmington, N.C., bound to Havana, with lumber; masts gone and other injuries. The

American ship John N. Cushing, of Newburyport, W.W. SWAP master, from Boston to New-Orleans, with a general cargo, arrived here on the 9th inst., with mainmast gone and fore top-mast wrung off and other damages. CHARLES M. HOIT, second mate, was washed overboard on the 3rd inst. British bark Lupeil, of London, GIBBUS, master, from Pensacola for Liverpool, was wrecked by being run ashore, leaking badly, on the 2nd inst., at Turtle Rocks, crew saved.

Brig 'Rival,' of New-York, J.R. MONISH, master, was totally wrecked at Moore's Island; abandoned. Was from New-York for Galveston with general cargo, which was partly saved and brought to Nassau. Wrecked on the 2nd inst. The crew and officers were saved, and composed as follows: J.R. Monish, Master; W.W. Delano and Roderick Dhin, mates, and Alfred S. Polk, Geo.T.Warren alias Mason, Joseph Allen, Dennis Canna, Arch. Addergreen and Neilsou, seamen. They all arrived here.

American bark S. Willis Rich, of Stockton, Me., J. L. PANNO, master, from Boston to Matanzas, with ice and general cargo, was totally wrecked on Gordo Aburo on the 2nd inst. Part of the wrecked cargo with officers and crew were brought to Nassau....Also, American brig 'William Henry,' Wm. BURNARD, master, from Portland to Havana, with lumber and shooks, was totally wrecked on the morning of the 2nd inst., at New Gordo Abaco. After striking, three of the crew were washed overboard and drowned, viz.: William Baker and William Jones, of Buffalo, New York, and James Brown, of Brooklyn, New York.

The other officers and the remainder of the crew were brought to Nassau with a small portion of their effects. The officers and crew arriving here are as follows: William Burnard, master, Thomas R. Ray and Charles Bishop, mates, and seamen Peter Derlem and Charles Johnson.

The British brig 'Grace Worthington,' DESSANT, master, from New York to Belize, Honduras, was towed to Nassau by wreckers Oct. 12, partially dismasted, with loss of rudder.

The American brig 'John R. Plater,' of Norwich, Conn., JAMES W. YALES, master, from New York for Havana, with a general cargo, was totally wrecked at Eleuthera, on the 1st inst. A portion of her cargo, with the officers and crew were saved and brought to Nassau. The officers and crew are as follows: Jas. W. Yates, master; Albert R. Douglas and Michael J. Nicholson, mates; John S. Bradley, R.M. Fowles, Chas. McPherson, Henry White and Patrick Moore, seamen.

The old American brig 'Baltic.' JOHN MADDOCKS, master of New York from New York for Galveston with a general cargo, struck on Eleuthera and was totally wrecked, on the 1ˢᵗ inst. A small part of her cargo, with officers and crew are as follows: John Maddocks, master; Francis R. Maddocks and Robert C. Wooster, mates, and Gilbert Sinclair, W.M. Boyd, John Morrison, Manfred A. Dyer and John S. Ferris, seamen.

American schooner 'Swam,' G.W. Mitchell, master, of Baltimore, was wrecked at Fortuna Island. The officers and crew arrived at Nassau on the 14ᵗʰ inst. She was wrecked on the 30ᵗʰ September. Her officers and crew are as follows: Geo. W. Mitchell, master; John D. Boyer, mate; Jas. H. Perry, Geo Johnson, Geo Vithul and John Brown, seamen. British brig 'Chile,' WHITEHEAD, master, from Nassau for Havana with coal, was totally wrecked at Andros Island on Oct. 1. 'American Eagle,' of Boston, bottom up at Cat Island, San Salvador; many dead bodies picked up on shore; she was loaded with brandy and wines, being brought here as derelict. It is reported that 100 dead bodies have already floated on shore, which would indicate that she was from European port, and had emigrant passengers on board. The owners of her cargo, if American interest should at once put in their claims to the proceeds of the cargo, subject to salvage and expenses of the Court here.

The American brig 'Joseph Baker' was abandoned and totally lost at Matthew Town, Inagua. American brig 'Julio,' BARTLETT, of Bangor, Me., from Nevassa for Philadelphia, was totally lost near Lantern Head, Inagua; crew saved with the exception of two men, who were drowned. Materials sold at Inagua. British schooner 'Laura,' of Annapolis, N. S. BISMARK, master, dismasted at Harbor Island. American brig J.P. Ellicott, of Boston, JONATHAN BRAY, master, from Bangor to Port au Prince with lumber, being dismasted, drifted on a reef at Harbor Island on the 16ᵗʰ inst., and is a total wreck. Her officers and crew arrived at Nassau, and are as follows: Jonathan Bray, master; Harvey Watson and WM Welch, mates, and Chas. M. Tripp, John Franis, James Donald and Patrick Farley, seamen. A French bark was towed into Mayaguana temporarily ragged and carried to Matthew Town, Inagua, loaded with logwood. A three-masted schooner was reported as wrecked at Grand Bahamas-cargo being taken into Green Turtle Cay, Abaco.

A large centre-board schooner was totally wrecked on Crossing Rock, Abaco. All hands were drowned; no name or nationality ascertained. Part of a clionometer-box marked "P.L. De Morey, New York," was picked up near the wreck, which may lead to her identity. She was loaded with coconuts, which were pitched.

A large vessel, whose name was ascertained to be the 'Race,' her port and nation unknown, loaded with lumber, is bottom up at Berry Island; all hands drowned. The schooner 'Advance,' formerly of Baltimore, transferred to Baltimore and Bahama Guano Company, was totally lost with her entire crew. Ten of her original crew on board at the time of the disaster supposed to belong to Baltimore.

The American schooner Union, of Harrington, reported in my last as having been driven ashore, will probably be afloat in a few days, as well as the British war-ship 'Nimble'.

This comprises all that has been ascertained up to this date, but I fear there are many not yet known. The crews now here will be forwarded to the United States at once.

CHAPTER ELEVEN

HURRICANE PREPAREDNESS

BE PREPARED BEFORE THE HURRICANE SEASON

- Know the storm surge history and elevation of your area.
- Learn safe routes inland and try not to wait until the last minute to begin your evacuation.
- Learn locations of official Hurricane Shelters.
- Review needs and working conditions of emergency equipment such as flashlights, battery-powered radios and cell phones (ensured that before the hurricane the battery is charged to 100% capacity).
- Ensure that non-perishable foods, can goods and water supplies are on hand and are sufficient to last for at least two weeks.
- Obtain and secure materials necessary to secure your home properly, such as plywood and plastic.
- Know the hurricane terms *Hurricane Alert*, *Hurricane Warning* and *Hurricane Watch* well in advance of an approaching storm and develop a clear and concise evacuation plans for your home, school, office or business in the event a hurricane threatens your area.
- Check your home for loose and clogged rain gutters and downspouts.
- Keep trees and shrubbery trimmed. Cut weak branches and trees that could fall or bump against the house and damage it in a hurricane. When trimming, try to create a channel through the foliage to the center of the tree to allow for airflow.
- Determine where to move your boat in an emergency.

- Obtain and store material, such as plywood, which are necessary to properly secure your windows and doors.
- Review your insurance policy to ensure that it provides adequate coverage and try not to wait until the hurricane season to take out or renew your policy because some insurance companies will not cover your home or business if the policy is taken out just before a storm and in most cases it takes some time for the policy to become effective but this varies from company to company so check with your individual company about this aspect of the policy.
- Take pictures of your home, inside and out to bolster insurance claims.
- Individuals with special needs should contact the local office of NEMA (Office of Emergency Management).
- For information and assistance with any of these items, contact your local meteorological office, office of emergency management, or the Bahamas Red Cross Society.

WHEN A HURRICANE ALERT IS ISSUED

- Monitor radio, television, and hurricane hotline numbers frequently for official bulletins of the storm's progress (such as the local 915 weather by phone).
- You should now begin your preparations for the approaching storm.
- Learn the location of official hurricane shelters
- Know the hurricane risks in your area, eg., determine whether you live in a potential flood zone.
- Find out where official hurricane shelters are located.
- Develop a family action plan.
- Review working condition of emergency equipment, such as flashlights and battery-powered radios.
- Ensure you have enough non-perishable food and water supplies on hand.
- Buy plywood or shutters to protect doors and windows.
- Clear loose and clogged rain gutters and downspouts.
- Determine where to move your boat in an emergency.

WHEN A HURRICANE WATCH IS ISSUED

- Be prepared to take quick action.
- Monitor radio, television, and hurricane hotline numbers frequently for official bulletins of the storm's progress (such as the local 915 weather by phone).
- Fuel and service family and business vehicles.
- Inspect and secure all businesses and homes.
- Prepare to cover all window and door openings with shutters or other shielding materials.
- Secure unanchored garbage cans, building materials, garden-tools and patio furniture immediately.
- Take down television, radio, and satellite antennae.

CHECK FOOD AND WATER SUPPLIES

- Have clean, airtight containers on hand to store at least a two-week supply of drinking water (about 14 gallons per person).
- Stock up on canned provisions.
- Get a camping stove with fuel.
- Keep a small cooler with frozen gel packs handy for packing refrigerated items.
- Check prescription medicines; obtain at least ten days to two weeks' supply.
- Stock up on extra batteries for radios, flashlights, and lanterns.
- Prepare to store and secure outdoor lawn furniture and other loose, lightweight objects, such as garbage cans, garden tools, and potted plants, which can be used as projectiles and missiles during the storm.
- Check and replenish first aid supplies.
- Have an extra supply of cash on hand.

WHEN A HURRICANE WARNING IS ISSUED

- Closely monitor radio, TV, or hurricane hotline telephone numbers for official bulletins.

- Follow instructions issued by local officials and leave immediately if ordered to do so.
- Complete preparation activities, such as putting up storm shutters and securing loose objects.
- Evacuate areas that might be affected by storm surge flooding such as coastal and low lying areas.
- If and when evacuating, leave early (if possible, in daylight).
- Notify neighbours and family members outside the warning area of your evacuation plans.

EVACUATION

Plan to evacuate if you:

- Live on a coastline, on an island waterfront or in an area prone to flooding.
- Live in a high rise such as a hotel or office building. Hurricane winds are stronger at higher elevations. Glass doors and windows may be blown out of their casings and weaken the structure.

When you leave:

- Stay with friends or relatives or at low-rise inland hotels or motels outside the flood zones.
- Leave early to avoid heavy traffic, road blocked by early floodwaters, and bridges impassable due to high winds.
- Put food and water out for your pets if you cannot take them with you or take them to the local humane society for safekeeping. Public shelters do not allow pets, and nor do most motels/hotels.
- Go to a hurricane shelter if you have no other place to go. Shelters may be crowded and uncomfortable, with no privacy and no electricity. Do not leave your home for a shelter until government officials announce on radio or television that a particular shelter is open. If you must leave your home for a shelter or to a family or friends, remember

turn off the main electricity switch and cut off your gas supply, as these can become fire hazards during the storm.

What to bring to a shelter:

- First aid kit, medicine, baby food and diapers, playing cards, games and books for entertainment purposes, toiletries, battery-powered radio, flashlights (one per person), extra batteries, blankets or sleeping bags, identification, valuable papers (insurance and passport), and cash.

IF STAYING AT HOME:

- Reminder: Only stay in a home if you have not been ordered to leave. If you are told to leave, do so immediately!
- Store water. Fill sterilized jugs and bottles with water for a two-week supply of drinking water. Fill bathtub and large containers with water for sanitary purposes.
- Turn refrigerator to maximum cold, and open it only when necessary.
- Turn off utilities if told to do so by authorities. Turn off propane tanks.
- Unplug small appliances.
- Stay inside a well-constructed building. Examine the building and plan in advance what you will do if winds become strong. Strong winds can produce deadly missiles and structural failure.

If winds grow strong:

- Stay away from windows and doors, even if they are covered. Take refuge in a small interior room, closet, or hallway. Take a battery-powered radio and flashlight with you to your place of refuge.
- Close all interior doors. Secure and brace external doors, particularly double inward-opening doors and garage doors.

- If you are in a two-story house, go to the basement, an interior first floor room such as a bathroom or closet, or under the stairs.
- If you are in a multi-story building and away from the water, go to the first or second floor and take refuge in a hall or interior room, away from windows. Interior stairwells and the areas around elevator shafts are generally the strongest part of a building.
- Lie on the floor under a table or another sturdy object.
- Be alert for tornadoes, which often are spawned by hurricanes.
- **If the 'Eye' of the hurricane should pass over your area, be aware that the improved weather conditions are temporary. The storm conditions will return with winds coming from the opposite direction, sometimes within just a few minutes and usually within an hour so it is important that you stay indoors until the weather officials give the 'All-Clear!!!'**

AFTER THE STORM PASSES

- Stay in your protected area until announcements are made on the radio or television that the dangerous winds have passed.
- If you have evacuated, do not return home until officials announce that your area is ready. Remember, proof of residency may be required in order to re-enter evacuated zones.
- If your home or building has structural damage, do not enter until officials check it.
- Avoid using candles and other open flames indoors.
- Beware of outdoor hazards.
- Avoid downed power lines and any water in which they may be lying. Be alert for weakened bridges and washed-out roads. Watch for weakened limbs on trees and/or damaged overhanging structures.

- Do not use the telephone unless absolutely necessary. The system usually is jammed with emergency calls during and after a hurricane.
- Guard against spoiled food. Use dry or canned food. Do not drink or prepare food with tap water until you are certain it is not contaminated.
- When cutting up fallen trees, use caution, especially if you use a chain saw. Serious injuries can occur when these powerful machines snap back or when the chain breaks.

CONCLUSION

People are fascinated by extreme weather events such as, devastating hurricanes which seems to be striking with even more ferocity and frequency than ever before. The most active and most intense hurricanes have occurred in recent times, and weather experts predict that they won't stop anytime soon as the planet is heating up. Here in the Bahamas, as in the entire region, more people are moving to hurricane prone places most notably the vulnerable coastlines in droves. Understanding how climate and human influence on the planet affect the weather is crucial to the unlocking the mysteries of these severe storms. Whether it's Hurricane Wilma in 2005, Hurricane Andrew in 1992 or this one in 1866, you can bet that there is more severe weather in the making. Knowing some of the most severe storms around the Bahamas yesterday and today will show you what tomorrow could bring and how scientists are working to better understand our world.

A hurricane is one of the most destructive forces of nature the Earth experiences. Every year between June 1 and November 30, hurricanes threaten us here in the Bahamas, the Eastern and Gulf Coasts of the United States, Mexico, Central America and the Caribbean. In other parts of the world, the same types of storms are called typhoons or cyclones. Hurricanes wreak havoc when they make landfall, and they can kill thousands of people and cause billions of dollars in property damage when they hit heavily populated areas. Hurricanes are severe tropical cyclones, which, though not nearly so frequent as mid-latitude cyclones, receive a great deal of attention from lay people and scientists alike, mainly because of their awesome intensity and their great destructive powers. Abundant, even torrential rainfall and winds of great speeds (from 75 to 150 mph or more) characterize hurricanes. Though these storms develop over the warm oceanic waters and often can spend their entire lives there but at times their tracks do take them over islands and coastal lands. The results can be devastating, destruction of property and sometimes even death. It is not just the rains and winds that can produce such damage to people and their surroundings. Accompanying the hurricane are unusually high seas, called storm surges, which can flood entire coastal communities. It would seem clear that people should avoid living in low coastal areas that are subjected to hurricanes.

Hurricanes are storms that are formed between the Tropics of Cancer and Capricorn in the Atlantic, Pacific and Indian Oceans. They have different names depending on where they are formed. In the Atlantic they are called hurricanes, in the north-west Pacific, typhoons; in the Indian Ocean they are known as tropical cyclones, while north of Australia they are sometimes called Willy Willies. To form, hurricanes need sea surface temperatures exceeding 26.5°C, moisture and light winds in the upper atmosphere. The hurricane season lasts from June 1 to November 30 in the North Atlantic, where approximately 12% of the world's total of tropical cyclones form. Hurricanes are enormous creatures of nature, often between 120 to 430 miles in diameter. They may last from a few days to a week or more and their tracks are notoriously unpredictable.

Earth's chaotic atmosphere can and often strikes at random with little or no warnings and the results can be quite devastating. This hurricane which struck the Bahamas in 1866 certainly proved this beyond a shadow of a doubt. The weather may very well be mankind's most widely discussed topic. Its effects are all pervasive, ranging from the trivial issue of whether we should wear certain colour clothing on a trip to the beach or whether we should take an umbrella to work, to tragedies that unfold during extreme weather events such as, devastating hurricanes or floods. The weather dictates the kind of life we live, the way we build our homes, the way we dress and to what we eat. In conjunction with the geological forces at work on our planet, the weather has shaped the landforms around us. It has also affected and shaped the variety of life here on Earth and it reflects nature's myriad solutions to the range of meteorological conditions that have occurred throughout history.

Among the many beautiful aspects of life on our planet, nature's resiliency is primary. After inflicting great damage, nature seems to begin to repair itself almost instantly. If nature's progress sometimes appears slow by our clock, it is in fact quite fast when viewed in the context of the millennia of evolution. There is nothing like them in the atmosphere. Born in warm tropical waters, these spiraling cloud masses require a complex combination of atmospheric processes to grow, mature, and then die. They are not the largest storm systems in our atmosphere or the most violent, but they combine these qualities as no other weather phenomenon does. In the Atlantic Basin, they are called hurricanes, a term that echoes colonial Spanish and Caribbean Indian words for evil spirits and big winds. These awesome storms have been a deadly problem for residents and sailors ever since the early days of colonization.

Today, hurricane damage costs billions of dollars but fortunately, people injured or killed during tropical cyclones have been steadily declining. However, our risks from hurricanes are increasing. With population and development continuing to increase along coastal areas, greater numbers of people and property are vulnerable to hurricane threat. Large numbers of tourists also favor coastal locations, adding greatly to the problems of emergency managers and local decision makers during a hurricane threat. It is important to add that hurricanes can't be controlled, but our vulnerability can be reduced through preparedness and education. The Bahamas geographic location persuades us to be more aware of the past hurricanes since history guarantees that they will come again with the same or greater fury than in the past. We can identify patterns and commonalities between storms just as human history helps us learn from our society's disasters and hopefully with this knowledge we can better prepare and adapt to the next big hurricane.

In late September, the *Great Bahamas Hurricane of 1866* quickly developed in the Atlantic and came to the attention of residents of the Bahamas in a big way. It quickly became apparent that this was no ordinary hurricane and it was developing into a strong Category 4 storm as it neared the Bahamas. The worst fears of our nation were quickly realized as the Bahamas was lashed from one end to the other by this massive and very destructive storm, leaving significant causalities in its wake. The Great Bahamas Hurricane of 1866 will not be the last to cause such massive devastation and havoc. A killer storm of similar strength could appear this year, next year, or 10 years from now, but there is no way to know when. The bitter lessons learnt from this storm have provided us with more than enough experience to survive the next big one. Meteorologists know that the science of meteorology will never provide a full solution to the problems of hurricane safety. However, with the rapid development of coastal regions, it has placed hundreds of thousands of people with little or no hurricane experience directly in the path of these lethal storms. It must be realized that the answer must be community preparedness and public education to save lives.

The hurricane challenge facing Bahamians in the twenty first century involves several components, knowledge, preparation and planning for these storms. Although we cannot control hurricanes, we can encourage better preparation and planning here in the Bahamas and in this region as a whole, so that similar tragedies can be avoided in the future. New concerns have also emerged in the Bahamas as coastal population growth and property development have exploded exponentially to help accommodate the ever-increasing tourism and new homes industries. Currently the Bahamas population increases are significantly largest in coastal communities. As a result, property damage costs due to hurricanes have skyrocketed in the last twenty years; placing the insurance industry on the brink of financial chaos should a major hurricane like the one in 1866 were to ever strike again. Today, many coastal residents are now finding it difficult to obtain insurance now. As a meteorologist, it is my hope and desire that this book will allow you to recognize and understand that the possibility exists that we may be faced with a major hurricane at some point in the future. It is also my objective that this book will encourage you to seek out additional preparedness information, not only for hurricanes, but for all types of disasters. It is the responsibility of both the government and the individual to be prepared for hurricane disasters, and to plan for a worst case scenario. As to what's going to happen in the near future, well that's anybody's guess, but the need to be prepared for all hurricane hazards should be a priority for every community, every family, and every individual.

SOURCES:

- *The Hurricane of 1866*-The Journal of the Bahamas Historical Society, Volume III, No. 1 pgs 13-14 (October 1981) by Nicolette Bethel.
- *"HURRICANE!"A Familiarization Booklet by NOAA, April, 1993.*
- *The Illustrated London News*, November, 24th 1866 pg 505 *'The Hurricane At Nassau, New Providence.'*
- Rawson W. Rawson, *Report on the Bahamas Hurricane of 1866*, Printed in Nassau, Bahamas 1868. From files at the Department of Archives, Nassau, Bahamas.
- *Blockade-Running in the Bahamas during the Civil War*, by Thelma Peters, A paper read before the Historical Association of Southern Florida at its meeting of May 5th, 1943.
- *The Bahamas Journal of Science Vol. 6 No.1 Historic Weather at Nassau*-Ronald V. Shaklee, Media Publishing Ltd.
- *The Bahamas Journal of Science Vol. 5 No.1 Historical Hurricane Impacts on The Bahamas, Part I: 1500-1749* Ronald V. Shaklee, Media Publishing Ltd.
- *The Bahamas Journal of Science Vol. 5 No.2 Historical Hurricane Impacts on The Bahamas, Part II: 1750-1799* Ronald V. Shaklee, Media Publishing Ltd.
- *The Bahamas Journal of Science Vol. 8 No.1 Historical Hurricane Impacts on The Bahamas: Floyd on San Salvador & Early Nineteenth Century Hurricanes 1800-1850* Ronald V. Shaklee, Media Publishing Ltd.
- *A Columbus Casebook-A Supplement to "Where Columbus Found the New World"* National Geographic Magazine, November 1986.
- *Harper's Weekly-A Journal of Civilization Vol. X-No 516,* Saturday, 17th November, 1866 *'Hurricane in The Bahamas.'*

- *The Philadelphia Inquirer, Saturday, October 6, 1866, 'Hurricane ravages Turks Island'*
- *The New York Times, November 13, 1866 'The Late Hurricane-Its Terrible Effects at the Bahama Islands-Report from the United States Consul at Nassau.'*
- *The New York Times, November 12, 1866 'TURK'S ISLAND: The recent Hurricane—800 Houses Completely Destroyed—3,000 People Houseless and Penniless—1,200,000 Bushels of Salt Destroyed—18 Vessels Wrecked and 20 Men Drowned.' Pg 3.*
- *The New York Times, November 29, 1866 'Settlements Are Almost Obliterated and Inhabitants Are Living In Caves.' Pg 4.*
- *The New York Times, November 17, 1866 'THE LATE HURRICANE.; Disastrous Effects of the Storm at Turks Island—Suffering Among the Inhabitants—Provisions Sent from St. Thomas.'*
- *The New York Times, November 9, 1866 'THE BAHAMAS.; Destruction of Shipping at Turk's Islands—Many Lives Lost.' Pg 4.*
- *The Mariners' Museum, Newport News, Virginia-'Bahamian Wreckers were a godsend to shipwrecked mariners.'*
- *The Mariners' Museum, Newport News, Virginia-'A Storm driving a ship onto a Reef.'*
- *Chronicles of the Sea, No. 58, December 15, 1838-The Mariners' Museum, Newport News, Virginia-'In the course of the salvage operations, particularly in rough weather, wrecking vessels suffered much damage.'*
- *The Illustrated London News, Vol. 17, 1850-'Wreckers removing valuable cargo from the inside of a wrecked ship.'- The Mariners' Museum, Newport News, Virginia.*
- *Sketch by S.G.W. Benjamin-Harper's Weekly, October 19, 1878-Florida State Archives-'Wrecking crew during a salvage operation.'*
- *Harper's New Monthly Magazine, Vol. 18, 1858/59, pg 577. Florida State Archives-'Wreckers at work during a wrecking operation.'*

- *Hurricane in the Bahamas-Nassau Half Destroyed-The National Library of New Zealand.*
- Bishop Addington Venables's account of the *Great Bahamas Hurricane of 1866*.
- *The Nassau Guardian, October 18, 1854 'Barometer Usage.'*
- *The Nassau Guardian, November 2, 1864 'Blockade Running.'*
- *The Nassau Guardian, October 3, 1866 'Hurricane in the Bahamas'.*
- *The Nassau Guardian-Lifestyles Section, February 17, 2005 'The historic development of the 'City of Nassau'-Part I & II Early Developments & Loyalist Impact.'* By Dr. Gail Saunders.
- *The Nassau Guardian-Lifestyles Section, November, 2005 'The historic development of the 'City of Nassau'-Part III Modern Developments.'* By Dr. Gail Saunders.
- *Bahamas Gazette 1784-1815,* John Wells, Editor. Nassau, Bahamas.
- *The Tribune, December 10 &17, 2009 'Rev. John Davey's account of the Great Bahamas Hurricane of 1866-The History of Religion in the Bahamas' by Jim Lawlor.*
- *The Bahama Herald,* February 18, 1862. *'Blockade Running.'*
- *Florida Historical Society: The Florida Historical Quarterly volume 65 issue 3*
- Adams, E.D. (1925) *Great Britain and the American Civil War,* New York, pg 266.
- Ahrens, D. (2000) *Meteorology Today, An Introduction to Weather, Climate, and The Environment,* USA, Brooks/Cole Publishing.
- Albury, P. (1975) *The Story of The Bahamas,* London, Macmillan Education Ltd.
- Allaby, M. (2000) *DK Guide to Weather-A Photographic Journey Through The Skies,* London, Dorling Kindersley Ltd.
- Barnes, J. (2007) *Florida's Hurricane History,* Chapel Hill, The University of North Carolina Press.

- Barratt, P. (2003) *Bahama Saga-The Epic Story of the Bahama Islands*, Indiana, Authorhouse Publishers.
- Buker, G. (1993) *Blockaders, Refugees, and Contrabands: Civil War on Florida's Gulf Coast, 1861-1865*, University of Alabama Press.
- Burroughs, Crowder, Robertson, et al. (1996) *The Nature Company Guides to Weather*, Singapore, Time-Life Publishing Inc.
- Butler, K. *The History of Bahamian Boat Builders from 1800-2000*, Unpublished.
- Butler, E. (1980) *Natural Disasters*, Australia, Heinemann Educational Books Ltd.
- Challoner, J. (2000) *Hurricane and Tornado*, Great Britain, Dorling Kindersley.
- Clarke, P., Smith, A. (2001) *Usborne Spotter's Guide To Weather*, England, Usborne Publishing Ltd.
- Craton, M. (1986) *A History of The Bahamas*, Canada, San Salvador Press.
- Davis, K. (2005) *Don't Know Much About World Myths*, HarperCollins Publishers.
- Fitzpatrick, J.P. (1999) *Natural Disasters-Hurricanes*, USA, ABC-CLIO, Inc.
- Gore, A.,(2006) *An Inconvenient Truth*, New York, USA, Rodale Books.
- Douglas.S.M. (1958) *Hurricane,* USA, Rinehart and Company Inc.
- Duedall, I., Williams, J. (2002) *Florida Hurricanes and Tropical Storms 1871-2001,*USA, University Press Of Florida.
- Durschmied, E. (2001) *The Weather Factor-How Nature has changed History*, New York, Arcade Publishing, Inc.
- Elekund, R.B. Jackson J.D., Thornton, M. (2004) *The Unintended Consequences' of Confederate Trade Legislation*. Eastern Economic Journal, Spring 2004.
- Emanuel, K. (2005) *Divine Wind-The History and Science of Hurricanes*, New York, Oxford University Press.

- Horatio, L.W. (1898) *The Blockade of the Confederacy*, Century Magazine, LVI pgs 914-928.
- Horvitz, A.L. (2007) *The Essential Book of Weather Lore*, New York, The Reader's Digest Association, Inc.
- J.D. Jarrell, Max Mayfield, Edward Rappaport, & Chris Landsea *NOAA Technical Memorandum NWS TPC-1 The Deadliest, Costliest, and Most Intense United States Hurricanes from 1900 to 2000(And Other Frequently Requested Hurricane Facts)*.
- Jones W. (2005) *Hurricane-A Force of Nature*, Bahamas, Jones Communications Intl Ltd. Publication.
- Kahl, J. (1998) *National Audubon Society First Field Guide To Weather,* Hong Kong, Scholastic Inc.
- Keegan, W., (1992) *The People Who Discovered Columbus-The Prehistory of the Bahamas*, Tallahassee, University Press of Florida.
- Kindersley, D., (2002) *Eyewitness Weather*, London, Dorling Kindersley Ltd.
- Lauber, P. (1996) *Hurricanes: Earth's Mightiest Storms*, Singapore, Scholastic Press.
- Lawlor, J& A., (2008) *The Harbour Island Story,* Oxford, Macmillan Caribbean Publishers Ltd, pgs 154-177, 203-226.
- Lightbourn, G. R. (2005) *Reminiscing I & II-Photographs of Old Nassau*, Nassau, Ronald Lightbourn Publisher.
- Lloyd, J. (2007) *Weather-The Forces of Nature that Shape Our World.* United Kingdom, Parragon Publishing.
- Ludlum, D. M., (1989) *Early American Hurricanes 1492-1870*. Boston, MA: American Meteorological Society.
- Lyons, A.W.' (1997) *The Handy Science Weather Answer Book,* Detroit, Visible Ink Press.
- MacPherson, J. (1967) *Caribbean Lands-A Geography Of The West Indies,* 2nd Edition, London, Longmans, Green and Co Ltd.
- Millas C.J. (1968) *Hurricanes of The Caribbean and Adjacent Regions 1492-1800*, Edward Brothers Inc/ Academy of the Arts and Sciences of the Americas Miami, Florida.

- Pearce, A.E., Smith G.C. (1998) *The Hutchinson World Weather Guide,* Great Britain, Helicon Publishing Ltd.
- Redfield; W.C., 1846, *On Three Several Hurricanes of The Atlantic and their Relations To the Northers of Mexico and Central America*, New Haven.
- Reynolds, R., (2000) *Philip's Guide To Weather*, London, Octopus Publishing Group Ltd.
- Rouse, I., (1992) *The Tainos-The rise and decline of the people who greeted Columbus*, New Haven, Yale University Press.
- Saunders, A. (2006) *History of Bimini Volume 2*, Bahamas, New World Press.
- Saunders, G. (1983) *Bahamian Loyalists and Their Slaves*, London, MacMillan Education Ltd, pg 2.
- Saunders, G, and Craton, M. (1998*) Islanders in the Stream: A History of the Bahamian People Volume 2,* USA, University of Georgia Press, pg 79.
- Sharer, C. (1955) *The Population Growth of the Bahamas Islands*, USA, University of Michigan Press.
- Triana, P.(1987) San Salvador-The Forgotten Island, Spain, Ediciones Beramar.
- Viele, J.(2001) *The Florida Keys Volume 3-The Wreckers*, USA, Pineapple Press.
- Wise, S. (1988) *Lifeline of the Confederacy: Blockade Running during the Civil War.* University of Carolina Press.
- www.noaa.gov
- www.nasa.gov
- www.weather.unisys.com
- www.wunderground.com
- www.wikipedia.org
- www.paperspast.natlib.govt.nz
- www.colorado.edu
- www.hurricanecity.com
- www.nationalgeographic.com
- www.weathersavvy.com

The writing of this book has been a highly satisfying project, made so by the subject itself but also by the people who have helped and assisted me in some way or the other, so here are the persons I wish to thank: -

My Father and Mother Lofton and Francita Neely
The late Mrs. Joanna Gibson
Ms. Deatrice Adderley
Mr. Andrew McKinney
Ms. Stephanie Hanna
Mrs. Darnell Osborne
Mr. Ray Duncombe
Mr. Neil Williams
Mr. Leroy Lowe
Mrs. Barbara Thrall
The late Mr. William Holowesko
Mr. Peter Graham
The Hon. Glenny's Hanna-Martin
Mr. Murrio Ducille
Mr. Charles Carter
Ms. Faith McDonald
Dr. Gail Saunders
Sir. Orville Turnquest
Sir. Clifford Darling
H.E. Arthur D. Hanna
Mr. Joshua Taylor and family
Mr. Stan Davis
Mrs. Patrice Wells
Mr. Brett Archer
Mrs. Ivy Roberts
Mrs. Jan Roberts
Ms. Jaffar Gibson
Mrs. Shavaughn Moss
Ms. Kristina McNeil
Mr. Ronald V. Shaklee
Mrs. June Maura
Mrs. Nicolette Bethel-Burrows
Mr. Coleman and Diana Andrews and family

The late Mrs. Macushla Hazelwood
Mrs. Suzette Moss-Hall
Mr. Rodger Demeritte
Mr. Michael and Phillip Stubbs
Mr. Orson Nixon
Mr. Neil Sealey
Mrs. Patricia Beardsley Roker
Dr. Myles Munroe
Dr. Timothy Barrett
Rev. Theo and Blooming Neely and family
Staff and Management of The Nassau Guardian Newspaper
Staff and Management of Media Enterprises
Staff and Management of The Tribune Newspaper
Staff of IslandFM Radio Station
Staff of the Broadcasting Corporation of The Bahamas (ZNS)
Staff of the Cable12 News
Staff of the Department of Archives
Staff of the Department of Meteorology
Staff of the Caribbean Meteorological Institute
Staff of NOAA and National Hurricane Center in Miami
Staff of Gemini Printing in Florida
Staff of Florida Printshop
Mr. Jack and Karen Andrews
Mrs. Margaret Jeffers
Ms. Kathy-Ann Caesar
Mr. Horace & Selvin Burton
Mr. Nigel Atherly
The late Mr. Conrad Knowles
Mr. Charles Whelbell

The good people of the Bahamas who opened their doors, hearts and minds to assist me with this project and provided me with overwhelming research materials, and many others too numerous to mention who gave me their take on this hurricane.

Contact Information:

Mr. Wayne Neely
P.O. Box EE-16637
Nassau, Bahamas
E-Mail: wayneneely@hotmail.com
      Or wayneneely@yahoo.com

I would like to sincerely thank each one of these sponsors below, both individual and corporate who assisted me financially and in other ways in making this book project a reality. Without them this book would have not been possible, so from the bottom of my heart I thank each and every one of you:

dive paradise with

East Bay Street
P.O. Box SS-5004
Nassau, Bahamas
Tel: 242-393-6054
Reservations: U.S. Toll Free (800) 398-DIVE
bahdiver@coralwave.com
www.bahamadivers.com

SUPER VALUE FOOD STORES LTD.

P.O. Box N-3039
Nassau, Bahamas
Phone: 242-361-5220-4
Fax: 242-361-5583
E-Mail: svfsltd@batelnet.bs

HIGHBOURNE CAY
EXUMA • BAHAMAS

P.O. Box SS-6342
Nassau, Bahamas
Phone: 242-355-1008
Fax: 242-355-1003
E-Mail: highborne@earthlink.net

WEATHER DEFINITIONS:

Advisory
Official information issued by a meteorological office describing all tropical cyclone watches and warnings in effect along with details concerning tropical cyclone locations, intensity and movement, and precautions that should be taken. Advisories are also issued to describe: (a) tropical cyclones prior to issuance of watches and warnings and (b) subtropical cyclones.

Air
This is considered the mixture of gases that make up the earth's atmosphere. The principal gases that compose dry air are Nitrogen at 78.09%, Oxygen at 20.95%, Argon at 0.93, and Carbon Dioxide at 0.033%. One of the most important constituents of air and most important gases in meteorology is water vapour.

Air Mass
An extensive mass of air with broadly similar properties, particularly surface temperature and humidity: for example, warm and dry, cold and humid etc. Different types of weather are associated with different air masses.

All Clear
All Clear simply means that the hurricane has left the affected area and all the Alerts, Warnings, and Watches are lifted but the residents in that area should exercise extreme caution for downed power lines, debris, fallen trees, flooding etc.

Aneroid Barometer
An instrument used for measuring the atmospheric pressure. It registers the change in the shape of an evacuated metal cell to measure variations on the atmospheric pressure. The aneroid is a thin-walled metal capsule

or cell, usually made of phosphorus bronze or beryllium copper which expands and contracts with air pressure changes. The scales on the glass cover measure pressure in both inches and Millibars.

Anemometer
An instrument used to measure the wind speed or force of the wind.

Anemograph
An instrument used to measure the wind speed and direction.

Atmosphere
The envelope of gases that surround a planet and are held to it by the planet's gravitational attraction. The earth's atmosphere is mainly nitrogen and oxygen.

Atmospheric Pressure
The pressure exerted by the atmosphere at a given point. It measurements can be expressed in several ways. One is Millibars, another is Hector Pascal's and another is in inches or millimeters of Mercury.

Barograph
A continuous-recording barometer. It normally consists of a rotating drum, a sensor and a chart to measure the atmospheric pressure on a continuous basis and typically the chart consisted of a daily or weekly chart or graph.

Barometer
A weather instrument used for measuring the pressure of the atmosphere. The two principle types are aneroid and mercurial.

Beaufort wind scale
A system of estimating and reporting wind speed originally based on the effect of various wind speeds on the amount of canvas that a full-rigged nineteenth century frigate could carry. Typically in 1866 this was the most common way to estimate the wind speed by most fishermen and spongers.

Best Track
A subjectively-smoothed representation of a tropical cyclone's location and intensity over its lifetime. The best track contains the cyclone's latitude, longitude, maximum sustained surface winds, and minimum sea-level pressure at 6-hourly intervals. Best track positions and intensities, which are based on a post-storm assessment of all available data, may differ from values contained in storm advisories. They also generally will not reflect the erratic motion implied by connecting individual center fix positions.

Calm
Atmospheric conditions devoid of wind or any other air in motion and where smoke rises vertically. In oceanic terms, it is the apparent absence of the water surface when there is no wind.

Cape Verde Islands
A group of volcanic islands in the eastern Atlantic Ocean off the coast of West Africa. A Cape Verde hurricane originates near here.

Cape Verde Type Hurricane
A hurricane system that originated near the Cape Verde Islands just west of the west coast of Africa.

Center
Generally speaking, the vertical axis of a tropical cyclone, usually defined by the location of the minimum wind or minimum pressure. The cyclone center position can vary with altitude.

Central Pressure
The central pressure is sometimes referred to as the 'minimum central pressure' and this is the atmospheric pressure at the center of a high or low. It is the highest pressure in a high and lowest pressure in a low, referring to the sea level pressure of the system on a surface chart.

Climate
The historical record and description of average daily and in seasonal weather events that help describe a region. Statistics are generally drawn

over several decades. The word is derived from the Greek klima, meaning inclination, and reflects the importance early scholars attributed to the sun's influence.

Climatology

The study of climate and it includes climatic data, the analysis of the causes of the differences in climate, and the application of climatic data to the solution of specific design or operational problems.

Cloud

A hydrometeor consisting of a visible aggregate of minute water and/or ice particles in the atmosphere above the earth's surface. Cloud differs from fog only in that the latter is, by definition, in contact with the earth's surface.

Cold Front

The boundary created when a cold air mass collides with a warm air mass.

Convection

The process by which warm air rises and cools, often condensing to form puffy cumulus clouds.

Coriolis Force

This is an apparent force observed on any free-moving objects in a rotating system. On the Earth, this deflective force results from the Earth's rotation and causes moving particles (including the wind) to be deflected to the right in the Northern Hemisphere and to the left in the Southern Hemisphere. It was first described in 1835 by French scientist Gustave-Gaspard Coriolis.

Cyclone

An area of low atmospheric pressure, which has a closed circulation, that is cyclonic (counterclockwise in northern hemisphere and clockwise in southern hemisphere). It is a particularly severe type of tropical storm with very low atmospheric pressure at the centre and strong winds blowing around it. Violent winds and heavy rain may affect an area of some hundreds of miles. The name applies to such storms in the Indian Ocean. 'Typhoons' and 'hurricanes' are other names applied to the same phenomena in the Pacific and Atlantic Oceans respectively.

Depression
It is a region where the surface atmospheric pressure is low. A distinctive feature on a weather map and the opposite of an anticyclone. Usually associated with clouds and rain and sometimes-strong winds. A less severe weather disturbance than a tropical cyclone.

Dew point
The temperature to which air must be cooled at a constant pressure to become saturated.

Disturbance
This has several applications. It can apply to a low or cyclone that is small in size and influence. It can also apply to an area that is exhibiting signs of cyclonic development. It may also apply to a stage of tropical cyclone development and is known as a tropical disturbance to distinguish it from other synoptic features.

Doppler radar
An advanced kind of radar that measures wind speed and locates areas of precipitation. It is like conventional radar in that it can detect areas of precipitation and measure rainfall intensity. But a Doppler radar can do more-it can actually measure the speed at which precipitation is moving horizontally toward or away from the radar antenna. Because precipitation particles are carried by the wind, Doppler radar can peer into a severe storm and reveal its winds.

Easterlies
Usually applied to the broad patterns of persistent winds with an easterly component, such as the easterly trade winds.

E.D.T.
Eastern Daylight Time

E.S.T.
Eastern Standard Time

El Niño
A Spanish term given to a warm ocean current, and to the unusually warm and rainy weather associated with it, which sometimes occurs for a few weeks off the coast of Peru (which is otherwise an extremely dry and cool region of the tropics). Several years may pass without this current appearing.

Equator
The ideal or conceptual circle at 0 degrees latitude around the Earth that divides the planet into the northern and southern hemispheres.

Extratropical
A term used in advisories and tropical summaries to indicate that a cyclone has lost its "tropical" characteristics. The term implies both pole ward displacement of the cyclone and the conversion of the cyclone's primary energy source from the release of latent heat of condensation to baroclinic (the temperature contrast between warm and cold air masses) processes. It is important to note that cyclones can become extratropical and still retain winds of hurricane or tropical storm force.

Eye
A region in the center of a hurricane (tropical storm) where the winds are light and skies are clear to partly cloudy.

Eyewall
This is a wall of dense thunderstorms that surrounds the eye of a hurricane.

Feeder Bands
These are the lines or bands of thunderstorms that spiral into and around the center of a tropical system. Also known as outer convective bands, a typical hurricane may have several of these bands surrounding it. They occur in advance of the main rain shield and are usually 40 to 80 miles apart. In thunderstorm development, they are the lines or

bands of low level clouds that move or feed into the updraft region of a thunderstorm.

Flood
Overflowing by water of the normal confines of a stream or other body of water, or accumulation of water by drainage over areas that are not normally submerged.

Forecast
A statement of expected future occurrences. Weather forecasting includes the use of objective models based on certain atmospheric parameters, along with the skill and experience of a meteorologist.

Fresh gale
Wind with a speed between 34 and 40 knots (39 and 46 mph); Beaufort scale number 8.

Front
The transition or boundary between two air masses of different densities, which usually means different temperatures. The several types of fronts bring distinct weather patterns.

Frontal Passage
It is the passage of a front over a specific point on the surface. It is reflected by the change in dew point and temperature, the shift in wind direction, and the change in atmospheric pressure. Accompanying a passage may be precipitation and clouds.

Gale
A gale is a very strong wind. There are conflicting definitions of how strong the winds must be to classify it as a gale. The U.S. Government's National Weather Service defines a gale as 34–47 knots (39–54 miles per hour) of sustained surface winds. Forecasters typically issue gale warnings when winds of this strength are expected. Other sources use minimums as low as 28 knots and maximums as high as 90 knots. Through 1986, the National Hurricane Center used the term gale to refer to winds of tropical storm force for coastal areas, between

33 knots and 63 knots. The 90-knot definition is very non-standard. A common alternative definition of the maximum is 55 knots. Typically in 1866 whenever a storm or significant bad weather was approaching the Bahamas most people said that 'Gale was travelling' which had no relation at the time to the true meaning of the word but essentially meaning that there will be severe weather to be experienced over that area to which they referred.

Gale warning
A warning for marine interest for impending winds from 34 to 47 knots.

Gust
A sudden brief increase in the speed of the wind, followed by a lull or slackening.

Hail
Precipitation that originates in convective clouds, such as cumulonimbus, in the form of balls or irregular pieces of ice, which comes in different shapes and sizes. Hail is considered to have a diameter of 5 millimeter or more; smaller bits of ice are classified as ice pellets, snow pellets, or graupel. Individual lumps are called hailstones.

Heat
A form of energy transferred between two systems by virtue of a difference in temperature.

Hemisphere
The top and bottom halves of the Earth are called the Northern and Southern Hemisphere.

High
The center of an area of high atmospheric pressure, usually accompanied by anticyclonic and outward wind flow. Also known as an anticyclone.

Hurricane

This the term used in the North Atlantic Region and in the eastern North Pacific Ocean to describe a severe tropical cyclone having winds in excess of 64 knots (74mph) and capable of producing widespread wind damage and heavy flooding. The same tropical cyclone is known as a typhoon in the western Pacific and cyclone in the Indian Ocean.

Hurricane Alert

A hurricane alert indicates that a hurricane poses a threat to an area (often within 60 hours) and residents of the area should start to make any necessary preparations.

Hurricane Season

The part of the year having a relatively high incidence of hurricanes. The hurricane season in the North Atlantic runs from June 1 to November 30.

Hurricane Warning

A formal advisory issued by forecasters in the North Atlantic Region when they have determined that hurricane conditions are expected in a coastal area or group of islands within a 36 hour period. A warning is used to inform the public and marine interests of the storm's location, intensity, and movement. At this point residents should have completed the necessary preparations for the storm.

Hurricane Watch

A formal advisory issued by forecasters in the North Atlantic Region when they have determined that hurricane conditions are a potential threat to a coastal area or group of islands within 48 hour period. A watch is used to inform the public and marine interest of the storm's location, intensity, and movement and residents of the area should be in the process of being prepared.

Knot

The unit of speed in the nautical system; one nautical mile per hour. It is equal to 1.1508 statute miles per hour or 0.5144 meters per second.

Landfall

The intersection of the surface center of a tropical cyclone with a coastline. Because the strongest winds in a tropical cyclone are not located precisely at the center. It is possible for a cyclone's strongest winds to be experienced over land even if landfall does not occur. Similarly, it is possible for a tropical cyclone to make landfall and have its strongest winds remain over the water.

Latent Heat

The energy released or absorbed during a change of state or quite simply, the energy stored when water evaporates into vapour or ice melts into liquid. It is released as heat when water vapor condenses or water freezes.

Latitude

The distance on the Earth's surface measured in degrees north and south of the equator.

Lightning

A sudden and visible discharge of electricity produced in response to the build up of electrical potential between cloud and ground, between clouds, within a single cloud, or between a cloud and surrounding air within a cumulo-nimbus cloud.

Longitude

The distance on the Earth's surface measured in degrees east and west from the Prime Meridian.

Low

An area of low barometric pressure, with its attendant system of winds. Also called a depression or cyclone.

Meteorologist

A scientist who studies and predicts the weather by looking at what is happening in the atmosphere.

Meteorology
The study of the atmosphere and the atmospheric phenomena as well as the atmosphere's interaction with the Earth's surface, oceans, and life in general.

Millibar
A unit of pressure, which directly expresses the force exerted by the atmosphere. Equal to 1000 dynes/cm² or 100Pascals.

Moderate gale
Wind with a speed between 28 and 33 knots (32 and 38 mph); Beaufort scale number 7.

National Hurricane Center
The National Weather Service office in Coral Gables, Florida, that tracks and forecasts hurricanes and other weather in the Atlantic, Gulf of Mexico, Caribbean Sea, and parts of the Pacific.

National Weather Service
The federal agency that observes and forecasts weather. Formerly the U.S. Weather Bureau, it is part of the National Oceanic and Atmospheric Administration, which is part of the Department of Commerce.

NOAA
National Oceanic and Atmospheric Administration.

Occluded Front
Also known as an occlusion, it is a complex front formed when a cold front overtakes a warm front. It develops when three thermally different air masses conflict. The type of frontal boundary they create depends on the manner in which they meet.

Precipitation
Any and all forms of water particles, liquid or solid, that falls from the atmosphere and reach the ground.

Prevailing Wind
A wind that blows from one direction more frequently than any other during a given period, such as a day, month, season or year.

Quasi-Stationary Front
A front which is nearly stationary or moves very little since the last synoptic position. Also known as a stationary front.

Radar
Acronym for **RA**dio **D**etection **A**nd **R**anging. An electronic instrument used to detect objects (such as falling precipitation) by their ability to reflect and scatter microwaves back to a receiver.

Rainfall
The amount of precipitation of any type, primarily liquid. It is usually the amount that is measured by a rain gauge.

Rain gauge
Instrument for measuring the depth of water from precipitation that is assumed to be distributed over a horizontal, impervious surface and not subject to evaporation and measured during a given time interval. Measurement is done in hundredths of inches (0.01").

Reconnaissance Aircraft
This is an aircraft, which flies directly into the eye of a hurricane to make a preliminary survey to gain information about a hurricane using advanced meteorological instruments.

Recording rain gauge
A rain gauge that automatically records the amount of precipitation collected, as a function of time.

Ridge
An elongated area of high atmospheric pressure that is associated with an area of maximum anticyclonic circulation. It is the opposite of a trough.

Saffir-Simpson Damage-Potential Scale
A scale relating a hurricane's central pressure and winds to the possible damage it is capable of inflicting and it was first introduced in 1971 by Herbert Saffir and Robert Simpson.

Satellite
Any object that orbits a celestial body, such as a moon. However, the term is often used in reference to the manufactured objects that orbit the earth, either in geostationary or a polar manner. Some information that is gathered by weather satellites, such as GOES9, includes upper air, temperatures and humidity, recording the temperatures of cloud tops, land, and ocean, monitoring the movement of clouds top determines upper level wind speeds, tracing the movement of water vapour, monitoring the sun and solar activity, and relaying data from weather instruments around the world.

Satellite Images
Images taken by weather satellite that reveal information, such as the flow of water vapour, the movement of frontal systems, and the development of a tropical system.

Schooner
A typically 2-masted fore-and-aft rigged vessel with a foremast and a mainmast stepped nearly amidships.

Severe Weather
Generally, any destructive weather event, but usually applies to localized storms, such as blizzards, intense thunderstorms, or tornadoes.

Severe Thunderstorm
A thunderstorm with winds measuring 50 knots (58 mph) or greater, ¾ inch hail or larger, severe thunderstorms may also produce torrential rain and frequent lightning.

Severe Thunderstorm Warning
A severe thunderstorm has actually been observed by satellite or indicated on radar, and is occurring or imminent in the warning area.

Shear
It is the rate of change over a short duration. In wind shear, it can refer to the frequent change in wind speed within a short distance. It can occur vertically or horizontally. Directional shear is a frequent change in direction within a short distance, which can also occur vertically or horizontally.

Shower
Precipitation from a cumuliform cloud. Characterized by the suddenness of beginning and ending, by the rapid change in intensity, and usually by a rapid change in the condition of the sky. The solid or liquid water particles are usually bigger than the corresponding elements in other types of precipitation and usually lasts less than an hour in duration.

Small Craft Advisory:
When a tropical cyclone threatens a coastal area, small craft operators are advised to remain in port or not to venture into the open sea. It is an advisory issued for marine interests, especially for operator of small boats or other vessels. Conditions include wind speeds between 20 knots (23 mph) and 34 knots (39 mph).

Sponging
This was an industry of the Bahamas in the mid to late 1800s thru the mid-1900s. This industry was the number industry in the Bahamas for many years before over-sponging; the introduction of synthetic sponges and sponge diseases killed it off in the mid-1900s. The fishermen went to harvest the sponges from the seabed and then sold them to the sponge exchange in Nassau.

Stationary Front
A front which is nearly stationary or moves very little since the last synoptic position. May be known as a quasi-stationary front.

Storm
An individual low pressure disturbance, complete with winds, clouds, and precipitation. Wind with a speed between 56 and 63 knots (64 and 72 mph); Beaufort scale number 11.

Storm Surge
This is the mound or rise in ocean water drawn up by the low pressure below a hurricane; it causes enormous waves and widespread damage if the hurricane reaches land.

Storm tide
The actual level of sea water resulting from the astronomic tide combined with the storm surge.

Strong gale
Wind with a speed between 41 and 47 knots (47 and 54 mph); Beaufort scale number

Swell
Ocean waves that have travelled out of their generating area. Swells characteristically exhibits a more regular and longer period and has a flatter wave crests than waves within their fetch.

Temperature
In general, the degree of hotness or coldness of a body as measured on some definite temperature scale by means of any of various types of thermometers.

Thermometer
An instrument used for measuring temperature. The different scales used in meteorology are Celsius, Fahrenheit, and Kelvin or Absolute.

Thunderstorm
A local storm produced by cumulonimbus clouds and always accompanied by lightning and thunder.

Tide
The periodic rising and falling of the Earth's oceans and atmosphere. It is the result of the tide-producing forces of the moon and the sun acting on the rotating Earth. This propagates a wave through the atmosphere and along the surface of the Earth's waters.

Tornado

The name given to a very strong and damaging whirlwind with a clearly visible dark, snake-like funnel extending from a thundercloud to the ground. The track of a tornado at the ground level is rarely very wide, but buildings, trees, and crops may be totally devastated.

Trade Winds

The very constant winds found over most oceans within the tropics. These winds blow towards the equator as the northeast trades in the northern hemisphere and as the southeast trades in the southern hemisphere. They were of great importance to shipping in the days of sail; hence the name.

Tropics

The region of the Earth located between the Tropic of Cancer, at 23.5 degrees North latitude, and the Tropic of Capricorn, at 23.5 degrees South latitude. It encompasses the equatorial region, an area of high temperatures and considerable precipitation during part of the year.

Tropical depression

A mass of thunderstorms and clouds generally with a cyclonic wind circulation between 20 and 34 knots.

Tropical disturbance

An organized mass of thunderstorms with a slight cyclonic wind circulation of less than 20 knots. It is a moving area of thunderstorms, which maintains its identity for 24 hours or more.

Tropical storm

Once a tropical depression has intensified to the point where its maximum sustained winds are between 35-64 knots (39-73 mph), it becomes a tropical storm.

Tropical Wave

An inverted, migratory wave-like disturbance or trough in the tropical region that moves from east to west, generally creating only a shift in winds and rain. The low level convergence and associated convective weather occur on the eastern side of the wave axis. Normally it moves slower than the atmospheric current in which it is embedded and is considered a weak trough of low pressure. Tropical waves occasionally intensify into tropical cyclones. They are also called Easterly Waves.

Tropical Storm Watch
A tropical Storm Watch is issued when tropical storm conditions, including winds from 39 to 73 mph (35 to 64 knots) pose a possible threat to a specified coastal area within 48 hours.

Tropical Storm Warning
A tropical storm warning is issued when tropical storm conditions, including winds from 39 to 73 mph (35 to 64 knots) are expected in a specified coastal area within 36 hours or less.

Troposphere
The lowest layer of the atmosphere located between the earth's surface to approximately 11 miles (17 kilometers) into the atmosphere. Characterized by clouds and weather, temperature generally decreases with increasing altitude.

Trough
An elongated area of low atmospheric pressure that is associated with an area of minimum cyclonic circulation. The opposite of a ridge.

Typhoon
The name given in the Western Pacific and particularly in the China Sea to violent tropical storms or cyclones with maximum sustained winds of 74 miles per hour or higher. This same tropical cyclone is known as a hurricane in the eastern North Pacific and North Atlantic Ocean, and as a cyclone in the Indian Ocean.

Warm Front
The leading edge of an advancing warm air mass that is replacing a retreating relatively colder air mass. Generally, with the passage of a warm front, the temperature and humidity increase, the pressure rises, and although the wind shifts (usually from the southwest to northwest

in the northern hemisphere); it is not as pronounced as with a cold frontal passage. Precipitation, in the form of rain, snow, or drizzle, is generally found ahead of the surface front, as well as convective showers and thunderstorms. Fog is common in the cold air ahead of the front. Although clearing usually occurs after passage, some conditions may produce clouds and rain in the warm air.

Weather
The state of the atmosphere, mainly with respect to its effects upon life and human activities. As distinguished from climate, weather consists of the short-term (minutes to months) variations of the atmosphere.

Whole gale
Wind with a speed between 48 and 55 knots (55 and 63 mph), Beaufort scale number 10.

Willy Willies
A colloquial Australian term for a violent tropical storm or cyclone affecting the coasts of northern Australia.

Wind
Air in motion relative to the surface of the Earth. Almost exclusively used to denote the horizontal component.

Wind speed
Rate of wind movement in distance per unit time.

Wind vane
An instrument used to indicate wind direction.

World Meteorological Organization (WMO)
This is the governing sub-body for meteorology within the United Nations made up of 185 member states and territories. It succeeded the International Meteorological Organization, which was founded in 1873. It is the United Nations system's authoritative voice on the state and behaviour of the Earth's atmosphere, its interaction with the oceans, the climate it produces and the resulting distribution of water resources.

ABOUT THE BOOK

Wayne Neely has once again produced a well written and well researched book about a major Bahamian hurricane and a sure best seller. In his book 'The Great Bahamas Hurricane of 1866', Wayne Neely, one of the world's leading authorities on Bahamian and Caribbean hurricanes, gives us an engaging account of this awe-inspiring meteorological event. He revealed how this hurricane literally devastated the entire Bahamas and actually altered the course of Bahamian history. *The Great Bahamas Hurricane of 1866* swept through these islands just as they were rallying from the effects of two years exhaustion by an epidemic fever, and by the sudden cessation of the vicious stimulus of the blockade era. The exact death toll is unknown but it was estimated that as much as 387 persons died in this deadly hurricane here in the Bahamas. This book also showed how this hurricane significantly impacted the wrecking and salvaging industry-the number one industry in the Bahamas at the time. Interwoven into this book is the compelling stories and vivid descriptions of one of the most powerful and deadly hurricanes to ever impact this country. Fortunately, casualties on the land were at a minimum but casualties at sea were astounding. A French boat was wrecked at Great Stirrup Cay. It capsized and went to pieces. All hands were lost. The boat *American Eagle* of Boston, sunk at Cat Island and San Salvador and many dead bodies were picked up on shore and it was loaded with a shipment of brandy and wines. It is reported that at least 100 dead bodies floated on shore from this boat and by looking at the bodies it indicated that it originated from a port in Europe, and had emigrant passengers on board. A large centre-board schooner was totally wrecked on Crossing Rock, Abaco. All hands onboard drowned. A large vessel called *Race* with an unknown port and nation, loaded with lumber capsized at the Berry Islands and all hands drowned. The schooner *Advance* formerly of Baltimore was totally lost with her entire crew.

ABOUT THE AUTHOR

Wayne Neely

Wayne Neely is an international speaker, best-selling author, lecturer on hurricanes, and a Meteorologist. Travelling extensively throughout the region and the world, Wayne addresses critical issues affecting all aspects of hurricanes, especially Bahamian hurricanes which are one of his central areas of expertise. The central themes of his books are always on hurricanes in general and the impact of hurricanes on all aspects of mankind's ever expanding society. He has a great passion for writing and does it in his spare time. Wayne Neely is a certified Bahamian Meteorologist and Forecaster working at the Department of Meteorology in Nassau, Bahamas for the last 20 years. Prior to working in the meteorological field, he majored in Geography and History at the College of the Bahamas in Nassau. He then attended the Caribbean Meteorological Institute in Barbados where he majored and specialized in weather forecasting. His love for hurricanes and the weather came about while growing up on the island of Andros where he experienced his first hurricane in 1979 called David. He also listened quite regularly to his parents, grand parents and other older residents within the community talking about a major hurricane which occurred in 1929 and devastated the Bahamas. That piqued his interest in hurricanes and got him started on writing his first book called '*The Great Bahamas Hurricane of 1929.*' He then went onto write his second book called '*The Major Hurricanes to Affect the Bahamas*' followed by his third book '*Rediscovering Hurricanes*' *(Foreword by Herbert Saffir)*. This was followed by his fourth book '*The Great Bahamian Hurricanes of 1926*'*(Foreword by Bryan Norcross)* and now this is his fifth book on hurricanes and the rest is history. Over the years, Wayne has written several articles on hurricanes and other severe weather events for some of the major local and international newspapers and magazines. He has regularly contributed and wrote the hurricane supplements for both *The Nassau Guardian* and *The Tribune.* He speaks quite regularly to schools, colleges, universities and frequently does radio and television interviews both locally and abroad about the history and impact of Bahamian and Caribbean hurricanes and hurricanes in general.